Spirit Rising

Spirit Rising

My Winding, Tumultuous Odyssey with Depression

DR. CINDY HOARD

For information about this title or to order other books and/or electronic media, contact the publisher:

Dr. Cindy Hoard
www.drcindyauthor.com
cindy@drcindyauthor.com

ISBNs:
979-8-9869199-0-4 (softcover)
979-8-9869199-1-1 (eBook)

Printed in the United States of America

Cover and Interior design: 1106 Design

Dedicated to Dr. Jeanie Thomson,
who walked every step of the way with me
to bring my book to life.
As a treasured friend and colleague, she often
felt more like a co-author.

CONTENTS

Contents

Contents

Contents

INTRODUCTION

As I wrote this book, one of the questions I continue to ask myself is "What is the hidden gift in this crisis called 'depression'?" I want you to know I don't have specific answers, but I do explore many possibilities throughout this book. With the hope that my words might alleviate suffering in the world for even one person, I share my journey of "Spirit" through depression and what it takes to get through each day. I recount avenues and resources I explored, especially for questions the answers to which I couldn't find. While I want to tell my story, be aware that my professional training as a psychologist slips in sometimes as opinions or my perceptions. My eventful personal journey is a story worth telling. This is an opportunity to witness my persistence despite my challenges; in so doing, I unveil my animated side, whether seen or unseen.

"Spirit," "Faith," and "Soul" have been overarching themes throughout my life, punctuated by my episodes with severe depression. My *lack of connection* with my "Spirit" and the searing desperation of depression appears over and over again in my journals. The felt distance from "God" is a mystery because there *are* episodes and outcomes that demonstrate my connection to my "Spirit" and "Soul," even though I did not *feel it* at the time. I grew up with a religion that provided me with an initial set of beliefs and values as a way to establish a foundation. As I matured and grew as a person, "Spirit" became my word for that part of my life. The word "Spirituality" emerged over the past few decades as a more all-encompassing term with multiple meanings for me. The notion of "God," the "Divine," or whatever one calls that which is greater than each of us is personal and threads throughout my life. On the journey of "Spirit" through depression, "God" became a source I begged and pleaded with because I felt abandoned. At times, I also felt connected to "God Within" based on spiritual happenings I experienced.

The unfolding and expansion of my "Spiritual Faith" are the context for the voyage I relate in this book and is not intended to proselytize specific beliefs. My stops along the way are deeply private, meaningful and painful, yet intertwined in my lifelong struggle with depression. Though words tell my story, it is evident to me that depression, "God," "Faith," the "Soul," "Spirit," the "Divine," "Spirituality," and even "values" cannot be put into exact words with common or shared meanings. My words reflect my perception, perspective, and experience of what took place in my life.

A chronology of my life as it relates to this journey ends this Introduction section. I chose to provide this chronology so that the reader might benefit from contexts that impacted the progression of the lessons I have learned.

I am an explorer and also someone who has literally *been "explored,"* as you will see. Please join me on this voyage that can be enlightening, painful, crazy, amazing, desperate, insightful, and many other things. If you find some kernel with meaning, or something that stimulates wonder about your own life's journey, I am grateful. I appreciate your willingness to join my voyage in written words.

Please note: Due to the emotions of the moment, journal entries may have grammatical and spelling errors.

✦ ✦ ✦

CHRONOLOGY OF SELECTED SIGNIFICANT LIFE EVENTS

Age	Year	Event
10	1964	A school counselor approached my mother with concern about how sad I seemed and thought I could benefit from some counseling. This was my first awareness of depression.
16	1970	Diagnosed with endometriosis* and received my initial treatment for what became a lifelong challenge. I was treated with hormone-based medications, which affected my mood as well.
17	1972	Chosen by my church to participate in an exchange year abroad with International Christian Youth Exchange (ICYE). I was placed in Germany for one year; I spent half of the year in a religious commune and the other half with a wonderful family in Worms, Germany.
18	1973	Faced challenges readjusting to the USA. Things changed personally during the exchange year, and I needed time to readjust and attend to my physical and mental health. During this process, I was "formally" diagnosed with depression.

---

* Endometriosis is a disorder caused when the lining of the uterus enters the abdomen and implants and grows on other organs and/or the abdominal wall.

22 1976 Initial laparotomy surgery for endometriosis. Multiple surgeries related to the adhesions from endometriosis followed (1977, 1981, 1982, 1987, 1988, 1989, 1990, 1995, 1999)

1977 Earned my BA in Special Education and started teaching children with special needs in Phoenix.

1978 Entered talk therapy with Dr. Mathilda Canter, PhD, Psychologist, and was referred to Dr. Harris Murley, MD, Psychiatrist, for antidepressant-medication prescribing.

1982 I entered graduate school in Tucson, Arizona, and earned a master's degree in Educational Psychology in 1984 despite my depression.

1983-1984 Surgical reconstruction of both ankles, with six weeks off for each ankle and then rehabilitation.

1985 Moved to Flagstaff, Arizona, to pursue my doctorate in Educational Psychology.

1986 Dr. Canter referred me to Dr. James R. Fredrick, Director of the Counseling Center at NAU (see page 185 in Talk Therapy)

1988 Doctors determined that I needed a hysterectomy. The endometriosis was so severe that they could no longer just use a laparoscope to treat me, as they had done several times. I had to take a semester off from graduate school to recover.

1992   I was awarded my doctorate in Educational Psychology, with a specialization in Early Childhood School Psychology despite my pervasive, raging war with depression.

1992   Began working at an agency that specialized in services for children younger than five years old, and their families.

1993   Broke my ankle at work, stepping down into a playground.

1993   Secured my license to practice as a psychologist in Arizona.

1998   Ventured into therapy with Dr. Marilyn Kieffer-Andrews, RNP, PhD.

2000   Surgery for bowel resection and lysis (cutting) of adhesions due to the effects of endometriosis.

2004   Started my private practice for children ages ten and younger.

2008   Severe depressive episode necessitated putting my license as a psychologist on hold and going on Social Security Disability.

2009   ECT (Electroconvulsive Therapy) (twenty-six sessions) was a requirement for participation in a study of DBS (Deep Brain Stimulation) for Treatment-Resistant Depression.

2009   Accepted into the DBS study and had surgery to implant DBS electrodes in my brain and device in my chest with annual surgical battery replacement required, in Atlanta, Georgia, at Emory University.

2009   Increased participation in my father's care.

2011   Breast cancer—lumpectomy surgery, followed by chemotherapy.

2014   Mother and I continued to live together after my Dad's passing.

2018   Second diagnosis of breast cancer, resulting in a bilateral mastectomy

2020   Opened a private practice for a second time, specializing in assessment and diagnosis of autism in young children.

PRELUDE TO MY JOURNEY

Beyond the chronology of events that impacted my journey, I'd like to share a bit more information and context that you might wonder about as you read my story. Many people, places, and experiences contributed to who I am. I highlight events in my early life and teens, my educational and professional paths, *curveballs* that impacted me, early long-standing coping strategies, and a crucial therapeutic relationship. These historical-background stories intersect with the journey I will tell. They comprise a prelude to the whole.

MY EARLY YEARS AND TEENS

I am the oldest of four girls in my family. I was born in Detroit, Michigan, but my family moved to Phoenix, Arizona, when I turned ten years old. "Goody Two Shoes" to my sisters, I self-imposed a lot of "responsibility" on myself, a persistent expectation I've carried throughout my life. As I acted this out, it affected

my relationships with my sisters. I helped my mom all of the time and tattled on my sisters. When I took on the "Mom" role with my sisters, they retorted, *You are not my mother!*" Though my parents always strove to treat us equally, my sisters perceived me to be the favorite. My need to contribute and take responsibility at home alienated me from them. In a broader view, my behavior reflected my preference to interact with adults over my peers. I played this out in a similar way at Girl Scout meetings and events, where I always volunteered to help in order to be with the adults.

Thirsty to learn something new every day, I excelled in school. My focus shifted to this domain in junior high and high school, where I strove to be a straight-A student, except for physical education. In addition, I committed myself to my music, specifically, playing the flute. My parents viewed playing an instrument as a choice and didn't nag me or my sisters to practice an instrument. My parents could not include private lessons in their budget. In junior high, I babysat for hours to save enough money to go to summer music camp in Flagstaff, Arizona.

During the rest of the year, I religiously practiced my flute. In high school, I earned a seat in the All-State Band, a huge accomplishment, given that all the other flute players competed with years of private lessons behind them. I qualified for the varsity school band, which was unusual for a freshman. I also played in the high school orchestra.

An outgrowth of my desire to assume responsibility, I strove to keep my commitments. Over time, this proved a gift but also a liability when depression drained my energy.

Beyond academics and music, church involvement filled out my life during these times. I quickly included "adult-like" responsibilities, for which I drew high praise from women from the church, whom I considered special and important in my life. I wanted to please them. I attended weekly choir practice and "Sunday School." Here again, curious and attracted to studies of contemporary theology and ecumenical activities, I sought out adults who led classes, not my fellow students. I also became "friends" with the Director of Christian Education and the Church Secretary (also my Sunday School teacher). While important to me, these two relationships created awkward situations with my mother. The Director of Christian Education and the Church Secretary considered my mother, the church's Preschool Director, as a colleague. Because I entrenched myself into my relationships with my high school Sunday School teachers, my only "friends" proved to be my parents and these significant adults in my life. Many years later, my Sunday School teachers shared their concerns about how I had not connected with my peers. Yet, at the same time, they recognized that I had different interests from my classmates'.

Thrilled to be selected to be an exchange student after graduation from high school, I couldn't wait to take off for Germany for one year. For the first time, I would live outside of the central sphere of my parents, my church, and others who I felt might judge me. Not knowing the end to this story, I had apprehension when I embarked on this move.

Instead, I discovered a *"Me"* I did not yet know, a "Me" I embraced. Because of those changes in me, I worried how my parents and other important adults in my life would react as I emerged from the previous year. I felt so different and did not want to rush and immerse myself in the culture from which I came. This bothered those who knew me as a *doer*, typically with a plan and action steps to forging ahead.

Curious to see in what direction I would head after my experiences in Germany, I started to explore lots of options, including junior college. Though my abundant inquisitiveness got me into trouble at times, through it, I learned more about myself and chose a post-Germany path: attend junior college. Essential for my mental health, I knew for certain that I needed time alone and would not be ashamed of my choice. I engaged in therapy as I started junior college, the beginning of my formal college education. Upon earning my Associate of Arts degree, I transferred to Arizona State University (ASU).

MY PROFESSIONAL PATH IN LIFE

I chose multiple paths throughout my professional life and earned four degrees along the way. My first was an Associate of Arts from a community college. In my next step, I earned entrance to Arizona State University (ASU) and received my Bachelor of Arts degree in Special Education. I then earned a Master's degree in Educational Psychology and a Doctorate in Educational Psychology, my highest achievement. Each divergent path arrived at important junctures in my journey.

Initial University Years and First Professional Position

I chose an emphasis on early childhood for my studies. My mother had founded three preschools, which inspired my choice, as did the years I babysat, which affirmed my love for working with children. I considered many possibilities where I could make a difference in the families of little ones with special needs. My Bachelor's degree prepared me to become a Special Education teacher, my choice among the myriad options I explored.

Ecstatic to welcome my first students into my initial class as a teacher in Phoenix, I quickly realized how much I still needed to learn! My classroom, labeled "Learning Disabilities," proved so much more than that. Children with significant emotional problems, communication problems, and learning and other individual differences shared our class. Here, I learned firsthand the wide range of developmental challenges children experience. I gained a reputation as the teacher who could *figure out* the needs of children with whom other teachers could not make headway. The longer I taught, the more interested I became. I explored the many different roles I could play with these children and their families. My research spurred me on to pursue graduate education in school psychology. I subsequently earned my Master's and Doctorate degrees, required to sit for licensure as a psychologist in the State of Arizona.

Earning My Master's Degree

I first moved to the University of Arizona (U of A) in Tucson to pursue my graduate work. I participated in influential coursework with a woman who, as a pioneer in learning disabilities, dedicated her work and research to early intervention for children younger than five. While I knew I wanted to work with preschool children, this experience drove home the importance that intervention begin as early as infancy. The earlier the better. Over time, the early-intervention multidisciplinary world delightfully expanded the focus of my professional work.

As a graduate assistant to a Psychology 101 course, I led weekly discussion sessions for groups of fifteen to twenty students to discuss the contents of their main lectures. My discussion sections included first-year freshmen straight out of high school, as well as women who'd had their children, raised them, and decided to return to school. That experience taught me so much that I value in my work today. Through my work with students of a wide range of ages, experiences, and levels of education, I gained an appreciation of the many different ways people learn. I also experienced a broad array of individual interests and diversity of thought.

During this time, I required two separate visits to the operating table for laparoscopic surgeries to slice endometriosis adhesions from my abdominal wall and organs. Although these were outpatient surgeries, they still involved anesthesia and recovery time. Some people told me that outpatient surgery should be a piece of cake—not my experience. Much later in my life, my double mastectomy was also performed as outpatient surgery, required months for recovery.

During this period of graduate work, I also endured surgical reconstruction of both of my ankles. Each procedure left me non-weight-bearing for six weeks and then required intense physical therapy. Beyond these major physical challenges I faced, I lived with the physical illness of depression. This double whammy erected hurdles I needed to dismantle in order to move toward the life goal(s) I had set at the time each challenge arrived in my theatre.

Toward completion of my master's degree, the faculty informed me they did not feel me capable of completing a doctorate degree. Sobbing, I headed to the home of a close friend for a cleansing cry. That same day, I drove to Phoenix for Thanksgiving with my family. Despite feeling dumped and discouraged, I intuited that this might be a good thing. The U of A faculty offered me pursuit of an Education Specialist degree, with all of the work of a PhD, but without preparation for the work I craved. This did not fit with my determination to earn a Doctorate and become a licensed psychologist.

Pursuit of My Doctoral Degree

Ultimately, the U of A faculty did me a favor! I quickly found out that the Educational Psychology Department at Northern Arizona University (NAU) in Flagstaff, Arizona, had started a cutting-edge Doctoral specialization in early-childhood special education/school psychology. I could not believe my eyes and the possibilities! In one week, I moved from Tucson, Arizona, to Flagstaff, Arizona. Without any guarantee I would get into the Doctoral program, I sensed a good opportunity when I found it. Despite desperation due to depression, I continued to set my sights on my goal to practice as a psychologist.

Accepted into the program I yearned for, I obtained a position of graduate assistant to the head of this department, Dr. Susanna Maxwell. My vast and varied tasks exhilarated me. I gathered information from across the country about various state requirements for licensing and the course content for specializations in the early-childhood field. In the process, I also developed a deep understanding of the federal laws that governed these programs. Everything excited me. Enlightened and inspired daily, I spent eight years in Flagstaff earning my Doctoral degree. From the Institute for Human Development at NAU, my subsequent Doctoral internship with the Indian Children's Program turned into a marvelous adventure, a highly privileged opportunity. I provided services on the Hopi and Navajo Indian Reservations. Possibilities opened up to me to secure future consultant contracts with the Navajo Head Start program.

Depression Accompanied Me Through It All—Every Step to My Degrees and Each Day of Internship

And *Not again!* Endometriosis injected more challenge into my Doctoral training; I required three additional laparoscopic surgeries for the endometriosis adhesions. Finally, a necessary hysterectomy debilitated me longer than expected and obliterated my chances to bear a child. I stopped my coursework for a semester to recover physically and emotionally. Then I started hormone therapies, which affected many aspects of my physical and emotional health; they stretched out the time it took to finish my doctorate.

> *5.12.1992: Yet, important and amazing, I did it!!! I persisted throughout my work to earn my doctorate. The insidious assault of depression diminished me and waxed and waned in severity.*

Post-Doctorate Professional Life Launched

With my doctorate in hand, I returned to Phoenix. I secured a position in an agency that specialized in a wide variety of services for children five years and younger, and their families. My exposure to early intervention in graduate school contributed to my draw to the position. Unfortunately, my first ankle break disrupted my new job within the first couple of months. After a second attempt at the licensing exam, I earned my license to practice as a psychologist in Arizona. With my licensing behind me, I explored and took an opportunity to develop mental-health programs at Head Start. Preschool children with special needs from public schools participated in Head Start. I evaluated the little ones to identify their strengths and needs, critical input into their educational plans. I also began to consult with the Colorado River Indian Tribes Head Start in Parker, Arizona.

It quickly became apparent that these programs needed more professionals who spoke Spanish. One of my very best friends, Ida Vigil, a teacher's aide with whom I taught, helped me bring my Spanish-language skills up to snuff over a period of time. With heightened enthusiasm and extraordinary pride, I could not only communicate in Spanish but also developed an ability to help complete assessments in Spanish and explain results to parents in their first language. Parents thanked me for helping them and their child. Children quickly communicated with me once they realized I spoke Spanish. I gained increased insight and understanding of children and families because I could relate to them and address concerns and provide explanations in Spanish. I could also educate parents in meaningful ways.

During my early post-doctoral years, autism gained increased attention, with new research that strongly called for professionals to diagnose children as early as possible. This research and the clear need for providers inspired me to develop and polish my skills in this area. As my confidence built, I chose to open my private practice. Evaluation of children under the age of ten centered my practice. I targeted this age group because I understood their amazing potential for improvement. Research revealed that the earlier intervention began, the greater the long-term benefits and future were for children. Fortunately, I knew a number of people in the early-childhood community in Phoenix, who opened doors for me and increased referrals to my private practice. To boost my practice, I became a disability examiner for the Social Security Administration. Even more importantly, I invested more time with the Arizona Early Intervention Program (AzEIP), which focuses on children birth to age three. AzEIP continues to dominate my professional work even in outlying rural areas of the state of Arizona. At one point along the way, I decided to see a few private clients for brief therapy.

And the Depression and Surgery Roller Coasters Continued
I required two more laparoscopic surgeries during this time. In 1999, a surgeon removed part of my large intestine due to serious adhesions from endo and the multiple prior surgeries.

My most serious and severe episode of depression disrupted my young private practice, a devastating blow. I had to stop working. My therapist and close friends encouraged me to apply for Social Security Disability status since my future was clouded because of uncertain outcomes related to depression. Taking care of myself took all my energy, and I didn't even do a good job at that. My family moved me back into my parents' home, the house in which I'd grown up. This helped relieve the demands of caring for my home and personal affairs, which were draining me. Though embarrassed at that time, I knew I was safe, loved, and cared for, so I could focus on my physical- and emotional-health needs. This move proved a forerunner for the emergence of my role as a caregiving partner, with my mother, for my ailing, aging father.

CRITICAL HEALTH CHALLENGES
ALONG MY JOURNEY

Depression
Severe depression permeated me, the longest, most pervasive, and debilitating health challenge, one which I continue to traverse. I will spend considerable time discussing my depression in future chapters. Beyond my depression, a brief overview of other

significant health challenges warrants introduction here. I call them unexpected *curveballs* that have relevance and penetrating repercussions throughout my journey with depression.

Endometriosis (endo)

At sixteen years of age, I was diagnosed with endometriosis. This debilitating condition involves the tissue of the lining of the uterus. The tissue leaves the uterus and implants itself in other places in the abdomen. As I noted earlier, I had more than seven surgeries in effort to remove adhesions that formed from the endo, including a hysterectomy. Besides the sheer physical pain created by the endo and adhesions, with each surgery, I knew that the chances of being able to bear a child were dwindling. The well of anguish and gloom grew deeper and deeper, and I felt emptier with each event. I elaborate on the effect of these surgeries in later chapters.

Breast Cancer

I had two different distressing bouts of breast cancer. The first instance required surgical lumpectomy and chemotherapy, followed by estrogen-suppression therapy (Aromatase Inhibitors), ideally to continue for four years. I could not tolerate these drugs and chose to stop this therapy. Seven years later, I received a second diagnosis of breast cancer, with tumors in both breasts; one of the tumors turned out to be a different type of tumor than the initial tumor. This time, I elected to go forward with a bilateral mastectomy.

Clear that a double mastectomy did not necessarily mean I would be totally cured, it was, nevertheless, an action that I could take. Besides, there were benefits for my "hooters," over which boys taunted me in the seventh grade. I would save $100 on bras I needed due to my size! The strain on my back—to the point of spasms—disappeared. More options for clothing sizes and types opened up. Wow! I remained calm and determined to take the necessary steps to have the more radical surgery.

A wide range of emotions is expected with any "Big C" diagnosis. Not *again*. "Why?" was the ever-present question when I encountered difficulties. I feared the unknowns, and I was angry, as I tried to figure out what led to cancer. Was it the hormones I had received at different times? Whom should I be mad at?

My amazing oncologist repeatedly focused my perspective. He treated me as a whole person, not just a patient with cancer. He recognized the potential concerns about the recurrence of depression and willingly collaborated with my other providers. He boosted my confidence as he patiently listened to and regarded me as an active partner. The various choices I had to make would, ultimately, be mine. I used all of the information I'd received and gathered. I pressed onward, with "Spirit" undergirding me, a support I appreciated immensely.

EARLY COPING STRATEGIES

For my overall wellness, I naturally engaged in some activities for as long as I can remember. The forty years of journals I kept to myself built part of the foundation for this book. On their pages, I processed my experiences, recorded my thoughts, and documented private feelings, writings I could not share with others. I questioned the validity of what I thought. Sometimes entries just detail what is going on in my mind, which my writing buddy refers to as a *brain dump*. The writing process delivers innumerable benefits. I have found reflection valuable, regardless of the subjective degree of the pleasantness of an experience. Continued learning bolstered me. The journals also act as a history of events and experiences that provide insights and reminders of how much I attained. Seeds of information from books, magazines, and articles inspired me to think about "Me" and my process in my journals. My thinking alternately expanded with ideas and insights or showed me what might need to be reined in.

Wellness Practices
From early on, in my quest for overall wellness, I exercised in some manner daily, ate carefully to monitor my weight fluctuations, and actively ensured adequate sleep on a nightly basis. My medical challenges and depression persistently affected the essential elements of my general physical health.

MY PERSISTENT SEARCH FOR HELP

I availed myself of traditional types of treatment for depression, such as medications and various forms of mental-health/talk therapy. As I became more and more distraught, my persistent little spirit girl intensified my research, certain there must be something additional to help me. I scrutinized different Eastern wellness practices. I also indulged my inquisitive mind and unearthed potential treatments considered cutting edge for depression.

My despondency left me willing to try just about anything! Perpetual exploration led me to something called Deep Brain Stimulation (DBS), formally under investigation at Emory University in Atlanta, Georgia. Even my closest friends and family thought brain surgery to implant the device was a drastic step, but I was in agony and determined. I did not believe I could feel any worse than I already felt. The requirements for selection to participate in the study included exhaustion of medication treatment, limited therapy progress, and ECT (Electroconvulsive Shock Therapy Treatments), the only criteria I didn't meet to qualify for the study. With apprehension, I endured twenty-six sessions of ECT, without any effect. With that result, I became eligible for the DBS study. I will describe the DBS processes, my experiences, and their important roles as my story unfolds.

CRITICAL LONG-TERM, TRUSTED THERAPEUTIC RELATIONSHIP

The critical role of a long-term, trusted therapeutic relationship and connection with my religion/"Faith"/"God"/"Spirit," were vital to my journey. Dr. Marilyn Kieffer-Andrews, RNP, PhD ("MKA"), psychiatric mental health nurse practitioner, "put up with me" for more than twenty years. In preparation to write, I investigated and discussed the experiences of key people in my life during my deepest episode of depression. I asked Dr. Kieffer-Andrews why she stuck with me when, from my perspective, I was going nowhere. Her reply was that she knew I would weather it, and she just wanted to see me through it. We've sometimes discussed how individuals seek her services when other therapists had given up on them or said there wasn't anything else they could do to assist them.

She created and built a deeply therapeutic relationship with me that provided a compassionate foundation. She never treated me as less of a person through the process. On no occasion did she tell me what to do or how to do it, unless I requested. She posed difficult questions and offered support in a vast number of ways. She advocated, respected, and stood with me, no matter what happened. As a lifeline, Dr. Marilyn Kieffer-Andrews literally kept me *alive* any number of times. I came to trust her and felt safe to express whatever I thought or felt. She appropriately shared copious resources from what she and other clients found helpful. I believe this enhanced our work together.

In my most desperate of moments, she listened, understood, and guided me to qualities and the wealth she knew I held within. She reminded me I still had a lot to live for and reassured me that I had the necessary patience to weather the challenges. She never discounted or dismissed the direness of a moment; rather, she brought me relief with her presence and acknowledgment of the seriousness of my difficulty. The therapeutic relationship with Dr. Kieffer-Andrews extended way beyond "just talking." She did not have a magic wand, but she fashioned a treasured cocoon for me to incubate and renew my willingness to endure.

The presence of a completely objective, supportive person to talk about *anything* is one gift of therapy. A therapeutic relationship between a therapist and a client can be so many different things. Someone to depend on. Someone to share scary questions and thoughts with, knowing I will not be judged.

Ideas raced through my mind. I did not understand them, and I lacked the ability to slow down and let them go. I needed help. I *knew* it was easy to get carried away with fears of "what-ifs." Despite my awareness or insight into the issues, I needed perspective about some things I was experiencing. I needed assistance to help reframe my thinking, especially my interpretation of the meaning of my problems. All of these things could be addressed in the therapeutic safety net Dr. Kieffer-Andrews and

I built together, in which I could be vulnerable and unafraid of what I would say or do. As time went on, I realized the depth and breadth of Dr. Kieffer-Andrews' vital role and contributions in my life. I named her my "Perspective Angel." She is a trusted guide on this, my depression journey.

✦ ✦ ✦

MY SUBJECTIVE EXPERIENCE
OF DEPRESSION

Throughout this book, I explore how my experience of depression impacted my connected world and me. It is important to note that 2020 prevalence statistics from the National Institute for Mental Health reported: *"An estimated 21.0 million adults in the United States had at least one major depressive episode. This number represented 8.4% of all US adults."* I am not alone on this trek.

I briefly describe "My Subjective Experience of Depression." Before I get started, here are a few basics about depression, from my viewpoint, to establish some background to that experience. I have come to embrace specific perspectives about depression in general and my depression in particular.

First, I believe there is a difference between depression related to common and extraordinary life events and depression that is a debilitating physical illness. I believe my biology is largely responsible for the depression I have experienced during my life—not that I'm naming that as a scapegoat, apology, or reason to accept depression. That belief allows me to avoid the idea that my body betrays me or that I bear some responsibility for my mental state. Instead, I am determined to embrace who I am—all of me, including depression! If I could not get rid of my depression, I wanted to acknowledge its presence. In turn, that allowed me to accept and integrate it more fully into my knowing of me.

I have come to appreciate that depression colors my reactions, insights, and understandings of situations, something I keep in the foreground to help me process experiences. I know there are people who have more serious depression and don't recognize it, and there are others who don't know what to do or have not yet decided to do something about it. This statement reflects the challenges many face and reminds me that I am not the first or the only person with severe depression. I previously mentioned several *curveballs* that socked me in the gut. These intrusions dramatically added to the already-complex and difficult challenges I faced due to depression. Through all of this, I decided I would not succumb to my depression. After I worked hard to overcome it, I realized I needed to integrate this medical condition as part of me to *feel* whole. This is the story I want to tell. I offer you next my "subjective experience of depression."

DEFINING MY DEPRESSION

Throughout the book, I frequently make reference to "not feeling anything" or "having no emotions" in one form or another. The one emotion that you hear over and over is *helpless, hopeless despair*. This gut *feeling* pushed out any other possible emotions or feelings for long periods of time.

Excerpts from an interview with the very patient and insightful Helen Mayberg, MD, the lead investigator for a clinical trial of (DBS) Deep Brain Stimulation in which I am a participant, provide some insights. She made similar important comments in an article that articulates the experience of depression:

> Most people think of depression as a deficit state, Mayberg says. "You're low, you're negative." But in fact, talk to a depressed person, and you have this bizarre combination of numbness and what William Styron called "an active anguish." "A sort of psychical neuralgia," he said, "wholly unknown to healthy life." You're numb, but you hurt. You can't think, but you are in pain. *Now, how does your psyche hurt? What a weird choice of words. But it's not an arbitrary choice. It's there. These people are feeling a particular, indescribable kind of pain. One patient noted what she most wanted was* "to hold her children and feel it." *Dr. Mayberg went on to note,*
>
> *"For those of us who've never known depression, recognizing it may help us see depression not as a dead absence but as a live affliction."*

When I returned to Phoenix during the clinical trial for Christmas celebrations, the depression overwrote the emotions I expected to *feel* (e.g., excited, happy, spine tingling, and feeling loved). Their absence while in Phoenix and when I returned to Atlanta only intensified the overwhelming *helpless, hopeless despair* that enveloped me.

Dr. Edwin Schneidman, who has been a pioneer in the study of suicide, talks about depression as a "psychache" that defies definition. But he goes on to describe psychache: "It is a stripping of one's humanity, character, being, and any meaning in life, which is hard to describe. There is a feeling of desperation that does not seem able to be touched by any 'words,' advice, writing, or thoughts, to move it in another direction. It is a pervasive feeling that is physiological as well as psychological. Sometimes experienced as pain/aching from head to toe in the body."

Over the course of my life, a torrent of struggles and roller-coaster rides—from peace and appreciation of life to wanting to end my life—prevailed. Some of my words:

I often thought I was in a tunnel without a light at the end, constrained, stuck, and unable to move forward.

I meandered aimlessly. I wished something would sweep over me and make me *feel* better. Doubt filled me to such a degree that I could not hold on to who I was, my gifts, my potential, or a sense of future. I wrestled constantly to find words that could effectively characterize or express how I felt. My desperation. My *helpless, hopeless despair.* My emptiness. My lack of desire for my life to continue. Worry about the judgment of what I might say or how I said it. I never found words to sufficiently represent my experience.

After many years of varied diagnoses that never fit, my team of providers finally agreed to diagnose me with *treatment-resistant depression* (TRD). It's clear that the professional fields do not agree on a definition of TRD. The primary indication that distinguishes TRD from other types of depression is that the person shows a lack of, or no response to, any treatment or combination of treatments over months or years. This may include antidepressants, anti-anxiety drugs, counseling, psychotherapy, electroconvulsive therapy, dietary changes, holistic approaches, meditation, and acupuncture. Individuals with TRD are at very high risk of suicide and often develop other problems as a result of the TRD. They also have a high relapse rate.

Alternatively, some providers use "Bipolar II" to describe it. I will describe the myriad treatments I received in more detail in later chapters. The core truth here remains that the current *medical* definition of depression does not get to the heart of the saga of TRD. Attempts at a scientific definition miss the deeply emotional, spiritual, and physical effects of depression. These impact and have a direct effect on my social life, day-to-day self-care, and every aspect of my *whole life*.

People who genuinely wanted to help me tried to get me to use *positive affirmations* or listen to motivational individuals they found inspirational. I suspect some denied my state or were frustrated and upset by my behavior. Others seemed to deny it because they did not understand. Most people only wanted me to feel better and turned to sharing personal sources of encouragement and passion. I realized the efforts were always well intended, but, deep down inside, I felt disbelieved and disregarded. I am certain that, unless someone traveled the road of such severe depression incapacitation, they would be unable to empathize no matter how or what I expressed. For my own sanity, I privately acknowledged their efforts and focused on their loving and caring intentions, despite my immediate internal reaction to feel dismissed.

A LOOK AT THE COURSE OF MY DEPRESSION

As I scan the history of depression in my life, I recall that I received brief services at age ten, after the school counselor told

Mom I seemed sad and struggling with something. This episode also marked my first recollections of feeling depressed. Our family move from Detroit, Michigan, to Phoenix, Arizona, cut these services short.

I mined my journals in excess of forty years that tell my story of depression as it has occurred over time. My brain stripped me bare of "Me." Constant questions threw me off balance. Where is "God?" Unimaginably troublesome days. Bed, my escape. Yet I embraced each day as a new one. I found many consistent themes in entries, though the actual words I used varied. I believe the following journal entry reflects a *big-picture* theme that repeated:

> *Today I am many days and months into an episode of depression. What does that mean? I was mowed down by a disorder of my brain that stripped me bare of all that I was and all that I knew. It has left me with many questions and few answers. I take each day as a new one. Knowing that I will walk, eat, drink, sleep, journal, and, some days have an appointment. I am very focused on what I don't have and remain stymied by the aftermath and where my life is headed. I feel if I had a connection with God, I would have hope and faith in myself and the future. My days creep by, and I find myself anxiously waiting for the time to go to bed. It is an escape. Many questions run through my mind all of the time.*

During the 1970s, fear and anxiety surged through me. Throughout high school, absorbed in my studies and activities at church and school, I developed a laser focus on specific, attainable goals that temporarily helped me avoid my depression.

My year in Germany following high school presented me a buffet of opportunities that invigorated me and allowed me to be and *feel* independent. The precocious, spirited child in me shined and opened many windows to my "Soul." I tasted a sense of freedom and full responsibility for myself. The sometimes-scary odyssey ultimately freed me to be myself! However, a quite dramatic change in me became apparent upon my return from Germany.

Stark evidence of this remarkable change became clear when I returned to the States. Withdrawn emotionally, I did not respond in any manner when my mother hugged me. It was like I didn't know how to respond. I had just come from a year immersed in German culture, where people rarely displayed physical affection.

My re-entry into my native culture was filled with feeling like an alien, with no idea where to head, what I could do with my life, or even how I would survive. I felt slammed by a sledgehammer of unknowns about myself that flattened me to the ground. Immobilized, I felt frozen, without a thaw in view. My clearly compromised state and vague physical symptoms concerned me. I requested counsel with my family physician. I explained. I did not want to be around other people, due to fear that those who had been the center of my universe would belittle the "changed me." I lived in a trance state, disconnected from the world surrounding me. Worthlessness, incompetence, and isolation consumed me. I feared new friendships and buried myself in doubt. Perplexed about what was happening to me and why, and consistent with my excessive sense of responsibility, I assumed the confusion and decline were my own fault.

The family doctor made a formal diagnosis of depression. He prescribed medication and therapy to treat my mood and anxiety. He contacted my parents to share his concerns, to which my mother replied she did not think there was anything wrong. In spite of my mother's reaction, the family physician reaffirmed his diagnosis to me! With his determination, the winding paths of serious treatment for depression began.

After the physician's diagnosis, and even with the start of medication, my ability to cope with daily demands continued to crumble. I still felt challenged about what to do in the transition time of re-immersion into life in my culture. My persistent, overdone sense of responsibility left me bereft and pulled me further under as I judged myself. I sought God's help.

6.3.2011: "God"—I didn't choose depression. It came into my life and doesn't seem to want to leave. I could certainly do without it. Help me out of this deep, dark place that has and continues to rob me of so much. I choose life with meaning, purpose, and direction, if only for the next few minutes, though I would love to see the bigger picture.

I found periodic moments of short-lived respite from my depression, though, most of the time, I felt a shroud of suffering enveloping me. The occasional instances of possibility flashed before me but never lasted long. I tried to hold on to those precious glimpses through journal entries and multimedia pieces of art I created as a visual reminder that the potential for change existed. I placed these treasures in constant view as keepsakes to continually embrace. On some level, I almost always carried an inkling that hope and possibility would return to me.

TIME TO GET MOVING ON

I eventually found my way out of this deep depression through junior college. I completed my Bachelor's degree in special education in the 1970s. I needed to commute to college for hours every day and work part-time as well. My busy schedule suppressed the depression and allowed me to successfully navigate this time. After I earned my degree and started to teach, depression again overcame me and required intense attention to my emotional needs. Despite my success professionally, I dove deeper and deeper into despair. I also had my initial surgery for endometriosis during this time, which also drained me. These challenges deprived me of critical sleep and my efforts to meet my dietary needs. My work, so important to me, suffered as my ability to attend and concentrate declined.

On my good days, my students filled me with wonder and excitement to figure out how to help them with their challenges. I saw each child as a distinct puzzle to solve. With my insight and understanding, I looked for opportunities to support and encourage individual children to succeed. Given these beautiful children, despair made no sense to me. I loved my fulfilling job; I owned my home and had secured my financial well-being. Slowly, however, I descended into ruin. Even things I enjoyed seemed unreachable. Again, disorientation filled my thoughts. My efforts to get *help* led me to therapy with Dr. Mathilda Canter, PhD, Psychologist. I hoped to grab hold of myself and make myself feel better. After early therapy sessions, I frequently ended up with my body collapsed in a puddle of tears in the stairwell. During these initial days, I cried myself out until I could regroup to drive myself home.

Despite work in therapy, my plunge continued. My very wise and experienced therapist introduced the idea to bring a psychiatrist into my care to assess my need for some medication. She hoped medication might make it easier for me to address the multitude of issues I faced. Even though I had taken psychiatric medicines before for a period of time, this solution frightened me—that I needed medication again. Could I really be that bad off? Could I possibly be helped? Why was this happening to me?

The psychiatrist, Dr. Harris Murley, an amazing person, approached me with understanding. He thoughtfully related that he really wanted me to understand what was going on in my brain with my neurotransmitters. With his care and explanation, he initiated the process to help me understand that I had a real physical illness—not unlike diabetes—over which I had virtually no control. Nevertheless, I soon experienced the ups and downs that the pursuit of optimal medication management of my depression required. I *had* to practice impossible patience and wait for the medications to take effect. I kept my diagnosis and medication a secret, within the circle of me, my therapist, and my psychiatrist. There was no way I felt safe, at that time, to tell anyone about being on psychiatric medications.

On into the 1980s with Dr. Canter, I endured ongoing talk and medication therapies, even though I still felt limited relief. I periodically had a few good days, but the overwhelming *helpless, hopeless despair* dominated. Ankle surgeries with considerable rehabilitation times stood as barriers to my efforts to get the physical exercise I needed to help my mood, energy, and persistence. I continued to teach. My enthusiasm for teaching took hits, due to my compromised mental and physical states. I had days when I had to call in sick, because I could not get out of bed or function. Despite my mental state, my curiosity helped me direct my attention to seek out and pursue going back to graduate school. I hoped another direction would let me provide more assistance to the children and families I loved.

THE ENDLESS ODYSSEY CONTINUES

Once in Tucson at the U of A to pursue my Master's degree, a psychiatrist monitored my psychiatric medications, though he did not provide actual ongoing therapy. During this period, I turned my concentration and attention to completing my degree. I do not recall why, but I stopped taking antidepressants toward the end of this time, before I transitioned to my Doctoral program in Flagstaff, Arizona, in 1986.

I'm grateful that my anticipation for the novelty and potential of further graduate work at NAU motivated and excited me. Unfortunately, within a couple of months of being in the program, the old, familiar state of depression raised its ugly head once more. I recognized the all-too-familiar *helpless, hopeless despair* coming on. Severe fatigue, immobility, and unbelievable effort to complete basic daily life tasks occupied my days. Fear struck mc hard.

My psychologist from Phoenix connected me with the director of the NAU Counseling Center, who agreed to see me for individual therapy. He embraced, supported, and integrated my spiritual life as inseparable from the process of my therapy, a first for me. In spite of my mood, my connection with "God" increased and reawakened that vital part of me. Dr. James Frederick helped me review uncharted aspects of my life, aware that, most likely, there were personal issues contributing to the intensity of the depression. He believed in me and acknowledged my strengths and gifts in efforts to support me, and potentially improve my pessimistic perspective.

Endometriosis continued to interrupt my life, with surgeries required to address my problems with adhesions. I felt exhausted with every surgery, and I became clearer that it had become unlikely that I could bring a child into the world. I knew in the back of my mind that the ability to have a child had progressively faded away. I cried inside as I sat in the gynecologist's office surrounded by pregnant women with three or four little ones running around.

Finally, I had the inevitable hysterectomy; the severity and the profuseness of the adhesions precluded further laparoscopic surgery to treat me. My depression amplified with each surgery, as my hopes for bearing a child dimmed. I needed more care and help from others for my surgical convalescence, which I didn't like to request. The hysterectomy required me to take a semester off from graduate coursework for physical and emotional recovery.

That I completed my Doctoral degree in the early 1990s can only be seen as miraculous, given the ever-present depression. I persisted, determined to be a licensed psychologist despite the continuous, sapping battle with depression. I found a gratifying job upon receipt of my doctorate, with a lot of real-world and stimulating responsibility. I developed mental-health programs and services for Head Start. The opportunity to make a significant difference in the lives of many children, families, and staff energized me intellectually. I sat for licensure and qualified as a licensed psychologist in Arizona. I achieved it against all odds. I coasted on my accomplishment for a little while, but, before long, my depression surfaced again.

MORE COMPLICATING FACTORS

The well-established progression of my depression incapacitation marched ahead, and my body, mind, and "Spirit" could not keep up, despite my achievements in the 1990s. A broken ankle further complicated things. It required me not to bear weight for weeks. That left me further dependent on others, without any way to exercise. I tried to focus on losing weight, which proved difficult, given my immobilization. With time, I sought out a dietician, who accurately noted my significant depression. With my gratitude to this day, this dietician referred me to Marilyn Kieffer-Andrews, PhD, RNP, Psychiatric Mental Health Nurse Practitioner, who would become my "Perspective Angel."

Together with Dr. Kieffer-Andrews, we endured treks through trials of various medications. Each required several weeks to take effect, in order to know whether the medication would make any difference. Getting through each day strained me. My feelings of incapacitation continued to expand, and *hopeless, helpless despair* prevailed.

> *4.12.1997: Maybe this is about breaking the crystal of my life into many pieces that will eventually be rejoined in a whole new configuration. What I lose depends on what or how I define my identity. It is like when one weaves. It can appear as a mishmash, without complements, integrity, or beauty. Even when you use exactly the same materials, the outcome can be something quite different. Actually, the materials may shift and change a bit, but the new construction exceeds all expectations.*

With this insight circling for a period of time, I tried to shift my self-concept and my current perception of my abilities and strengths. I came to view chaos as a necessary element, required to regroup and embrace the unknown. Options and refreshed possibilities might be available. My creativity briefly surfaced amid my daily meditations and devotions, and I had an important insight.

> *5.27.1997: An image to work with—a dried-flower arrangement that holds intricacies, hidden aspects, and wondrous construction. Many little facets peeked out and reassured me there is richness within me as well. This is another adventure with many unknowns, and yet part of those unknowns are sure to be rich.*

What an amazing realization in the midst of the madness and unpredictable gyrations in my depression. I cherished such moments and worked to hold on to them in my own best interest. Alas, the depression, had, unfortunately, not gone away; rather, it briefly overshadowed my insight. I continued to attend to my daily wants and needs. As I prepared for a private retreat to nurture my "Soul," I envisioned and wrote the following:

> *6.21.1997: There is a waterfall deep within me that is waiting to flow. The deep, dark pool holds many treasures. It is only by trusting the process and entering the unknown that I will find the hidden treasures.*

REVIVED DETERMINATION

Filled with a renewed sense of confidence following my retreat, I figured out that I wanted to see all life events as part of a bigger picture that would tell a story that embraced all of the ups and downs of my existence. Even when depression seemed all-consuming, this concept helped me. I gathered ideas to help myself cope better day-to-day. Of greater importance, I started to invite and integrate the overwhelming depression into my whole being. I shifted my attention to consider the gifts of depression I'd gained, like practicing patience. I *still* felt *helpless, hopeless despair*, but I saw it on a continuum, which seemed to help me keep my depression in perspective versus solely as a view of me being torn to shreds.

In this time, I decided to increase the amount of time I dedicated to meditation. With this increase, I found I experienced the possibility of allowing panic to float through me when I meditated, no matter where I meditated. This freed up space for chances that creativity, inspiration, and growth could also be part of the parade of thoughts in my mind. The mood of depression did not end with more meditation, but it shifted my attention to recall the healing I was doing for children and families in my professional life. I reminded myself to hold on to the role of healer as a predominant part of my being. I came to see that the pain of depression could be a teacher. I could derive benefit from my painful experiences, even if I could not articulate it.

Mother Teresa shared, "There is no way of describing what you feel . . . It's just total conviction that you have done the right thing and you're in the right place."

I held Mother Teresa's words close. I worked hard to hang on to even the smallest awareness of change, to help me move toward a healthier space of mind. Without my conviction to stay aware of change—even snippets of change—I had no reason in the world to keep striving to wind my way out of my exhaustion of depression. Despite my insights into depression, I faced more problems with the endometriosis adhesions. There were physical limitations, physical pain, exhaustion, the uncertainty of the outcome, and necessary vigilance to my physical well-being. All of this led me to pull in emotionally, quite literally to survive!

These adjustments did not make my depression disappear, but how I thought about depression and its impact on my life changed. I actively let myself slide into the present moment of whatever I was experiencing. I found that, when I stayed in the here and now, I felt at least temporary relief from depression's undertow. Brief moments of relief from the devastation effectively reduced the actual amount of time I felt drawn into despair daily.

The 2000s started off with one more chapter in the endo story. I did not feel well at all. I experienced physical pain and physical problems because my intestines were sitting in a tangled mess in the bottom of my pelvis, immobilized. The resurgence of unbelievable pain caught me off guard, and another surgery became the only solution. I required surgery to resect my large intestines (cut out a portion of the intestine and sew it back together). Surgery meant time off of work—*again*—and the need to be with my parents for help during recuperation. Embarrassment raged through me as, once again, I had to move home with Mom and Dad for a while. Needless to say, my mood took another hit in the midst of the extended healing process. Hormones were prescribed to try to prevent adhesion recurrence, which added to the continued convoluted mystery of regulation of medication for my depression.

More than ever, I needed to pay attention to messages from my body about adequate rest. I learned anew the importance of limiting my commitments, refocusing on my exercise, eating, sleeping, meditating, and reflecting. I strove to regain my bearings and explored new ways to define my identity.

As I recovered, I saw the fury of anxiety erupt out of what seemed like nowhere. Physically, the sensation of anxiety surged through me like I had my finger in an electric socket and created static that drowned out any connection with reality. No matter what, I seemed unable to do anything or to feel competent in any manner. My world spun out of control, fear escalated, and old, familiar self-deprecation ruled. My search for my "Soul" intensified through reading, writing, and meditating, hopefully, to achieve minuscule spurts of relief. I knew I could not make all of the pain go away, but even a few minutes for healing reflection helped. Incredulous, I found myself in this awful place again, which added to my feelings of being overwhelmed.

Connection to my "Soul" and "Spirit" appeared like it could become a refuge from the dark cloud. I recalled previous times in my life when I'd immersed myself in my "Soul" and "Spirit" and felt embraced in a cocoon. I craved that special space. I still wanted to know why this dreadful place was hounding me again, when I tried so hard daily to keep my emotional head above water.

There came a time when I railed against my depression with anger. My incapacitation made everything seem harder and led me to withdraw. My isolation, in turn, limited how I functioned, turned me in on myself, buried me in malaise, and scattered my thinking. I still thought I should be able to control it, minimize it, or keep it at bay. *Not!!!* My acute awareness of society's lack of acceptance of depression as a real illness further frustrated me and restricted my ability to talk with others about how I felt.

MY DEEPEST EPISODE OF DEPRESSION

My tumble into my worst episode of depression lacked an obvious trigger by any single event or challenge in my life. I worked hard and persistently to keep my body and "Soul" together, carry out daily responsibilities, and be positive, but it simply did not matter. My confidence melted away. My self-perception of capability with many aspects of daily life evaporated. I was caught in a tornado whirling faster and faster, which generated profound obliviousness and yanked me into obscurity. The state of *helpless, hopeless despair* succeeded. It barricaded any way out of my misery.

> *In the past it (depression) had taught me lessons, unleashed creativity, and brought me into a deeper relationship with God, but none of that was present now.*

Indifference and lack of emotion, besides *helpless, hopeless despair*, grew and overcame me. I tried to ignore or deny the presence of my psychological state again. But it had me. "God" seemed gone again, furthering my isolation, as the air in the bubble of my life escaped. I needed help, and a change of medication was likely. I sought out a restroom stall anywhere, as a place to close out the rest of the world and achieve total silence for a little while. The ruler I created to help me figure out what I needed in a given time involved basic questions. Would an activity I selected improve my depression and overall wellness? Did an activity give me enough time to rest? Would the activity make money to pay my bills? My deep depression left me in a place where I had to seriously consider caring for myself financially, and I did not want financial survival to rule my life.

As long as I was able to stay at work, I was better able to pull out of myself and stave off the effects of depression and fear temporarily. In reality, when the seriousness of my depression increased, I could not work. I couldn't focus. My ability to organize things crashed. I found conversations difficult, and eventually, my ability to interact with others in almost any manner disappeared. In fact, I lost sight of the complexities I faced, each with its own demands of personal care and energy. As these factors multiplied exponentially, my ability to function day-to-day collapsed. As my chaos increased, making daily decisions seemed impossible. I needed a lot of help with perspective. Most importantly, I required assistance to help me focus my attention and to encourage me to realistically consider what I could do, not what I thought I *should* do!

Pervasive exhaustion from fighting depression reigned. I did not care about myself or others, which began to show in my grooming, attentiveness, and engagement. I cried, without relief or a sense of release. Nausea never abated. Any proactive actions from my past experiences were inaccessible. Life reduced to mere survival, and persistence, even at that level, seemed impossible. I wondered if depression would shorten my life. I initiated an email thread for those closest to me, to share my emotional status because I could no longer tell individuals over and over again about my despair. I quit driving due to lack of concentration and distraction from the torrent of thoughts in my head. Slowly and reluctantly, I wrote my parents a letter about my experience of depression and how it affected me. I needed them to stop asking me, "Are you feeling better?" or telling me I sounded better. These comments resulted in guilty feelings because I could not say, "Yes, I am better."

Input and support from my closest colleagues and therapist exposed my inability to successfully engage in my precious work with children. A treasured colleague reviewed videotape of a session with a child, and it clearly revealed that I'd missed key abilities of the child that would ordinarily jump out at me during a child's evaluation. The time came for me to send in paperwork to put my psychologist's license on a temporary hold. Would I ever be able to practice as a psychologist again? Would I be able to make enough money to support myself? Was there any hope I could get better? Yet another of many preludes into the ever-present descent into total darkness. The question "Can I afford to take time off?" became the knowledge that I could "not afford *not* to take downtime" if I hoped to get well and stay alive.

Dr. Kieffer-Andrews, my therapist, felt it critical to call a family meeting to help them better understand my current state. While physically present, I was ashamed of my predicament. Marilyn fielded questions from my family members that did not have answers. Her message encouraged them to listen to me, not expect anything of me for a while, and to love me.

Favorite music, chanting, television, poetry, reading, eating, sleeping—none of them made any difference. Overwhelmed within the full throttle of anxiety, I talked myself out of suicide. Many medication changes followed. I tried previous strategies from the past that had helped my obliviousness, but they made absolutely no difference!!!

I quit working and applied for Social Security Disability with the help of my therapist. It would provide a little income for me to subsist on, although I questioned if I would ever be independent again. Shortly after that decision, my family moved me out of my own home, and into the home of my parents, so that they could care for me. What was left in life? Was there any reason to want to go on living? I had to rest, exercise, pray, meditate, and journal when I could muster the energy.

At the time of this most severe episode, I frantically combed the internet for additional options for treatment. I learned about the study of Deep Brain Stimulation (DBS) for treatment-resistant depression at Emory University in Atlanta, Georgia. Selection for participation in the DBS study involved a detailed application process and medical review for exhaustive history of medications, degree of progress in therapy, and ECT (Electroconvulsive Therapy) treatments. ECT sounded drastic in my mind and begged the question of whether I should just give up. With trepidation, I embarked on a series of twenty-six ECT treatments. Following the completion of the ECT without any results, they selected me as a patient for the DBS study.

Toward the end of that year, I had Chinese food with family, and my fortune cookie read, *"Your infinite capacity for patience will be rewarded sooner or later."* Maybe hope existed for me and a return to health. This belief helped me persist and continue.

There continued to be a lack of improvement, even with all of the different strategies I explored. As a result of acceptance into the DBS study, I essentially moved to Atlanta, Georgia, for six months to prepare to have surgery to implant the DBS. My medications and therapy did not require a change to become a participant in the study. I continued therapy by long-distance phone with my therapist.

I was skeptical even as I had the surgery. I wondered whether it was possible that anything else would decrease the impact of the depression. I stayed in a holding pattern, took daily walks, journaled, and crocheted in between appointments at the Emory Medical Center. It was a very difficult time for me, since I had to work with the psychiatrists in Atlanta as part of the study, and the fit proved not to be a good one. I did not feel that communication with the initial psychiatrist meshed with who I was and what I needed at that point. This felt unfortunate and contributed to my reluctance to share my thoughts and feelings with him. I would not be aware of any benefits of the DBS for months or maybe years after the surgery.

One of the psychiatrists in Atlanta expressed concern that I might be getting in my own way because of constant thought about trying to help myself. On a different occasion, a doctor in Atlanta told me he did not believe I could *think my way out of depression.* To refocus my attention and reduce repetitive thoughts about my depression, I began to pay attention and reflect on the changes in thinking documented in my journals. The notion of writing a book crystalized, and I began in earnest to review, reflect, and organize my thoughts about my possible exodus from depression.

During this ongoing time in Atlanta, I asked the question, "How can I *feel* whole, with my woundedness?" Did it make any sense to think I could feel whole when so many things had happened to me that compromised my wholeness? I looked for what was marvelous in my life. I searched to recall the gifts of my life even as I was cloaked in depression. Blessings abounded: a loving and supportive family; a safety net of friends who listened and checked on me; my contributions to many as a healer; copious creativity; an undeniable "Spirit" of persistence; openness to getting and accepting help; my faithfulness to commitments; my reliability; and, of course, my ever-present "Perspective Angel."

I wanted to make something out of the suffering. I put energy into a new and different direction.

A CURVEBALL I COULD NOT AVOID

A few years later (2011), as I continued to receive support from Atlanta in my DBS journey, a routine mammogram found a tumor, which required further studies and biopsy in order to diagnose breast cancer. Wow! What a curveball to hit me in the middle of my efforts to move my perception of depression into a different direction!

> *4.27.2011: Many old questions came pouring back. Why must I endure something new? I have endured enough with the depression, and it is not moving out of my life with any significance. Where am I? Is this all just a nightmare that will pass? It is all just questions and, of course, "Why me?" is in there among them. There is no way to predict what treatment I might need. Oh, this is all absurd. There is nothing I can do about it. I can remind myself not to get ahead of myself, and to not bring on stress that I don't need to bring on. Enough already.*

(Yes, I was still depressed!) I did not shed any tears or experience reactions to the biopsies, blood work, further mammograms, and a plan for surgery. Not even one emotion or feeling different from the *helpless, hopeless despair.*

Depression with a cancer diagnosis and treatment affects most people at least for a while, but with treatment-resistant depression, the dangers for a further dive in my depression were magnified. To the surprise of many around me, concerns about cancer surgery and chemotherapy were no big deal compared to the potential of another awful episode of depression. The treatable status of Stage I cancer brought hope that I would survive. The knowledge of my vulnerability to depression and additional episodes dwarfed my optimism.

In 2011, I endured a lumpectomy to remove the cancerous tumor, followed by chemotherapy, which necessitated a focus on my physical needs and healing. I still lived in my parents' home, since I needed ongoing care. I thought maybe this physical concentration on healing offered me an opportunity to at least push depression out of the way briefly. That did not happen. I acknowledged to myself the multitude of physical problems I'd already faced and conquered admirably. The seemingly impossible load of depression lightened gradually from the DBS, and I was labeled a "late responder" by the doctors in Atlanta. Yet, I still felt buried and lost in depression, without any direction. I was enveloped in disbelief that the despair could still exist, given all of the things I had done—and continued to do—to improve the quality of my life.

The year 2018 brought a second diagnosis of breast cancer that left me in another cloud of incredulity. Depression always loomed in the shadows, ready to strike. With the second bout of cancer, I knew I could not endure another round of chemotherapy and years of mammograms and biopsies. My fear of new levels of depression magnified. While it was clear to me that a double mastectomy did not necessarily mean I would be totally cured, it was at least some action I could take—something over which I had control. Taking action let me feel like I was *doing something about* the cancer! Wow! Twisted as that may seem, this view dampened my tendency to catastrophize about cancer and allowed me to make necessary preparations for the double mastectomy.

Amidst my meditation and contemplation, I created moments of peace in the sea of depression. Intellectually, I experienced a spaciousness filled with possibilities and tried to keep focus on positive outcomes. I banished guilt about asking my sister to take care of Mom while I recovered from my second surgery. I withstood profound emptiness. My emerging and changing perspective on depression let me view this emptiness as an opportunity to listen, wait, and see what would emerge to fill the emptiness. To reduce my stress, I adopted the idea to let go of unhealthy expectations about the end of depression. A focus on staying present in the moment replaced the dirge of depressing thoughts in bits and pieces and reduced the length of moments caught in depression. The breathing part of meditation also supported my inhalation of the "Spirit" of Life, a reconnection with "God."

ANOTHER CURVEBALL TAKES ITS TOLL

In the meantime, my Father's health deteriorated. I still remained with my parents, who had so willingly welcomed me back into their home and cared for me. I knew it was my turn to help my mother with his care. One would think that looming task might dominate my thoughts, but the depression overwhelmed every other thought! I attempted, without success, to convince myself that I *should* feel grateful for all my parents' efforts and that now it was my turn to help them. The physical and emotional demands to support my mother in caregiving took their toll on me, despite the continuation of therapy and medication to treat the depression. My personal financial independence and survival preoccupied me. How could I survive without an income-earning job? Social Security Disability would not pay all of my basic bills.

In spite of my caregiving responsibilities, I began efforts to inch my way back into my work as a psychologist. I observed my colleague, and he encouraged and mentored me. Even as I re-entered the work I loved, I faced relearning and refreshing my professional skills, as well as rebuilding my confidence. My stamina in short supply, I restricted work periods to a couple of hours at a time while I tested my concentration. Regardless of ongoing, repeated waves of depression, I continued to increase the time I spent at work, knowing that full-time work was absolutely not a possibility. I was much too fragile. To this day, I require daily naps or rest periods to be able to get a few more things done at night.

Throughout the development of my increased capacity to work, I continued to cycle through episodes of depression year after year, sometimes a couple of times a year. Fortunately, none of those periods of depression reached the gravity of the worst episode, but they were still frequent. Disbelief initially strikes when I feel an episode coming on. In light of my history with depression, one would think I would be better able to cope with depression. In some ways, I held onto the familiarity of depression and felt I would get through another bout. On the other hand, this insight did not decrease or minimize the experience of *helpless, hopeless despair*. When a pall started to consume me, it was time to make sure I took my medication, got enough sleep, meditated, exercised, ate well, and continued to journal. I know all too well I have to focus on myself, listen to my body, prioritize, back off of some engagements, and be aware of the amount of work I accept. The alternative is to completely go into a shell and disengage from everything and everyone—even such disassociation does not help me. I live with depression, as an ever-present condition. I maintain my sanity by acceptance of depression as a part of my life and determination not to succumb to it.

AND THEN THERE WAS FEAR

Fear is perhaps one of the greatest challenges I have faced at different times throughout this trek. It became part and parcel of these cyclic dives into depression. I wondered if I would become suicidal again. Other times when it raised its head, I felt *out of control* or overwhelmed and concerned that my depression would lead me down into the deep, dark hole of emotional anguish. My "Perspective Mentors" helped me for such a long period of time that they recognized when the irrational *What if* . . . signaled the probable return of depression. I'd become hypervigilant about feeling down and fearful, wondering whether the feeling is the beginning of an actual depressive episode. My degree of an entrenched fear of the return of depression became most obvious with my diagnoses of breast cancer. I knew the chances that my depression would raise its dreadful head multiplied with such a physical threat. The fear that depression might return grabbed my attention and energy more than the notion of having cancer. Often, in the throes of fear, I would wonder, "Is there a God?" "Where are my 'Soul' and 'Spirit'?" or "Where is 'God'?"

Much of the time, I was plagued with a kind of stationary inertia and felt like I had a boulder inside my gut that kept me from moving on. One journal entry follows my line of thinking as I grappled with having a *disabled* mind:

11.12.2008: On Sunday, I watched one of my favorite programs, Extreme Makeover Home Edition. I am again struck by how physical disabilities are the recipients of deserving families and services. Here I sit, disabled by a mind that has different ideas than I want or wish. Somehow, the physical disabilities are present, but so are supports. Mine is a physical disability, but those of us with mental illness are physically ill and unable to work and live life to its fullest potential. What is the bridge between me and those whose brains can heal and become more functional, happy members of society with the will to live and an honorable purpose as well?

Yes, many fears live inside depression, but the prospects of people finding out about my mental illness encompassed and further exacerbated related fears. Will society judge me? Will people see me as somehow less of a person? Will my illness, when revealed, outrightly isolate me from the rest of the world?

THE QUANDARY OF DEVOTION

Caregiving for my Father was hard and took me through wide ranges of feelings. He finally died of his congestive heart failure, in hospice. On that day, my mother and I realized what relief we felt. We had cared for him for so many years; we knew he was now at peace. We needed time to recover from the sheer physical and emotional exhaustion we seemed unaware of until he passed.

At the time of his passing, I had begun to emerge from the most extended depressive episode. His death plunged me into new demands and responsibilities, which included: management of my parents' finances and emotional support to my mother. On top of these issues, Mom fell and seriously broke her wrist, which required surgery and immobilization of her dominant, left hand. To add to the chaos, we bought a townhouse, cleared out the house we had lived in for more than fifty years, and moved. She had previously declared that she did not want ever to live alone. The physical and emotional reality of her statement hit me hard. My sisters and I had promised Dad that we would not leave Mom alone, and I was the one to move in with her. I was still on Social Security Disability and limited as to how much income I could make, and, so, I also needed some financial support. Consistent with my ongoing experience of depression, I rose to the occasion. While this responsibility seemed to briefly push the depression aside, eventually I suffered consequences of the temporary diversion with a progression of depression.

From that point forward, my mother and I lived together. Her "Spirit" was bright, and she was excited about our new home. However, she had her own set of physical challenges that demanded my time and attention. She no longer drove a car and had a couple of labor-intensive, long-term health problems that required many doctor appointments. Her hearing took a dive. We finally convinced her to get hearing aids, which she basically would not wear. This created continued difficulties with her because she did not understand or misunderstood things that were said to her. It also became more and more difficult for her to retrieve words and complete sentences, or remember what you told her five minutes prior, and was often confused about the time and day of the week. She was eventually diagnosed with

Alzheimer's/dementia by a neurologist who had followed her for more than ten years following a mild stroke.

I walked a tightrope between allowing her to do as much as she could for herself and the need to do things for her, with the changes I noticed. I remained committed to Mom's care with happiness and willingness to do whatever was necessary. She had a couple of groups of friends who would come and take her to lunch once a month. which she loved. I appreciated them because they briefly freed me up to attend to my personal needs and obligations. At the same time during those momentary respites from my ever-present obligatory support, I never felt completely relieved of my duties to oversee her health and welfare. The associated weight of responsibility and commitment blocked any personal progress I made against my own illness.

At one point, the demands to care for my mother seemed to drain all of my energy for things I wanted to do. I was overwhelmed with a deep-felt hopelessness, simply because I had no idea how long the caregiving would last. Sure, Mom would die eventually, but how long would that be? Would I be held captive for a day, week, years before I could take the time and energy to heal myself? In the midst of all of those feelings, I recognized that I was not experiencing any personal pleasure in any aspect of my life. My sleep was continuously disturbed, and, consequently, my energy and coping ability were sucked right out of me. I felt guilty because I told my sisters I needed a break from caregiving, in the interest of the health of both Mother and me. Looking back, no single thing left me in that state of mind. I *knew* a combination of factors at that time, but I also felt I should be able to handle them. I was strong. I was capable. I was smart. While I worried that the depression would raise its ugly head, I realized I had nothing to lose and everything to gain if I saw it through, based on how I'd grappled with so much over so many years. *Not again!!!*

Ultimately, my sisters took brief tours of duty with Mom, because she literally could not be left alone. My own physical- and mental-health issues continued and diminished my ability to cope over time. I asked one sister who cared for Mom while I had my mastectomy to please keep her a little longer as I continued my recuperation. This started a slow downhill slide for me. I felt regret that I could not care for my mother any longer, though not guilty because I had already done a lot for her. This meant talking with my sisters about next steps for our Mom's care.

> *1.6.2019: Today was awful in so many ways, but I guess it had to happen for me to move on. I knew as I was walking my dog, Sugar, taking a shower, and getting ready to go to meet a family friend, that I was at a breaking point. I respect the breaking point I hit today. I have to hold myself in a warm blanket. Give extra care. I got validation from people around me ("Perspective Mentors" and my "Perspective Angel") who understand what is going on. I have paid a price and will not let it continue to go on. I believe this is all for the better!!! My body is saturated with anxiety—I feel it everywhere. Keep breathing.*

It all came swooshing down on me. I was caught between a place of self-compassion, feeling hurt, feeling judged, and thoughts I should have the capacity to *not* be affected by the rushing stream of things that had happened to me recently. My confidence plummeted, as my sisters bombarded me with many questions and comments about our Mom's needs, and I broached the subject of my inability to continue as her full-time caregiver. I felt regret after I got off the phone with the decision made and expressed that I could no longer be a full-time caregiver. Was it guilt, upset, or letdown? I didn't know why I suddenly felt so bad. A horrible headache wrapped across my forehead pressed my temples like a vise and reached its fingers of pain down my neck. I could not rally to do anything the rest of the day. I decided that it was OK to just take care of myself, breathe, rest, and meditate.

Continued conversations with my sisters about Mom's care took their toll on me and on my relationships with my sisters as we tried to make decisions about our Mom's care. I knew from experience my mother needed to enter assisted living before my sisters even acknowledged our Mother's failing memory, frailty, and level of care needed. Given my previous need for my parents' assistance, I believe my sisters saw me in the role of primary caregiver to Mom until her death, as did I initially at that time, hence my increased regret. It's not unusual for the closest-proximity sibling to initially assume that role, but once assumed, it's hard to shift more responsibility to other siblings. And so that's what transpired among us sisters. In their denials of Mom's condition and care needs, they lobbed understandable but hurtful suppositions and aspersions my way. Grateful my sisters eventually agreed to take turns hosting Mom in their homes in California, Washington State, and Phoenix, Arizona, for varying periods of time, I also felt frustrated that they continued to resist assisted living as a viable and—from my perspective—necessary solution for Mom and for us.

Finally, a decision about Mom's care was made when she said she did not like moving from place to place between me and my sisters, and wanted to go into assisted living in Phoenix, where she could still see her friends. Because it was her choice, my reticent sisters finally agreed. She moved into the campus where our Father had spent his last days in hospice and where she had friends. I continued to endure responsibilities for her care, appointments, medical supplies, and medications. It all took time, but I was finally able to sleep through the night and begin to regain my own physical and emotional strength.

Once arrangements were in place, I noted the following:

> *7.21.2019: Today, I feel lost! I don't get it. I have freedom. I can do whatever I want whenever I want. This is difficult. I hope the depression is not raising its ugly head. It has been a few weeks since the Wellbutrin was reduced. I want so much for me to use fewer meds, though I know that may or may not happen. I am on a path for mindfulness and my eating, which is going well. It is good not to have to worry about Mom for a while.*

With time, I decided it was okay to just *be* and not really do anything. From my position of self-imposed responsibility, I felt like I should be doing something for myself with my newfound freedom. I felt like I was in a fog, and that was frustrating. I needed some time to rest and heal. I include this recent part of the story to illustrate how difficult it is for someone with treatment-resistant depression to find the space in their life to make self-care for their own physical and psychological well-being their most important responsibility. It, indeed, took a long, arduous process for me to learn this lesson. I now know in my bones that, if I want to continue to live my life with depression, I must take care of myself first and foremost.

This continues to be a difficult lesson to honor. In my core, I'm a person who picked a profession of service and am a giver in my heart. When demands for my attention increase, I need a lot of self-reminders to put my self-care first.

In the chapters ahead, I hope you find story moments, strategies to cope, or anything else that might speak to you or make life a bit easier. With gratitude that you opened my book and are curious to continue, I present the rest of my story.

✦　✦　✦

PATIENCE

The fabric of my life has been ripped and torn into pieces by episodes of depression. I can't even decipher some of the pieces. Review of previous lessons in the present moment increased my determination to weave a new and magnificent tapestry more beautiful than the tattered-and-torn version. Efforts to reweave them revealed my inability to retrieve valuable attributes and insights. A look at my past served as a foundation and reminder of hope for my future. Reweaving the tapestry can be accomplished only with endless patience.

PATIENCE REQUIRED!! What a surprise! This is present throughout my journey, a demand I have to respect, as it keeps me safe in times of anxiety and fear. Much of the discussion of patience in my writing pertains to my efforts to understand, support, and withstand the numerous people, situations, and circumstances I encounter. Patience is not just *waiting* with anticipation for something to happen. Endurance requires self-compassion and lovingkindness—especially in the throes of chaos. Awareness of a given moment offers the opportunity to breathe and be mindful of what is happening in and around me.

Experience of the sweet, savory flavorful taste of an onion requires patiently peeling away layers of skin. The practice of patience with the various challenges I faced has given me time and space to explore the potential emergence of goodness. Tears come as the challenges are peeled away; they sting in the moment but heal as they open up and free my mind, heart, "Soul," and "Spirit." The process does not follow a straightforward path.

Living in patience and surrendering without expectations of how to respond can carry me far. Without anticipation or expectation, I will listen. Responses may be in the form of a mustard seed—the planting of ideas not fully expressed or explained. Beginnings of responses will unfold as the seeds germinate. No lightning strikes or strokes of genius, but seeds. This could be happening even as I write this. It may be very subtle and not revealed for some time to come. Surrendering feels like giving up, yet it seems I am working too hard for naught. Surrendering does not have to mean giving up. I had to let go of the notion that I could think or reason my way out of depression. Surrendering those notions offered some relief and opened up other possibilities.

A POWERFUL EXERCISE IN PATIENCE

I was in a "brownout" because I had to direct my energy to my overall health and upcoming surgery for endometriosis. But my energy was waning from anxiety, which was trying my patience. How could patience help me in those moments? My energy was consumed with waiting, and I could not call on the knowledge that patience could guide me through this difficult time. I had no control over what was happening, and the "unknown" of that was so hard. The "brownout" characterization suggests that I knew patience was present at some level, not blacked out—just not accessible.

THE CONTINUUM OF PATIENCE

Often the road I traveled was too familiar. Every instance helped me practice patience despite the ongoing battle that drained me. Helplessness overwhelmed me, I felt on edge, and my anxiety soared. I thought I was at least a little better but thought I should feel more (sic) better. Then I wondered how I would know I practiced patience. Without a plan for the future, progress toward the future eluded me and consequently was immeasurable. This demanded attention to even tiny signs of improvement versus the expectation of some realization that would stun and startle me. Attunement to and appreciation of even the smallest of steps was essential to head in a healthy direction. Worrisome thoughts about if and when I could return to work and survive financially swirled around me. They were legitimate concerns but not pertinent at certain times. Nothing was accomplished with the pressure that I'd put on myself that "*I should be feeling better.*"

When I remain patient, I realize I *will* feel better with time. To me, this was an important reminder that "I am *not* helpless." The process and progress cannot be forced.

WAITING PATIENTLY FOR
DIFFERENTIAL DIAGNOSES

Diagnosis of various conditions was among the difficult patches on my road to physical and mental health. Conditions such as endometriosis, breast cancer, and nailing down a psychological diagnosis presented repeated opportunities for me to practice patience. Diagnosis is an art—there is an inordinate number of factors that do not fit neatly into each puzzle. The establishment of a differential diagnosis is essential to the development of the most beneficial management plan or, at least, a starting point for treatment.

Physically, the repeated surgeries for endometriosis were each their own trial. Every time the doctors believed they had surgically removed the problematic tissue, it reappeared and required further treatment with drugs and additional surgical procedures. The complex quandaries of treatment of endometriosis were themselves never-ending trials of patience. Doctors used surgery or lasers to *get rid of* obviously abnormal tissue.

The problem, even after a hysterectomy, was that there were still microscopic implants that continued to grow even without a uterus to supply more tissue into my abdomen. Hormone treatment is common after a hysterectomy, but those hormones fed the random microscopic implants. More surgery was required, and, finally, hormones were stopped, which had additional adverse effects. Despite the initial accurate diagnosis of endometriosis, as the complexity of the disease spread, it created more medical concerns. Endometriosis was a roller-coaster ride that spanned more than fifteen years.

Suspicion of breast cancer after routine, annual diagnostic mammography triggered a shower of more testing. More mammography photos were required. Then ultrasound provided additional views of areas of concern that suggested the type of growth. Further suspicion was generated, and extraction of breast tissue followed. Numerous steps, each designed to shed more light on the lump in my breast, were necessary to determine whether there was cancer in my breast. There was nothing I could do to speed up the process. I had to be patient minute-by-minute, day-to-day. Testing revealed two distinct kinds of breast cancer, which meant layers of consideration, and decisions had to be made. Each effort to make a more definitive diagnosis was necessary, but it also prolonged the process and made patience and endurance increasingly difficult. Even as I faced various physical problems, the nagging undertow of depression remained.

Psychological diagnosis is complex, even with the criteria and details outlined in the DSM-5 (*Diagnostic and Statistical Manual of Mental Disorders—5th Edition*), published by the American Psychiatric Association. The DSM-5 is a guide for diagnoses for insurance purposes. There are numerous types of depression distinguished by distinct characteristics or symptoms. My predominant diagnosis was depression—although, during the DBS study, another doctor thought Bipolar Disorder was a more appropriate diagnosis. My persistence and tireless efforts to obtain care were interpreted by a psychiatrist as evidence of "mania." Consideration lacked with regard to who I am, my dedication to my work, and what I saw as required by my family, society, and even "God." On the one hand, it did not matter what it was called, but, on the other hand, the prognosis and preferred treatment differed. The Bipolar diagnosis bothered me because I never felt I had a manic episode. My therapist of more than twenty years believed that treatment-resistant depression was the most apropos diagnosis. A change in diagnosis could have meant a change in medications, teeming with their own difficulties, and a wait for a new medication to take effect.

One integration of the idea of patience was appreciating that patience is powerful awareness that, in each moment of time, calm can be experienced. For my own well-being, I must remain in a state of "patient endurance." That could take many forms, but the most important thing was to remember to wait. Waiting is the opportunity to let go of stress and expectations and appreciate what is taking place in the moment, instead of focusing on what has been hard or what might happen down the road.

Regardless of the wait for a differential diagnosis, time was both a friend and an enemy. When I let myself *just be*, it prevented the use of time as a yardstick of the speed of growth and recovery. I constantly reminded myself that there was no way to know how long it would take me to move to unusual places on the trek. Putting a time limit on my change built unrealistic expectations that would be shot down and contribute to my disappointment.

PHYSICAL ASPECTS AND REACTIONS

Physical problems have been part of my story for many years. I can't *blame* the depression solely on my biology. I have to give myself space and not expect to be invincible or attempt to create a reflective protective shield. Waiting times for services and answers varied in length, and were affected by events beyond my control. The thing I had control over was to nurture myself and find—or build—a nest to buffer me from the adversity of that particular stop in the odyssey. Attention to what was happening in an immediate instant distracted me from rumination.

6.3.2011: Why am I challenged by so many things? Is it a test to see how much I can handle? Is it a test to see if I can let go of control? Is it a test of patience? My energy goes to healing at this point. The time will pass, and I will get through all of this.

Sometimes I asked myself, "*Is the darkness a physiologically necessary time out?*" The biological aspects of depression are addressed in part by medications, which is a touchy balance to achieve. If I admit that I am "human," it is not surprising that I was adversely affected by cancer, endometriosis, full-time caregiving, etc. The saga of my physical problems could have drowned me any number of times. But I persevered and realized I needed to listen to my body so that I could minimize the physical impact. It is OK to rest, take a break, regroup, and re-emerge in a stronger, more confident place. My body was affected by a combination of actual biological problems and the physical impact of depression. The battle against myself served no particular end. There would never be a total end to the darkness of depression. I presented mysteries:

1.11.1980: During this time, there was a process of trying to determine if I had a physical problem, and I was diagnosed with Valley Fever. However, there were a lot of tests, hospitalizations, etc. I had had surgery; my depression was so bad that it was hard to sort out what to attend to and whether the problems were physiological or psychological (probably a combination).

A review of my journals revealed the pervasive theme of my essential need to practice patience. I needed to create space to nurture my patience, especially because I did not have control over aspects of my own health. One result of the ongoing examination was the following meditation on patience, which speaks for itself.

[*Read this to yourself more often, Cindy—it's good stuff!*]

A MEDITATION ON PATIENCE

Life brings challenges of all different kinds and sizes.
Patience or lack thereof is tried in many of these challenges.
There are many wise words spoken about patience.
But it is a quality I so badly need and that is so elusive.
I know it is a virtue I must cultivate because impatience is
    very wearing and can be harmful.
Yet without a sense of direction or purpose,
Which I feel I need/want—what remains?
It feels like nothing. I talk often about how "patience-less"
    I am, yet it is something I desperately need.
If only I felt some sense of hope or future,
I think I could be patient,
But those, alas, are not there, either.
Must I merely sit back and wait? Is that giving up? How do
    I stay active without purpose or direction?
It seems like it is just surviving, not living.
I don't feel like I have a life.
I feel like, maybe, if I could be patient, my anxiety might
    decrease, and guidance would come if I would quit fighting
    it with impatience.
I am working at cross-purposes with myself.
I need to truly practice patience.

HOW I USED PATIENCE DURING
TIMES OF STRESS

Times of waiting varied in length, with effects beyond my control. I could control the design of a "waiting space" to ride out a particular stretch of the interminable journey. There was not anything to *do* but note the passage of time. My ability to stay present in the moment was a perfect escape from worry and fear.

6.3.2011: Preparation for surgery for my double mastectomy followed a second diagnosis of breast cancer. My emotions from one day to the next were unpredictable. Fortunately, I went through more ups than downs, and I recorded this reflection in the midst of waiting.

It feels good to not have guilt and regret weighing me down. Not having the weight of that negativity is awesome. So, even in these moments of uncertainty and frustration, I am not going down the rabbit hole.

It is evident that I faced multiple stressors. It is wondrous that I was fortunate to take the situations in, reflect on them patiently, and gain important messages from each of them.

The events that took place over years (e.g., treatment for endometriosis, searching for treatment for depression, cancer, caregiver in my parents' aging process) were the most difficult to sustain. The rides were unpredictable, but each event forced me to increase my patience to avoid more craziness than I already felt. Sometimes patience was a minute-by-minute challenge, which marked the time without a sense of forward movement. On occasions, I hoped I helped those around me with patience with me and my challenges. They wanted answers and directions to help me that were not readily evident.

One fleeting thought: if I got really upset and had a good, hard cry, my frustration could be released, and I might free myself from a past of crazy overdoing. It also occurred to me that it might jump-start the lack of emotions and feelings that I was experiencing. What did I have to lose if I had a good cry?

PATIENCE AND SURRENDER LED TO THE LIGHT OF "SPIRIT"

Over time, patience paid off again and again. Sometimes I had to relearn a lesson, but that was OK because it brought a new wrinkle to my insight and understanding that felt good. I knew I would not go back and relive my previous way of life, even though the particular moment may have been painful. I realized I needed to let go of perfection, which freed up a lot of energy. A little bit of frustration crept in as my understandings deepened. One aspect of my frustration consisted of my inability to *clearly* express in words how I felt. I lived my life by example and planted seeds for others wherever they were on their journey. I knew I must reinvest myself in patience daily. Patience allowed me to hold questions and resist the endless search for answers. That is patience. Robert Frost said,

"The only way out is through." Oh, how true.

Gradually I grasped that what I do day-to-day allows time for the incubation of my Being, to fuel the fire of inspiration. It is *how I am*, not *what I do* that matters. My struggle is the dichotomy between my cognitive understanding of what is going on and my subjective experience. I discovered the cognitive did not adequately change and affect the subjective experience of patience.

I carry so much anxiety for the future. If only I could let it go, release it, let myself be. I need to rebuild myself from where I am right now—not where I think I should be. Let go of the future. It will unfold, and I will know when my effort is required. I will be God's partner in the unfolding rather than feeling like I need to be in charge. Surrender to the need to know the future, and release the pressure and anxiety. Be with the unknown in the present moment. Let it be. Being present in this moment is sometimes filled with wisdom.

Periodically a wait threw open doors to other parts of my Being; reconnection with the goodness inside followed. This piece flowed so beautifully, without any judgment or worry about the grammar, wording, or correctness. It is a true expression of my "Soul."

2.11.2017: Dearest Cindy—

*You are full of ideas that have value to be shared. You have already touched other lives with things you have learned and know you can share with many more! You **are** a teacher, which means you communicate effectively. You have a way of connecting with your teaching that brings insight and understanding to others. You will never know how you impacted some, but your heart and "Soul" will know you have made a difference. Don't worry about whether you have said things correctly (grammar). You are a messenger and **do** know what to say and how to say it. Your message(s) is crystal clear deep down inside. The foundation is* *there, and you will elegantly and creatively express them. Let them unfold! The words and ideas **will** flow—maybe not as quickly as you impatiently want—but you are a master student of patience. Now you have the opportunity to use it in a special way and by example **do/write!** Remember, your expectations get in the way and sometimes prevent you from the grace of experience. You see, it is not usually going to be what you expect, so trust yourself!! **Know** it will unfold with elegance. **You are** a teacher who brings the enrichment of real experience to undergird what emerges in your writing.—Your Vigilant Angel*

Amazement emerged at some of the things that I said. There was no judgment of what was/was not appropriate, too snobby, or characteristic of the self-judgments I generously give myself.

I create a nest for myself to be quiet, feel safe, reflect, and practice patience. I realize that patience is a life preserver, a manifestation of "Spirit" which reminds me that it is always available and is a reminder of "God Within Me."

Patience is a candle I need to light within. It needs to be an enduring quality that is never snuffed out. I may be looking at months without any guidance, but hopefully that means good things are germinating within to be revealed.

✦ ✦ ✦

STAYING PRESENT
IN THE MOMENT

Welcome to an important element of my journey, in which I share the restorative impact of *staying present in the moment*. This is a totally free, available 24/7 blessing and one of the most beneficial, rewarding, inspiring, vital elements of my overall wellness, being, and healing.

Many respected writers have shared that some of life's richest experiences occur when we are just in the state of present-moment *being*. What does that mean? Very early on, I was encouraged to *just be* to try to quiet down the demands in my mind. It was difficult to grasp this concept, and, consequently, there were introductions and suggestions for direct practice. The core issue is a willingness to let go of the idea that *I had to be "doing" something all of the time! Not!* I needed to step back, listen, and even do nothing! My understanding of the concept expanded over time. With my curiosity piqued, I diligently explored ways to try out staying in the present moment.

2.17.1997: My exercise of staying in the moment is so contrary to my life to this point. I began to gain insight into the process which carries me with each step away from the known, the comfortable. On the one hand, I have nothing to fear. On the other hand, entering the unknown is an incredible risk. I cannot deny the journey. It is powerful, it is strong, it transports me where I know not, but the more I release myself from the certainty of the past, the greater my chances to soar to heights I have never known.

Staying present in the moment took on multiple forms and has been woven throughout this whole odyssey. What it is called varies from modality to modality, belief to belief, and tradition to tradition. But the key is the integration of this element often missing from our current daily life. How can I create a way of life that incorporates "staying present in the moment"? There are different ways to combine, integrate, and sustain this notion. I integrated ideas from various religious traditions, "New Age" exploration, and practices imported from Eastern thought and adapted for use in Western culture. Ultimately, the applications came together to provide an infinite cocoon of safety, reflection, calm, insight, renewal, and a sense of peacefulness. There is always something new to realize, explore, and appreciate.

Methods of prayer and some form of meditation have always been present in my life. These practices evolved over time and grew in depth, richness, and meaning. There is much talk of intuition or *knowing what we cannot explain.* I believe that intuition is present, and I sensed there was something greater to attend to in life, impacting my evolution from early on. Even though I was not always clear on "why" I prayed and meditated, it seemed second nature. The metamorphosis of this aspect of my life moved through the expansion of prayer to various forms of meditation and contemplation.

CONTEMPLATION/MEDITATION/ MINDFULNESS/PRAYER

The definitions for each of these terms depends on the orientation of the person, tradition, philosophy, or practice with which one associates. Various religious traditions, such as Catholicism, view contemplation, meditation, and prayer as various forms of prayer with different foci. There is much overlap between these terms, and what finally matters is what I integrate into my daily habits and belief. Mindfulness is often considered a subcategory of meditation, which is often identified with Buddhism, though is not restricted to that belief system. Learning about the nuances, experiences, and ideas of the various traditions offers new insight or even a twist on their previous knowing. This can bring them closer to reality and broadens the view of my understanding. It is interesting that meditation and contemplation are expressed as synonyms of each other in some traditions.

Consider what approach works best for you. Create your own practice. These words have many similarities and overlap in meaning. Keep in mind you can blend aspects of the various approaches and practices, and craft your own eclectic habits. Be patient with yourself. Practice consistently. Consider what you want to intentionally cultivate in yourself. Explore the many options and shape your own routine.

Sharon Salzberg, a highly respected teacher of meditation and Buddhism, talks about meditation being like a tightrope walk, but if you fall off, you land safely on another tightrope to continue your journey. Meditation consists of concentration on your breath, a symbolic object, or a religious symbol for a personally determined period of time. It can also be paying attention to your inner life once you establish a steady breathing pattern.

I became a serious student of mindfulness, meditation, and contemplation. Meditation increases body awareness, focuses on breathing, and lets thoughts/ideas pass by without trying to catch any of them. There is no need to take a *deeper* look in hopes of finding an *answer*. The only *work* of meditation is to center on my breathing without a goal. A quieting of the mind and body. There is usually still a stream of thoughts interlaced in and out of the focus on the breath, but I have learned to just let them float by. If a thought is important, it will return at a later time, when I can put energy behind it.

There are many ordinary uses of meditation that can be part of a healthy regimen for *anyone!* These notions blended together for me over time. There are a number of individuals who influenced the development of my meditation routine. A sample of dedicated practitioners and teachers includes Thomas Moore, Sharon Salzberg, Jon Kabat-Zinn, Dan Seigel, Zendel Siegel, Joseph Goldstein, Judson Brewer, and Jack Kornfield. As I encountered each of these people of wisdom, they broadened my perception and experience of contemplation, meditation, and mindfulness.

Clearly expressed by Jon Kabat-Zinn, "*Mindfulness means paying attention in a particular way; on purpose, in the present moment and nonjudgmentally.*" This is a common definition that is simply stated in different ways but includes components that are found across various definitions. Mindfulness helps me see with greater clarity how I may approach my moment-by-moment experience skillfully. It includes taking more pleasure in the good things that often go unnoticed or unappreciated, and dealing more effectively with the difficulties I encounter, both real and imagined. One of the mysteries is that words cannot adequately represent or explain what happens in moments of mindfulness. It is just a different kind of experience that does not require any response or action. It is about observation. It *does* require practice, practice, and more practice! There is nothing to master or a specific goal to reach. It is about the experience that takes me to places about which I may not have given any thought. There is not a specific goal—it is about *Being*, as opposed to our major emphasis in life of *Doing*. It is therefore about *letting* something happen rather than attempting to *make* something happen. It can start with just being aware of everyday activities, drinking your coffee, eating a meal, or taking a walk. Specific definition is elusive and ultimately does not matter. The custom is about the experience of being present in the moment.

One of the earliest lessons I learned about meditation and contemplation is that there is no such thing as *clearing my mind*. This is not possible, because we are thinking people, and there are always things racing through my head. Many different metaphors describe the process/experience of meditation. Their familiar theme is that I cannot stop the thoughts, but I *can* just watch them float by without responding to them or feeling like I need to do something about them. This allows other thoughts, ideas, and experiences to come to the surface. With expanded alertness comes calm and release from the compulsion to do something about one or more of them.

Wow—meditation is not a complex or complicated process.
When I can "BE," it is second nature. Being in a meditative space
is freeing; physically, it gives me a feeling of being lighter. It
seems effortless. This shows the integration of how the "threads
of meditation" have permeated my life.

Perhaps specific, observable definitions are not critical, because each different twist to any of them has similarities with the others. There is definitely repetition or rewording of concepts across all of these ideas. Insights into these concepts as well as "Faith" and wisdom do not come from one single source. Learning *within* a particular religion or tradition led to my curiosity about other religions, traditions, and sources of inspiration. Over time, I understood that formal religions concentrate on *what to know* instead of *how to know*. The "how" is not black or white, and cannot be taught. It is the encouragement to explore thoughts and ideas for personal meaning.

As my understanding of the notion of centering and grounding grew, I moved with curiosity to ponder more formally *Being* through prayer, meditation, contemplation, and mindfulness. Eastern thought in "Spirituality" has gradually come to our Western society and has opened up other ways to engage and sustain connection with "God" or "Spirit." Perhaps at my core was my ability to experience "God Within," something I was born with and which morphed many different ways over time. I was always amazed there could be moments of relief, peace, and quiet in the present moment. But, in the blink of an eye, I could be drowned in *helpless, hopeless despair.* Meditation became second nature to me and was important enough that I constantly weighed and reflected on where I was and how I wanted to expand my pursuit.

THE ENRICHMENT OF
MINDFULNESS MEDITATION

A concept that Jack Kornfield talked about was the notion of "Mind Like Sky," which originated in the Buddhist tradition. If I view my mind as similar to the sky, there is vastness, infinity, and boundlessness, and this image creates a space where I feel tranquility and spaciousness. My ability to maintain "Mind Like Sky" gave me a sense of hope and a future. During my exploration of numerous "methods" in this realm, I encountered a variety of approaches. In a set of activities on CD by Joseph Goldstein, meditations were focused on transformation through the gifts of objects from icons of various traditions and religions. He included religious figures and opened the door to experience gifts from different sources.

6.10.2011: (In anticipation of breast cancer surgery). Totally pre-occupied with whether they will give me a general anesthetic and whether they will give me a strong-enough pain medicine. In the vastness of "Mind Like Sky," I find refuge. I am able to step out of my physical body and mental misery. With the vastness, it seems like there should be infinite possibilities. That there should be a future that will fulfill me in some way. Right now, my immediate future is the cancer, the surgery, the pathology, the oncology—all of the steps in diagnosing the cancer and moving toward healing.

Goldstein characterized Jesus' transformation:

As the object of Wisdom who came to me. He showed me I could walk down whatever plan, or path, that is given to me. That I don't have to surrender to cancer but can be present to the healing that can come with it. I am strong and have continuously weathered the storm of depression. The gift that Jesus gave me was a beating heart. It represents all of the love and support that surrounds me and will continue to surround me as I walk the path through cancer and beyond.

When it came to Buddha's transformation:

An angel gave me a feather to represent patience. An eternal message for me . . . Patience.

In another Buddha transformation of difficulties:

The Angel of "God" came again. She came into my body and acknowledged the heaviness and vastness of the depression. She cradled my "Soul" and said it could be healed, that I have the fortitude to survive and thrive from the experience. She gifted me a pyramid prism to scatter bits of light throughout the depression to lift me closely but gently up for healing. I want an all-or-nothing solution, and the message was that it is gradual.

Quan Yin (Goddess of Compassion):

Quan Yin entered the continued worry about whether the cancer would be gone. She gifted me a trumpet to blow away the worry to declare that there are infinite possibilities for my life in addition to or other than the recurrence of cancer.

Many new doors for exploration opened wide for me and offered new topics for dialogue with others. When I read other authors on mindfulness or meditation practice, I began to see the commonalities that are present among traditions. Contemplation is used often, especially in Christian literature, by authors who may have lived a monastic life. I often wondered if these individuals were not just cut off from the world. How could they speak to the day-to-day experiences of many? Having the time for meditation/contemplation is evident when you are a monastic. However, I learned there are many people who have active, socially integrated lives, and view their meditation/contemplation as a source of strength in some of the most difficult times in their life. In one of her early works, Caroline Myss talks about *mystics without monasteries*—the notion that anyone can live a life of contemplation anywhere, which is enriching. You don't *have* to go away to a monastery to incorporate these practices into your day-to-day living.

I also used CDs with meditations and narratives to move me through relaxing my whole body. Using the CDs, in the beginning, helped me stay focused on my breathing, and the relaxation process throughout my body. This translated into a practice that is available anytime, anywhere. I work with my breathing, slow down my racing thoughts, and bring myself to the present moment. What the sages of the ages say is that, if you practice meditation regularly, you can actually find yourself meditating throughout your day. Monks talk about how *everything* they do is an opportunity for meditation. Even tasks that used to frustrate me are much easier. I love making tapioca pudding from scratch, but I always hated having to stand and stir it the whole time. Now, I see it as an opportunity to quiet myself and meditate, and it feels like it takes much less time.

Over and over again (repetition is usually required to learn just about anything), I experienced the painless passing of time. Meditation keeps me present in the moment and affords me transient possibilities of calm and time devoid of preoccupation with depression, cancer, ankle problems, and many other things. Tranquility never seems to last long enough, but then again, suffering never comes to an end. Suffering is the other side of the peacefulness coin, and I cannot perceive peace and contentment without periodic suffering. (I often think that if I could always remain in a state of being present, life would be so much easier.)

The minister for most of my life was Reverend William O. Smith (founding minister of Shadow Rock Congregational Church, affiliated with the United Church of Christ). In one sermon, he noted, "*to mourn is to really cry because it heals. Then go on and face what it is. Don't run away. If the suffering will heal or comfort, then do it, as long as you know you will be better.*" Rev. Smith was giving me permission to cry, feel my pain, and then let it go.

WHY DO I PRACTICE MINDFULNESS MEDITATION?

I have asked myself repeatedly, "*Why am I practicing mindfulness meditation?*" It was recommended to break up my thinking and rumination. I hoped it might also serve as a way to reconnect with "Spirit," since prayer didn't seem to be working. It is another way to practice that elusive and tenuous patience. I am not an *expert* at mindfulness meditation (many practiced individuals do not ever consider themselves "experts," as they see this as a practice that continues to grow and evolve throughout life). I learned that it makes a difference in many ways, such as reducing anxiety. As someone with depression, I accessed observations, knowledge, and experience over many years. The impacts they had on me were understanding the pervasiveness of depression and realizing there are many wrinkles, twists, and turns to depression; acquiring a *knowing* based on the experience of depression on many levels that eludes description with words; depression created space that is often unpleasant; mindfulness expands that space and lets in a myriad of ideas, thoughts, and possibilities. Mindfulness meditation allows an enlightening dive to the depths without baggage.

Mindfulness meditation is one of many forms of meditation. Mindfulness is like turning a camera on "zoom" with attention to my breathing, as well as awareness of my body and mind. It combines acceptance of my thoughts with the realization of my feelings and physical sensations. The process is done without any judgment, solely observation of what is passing by. Paying attention to my breath is the beginning of building a mindfulness practice. Breathing happens naturally and automatically unless I intentionally try to stop it. Becoming aware of my breath is as simple as paying attention to where I am physically, feeling my breathing (nostrils, chest, and/or abdomen), how long I spend taking in a breath (something I can control), and how long I take to release a breath. The deeper I breathe, the more I slow down my heart rate and am enveloped in release and calm. I can do this anywhere! Standing in line at the grocery store, sitting in traffic that is not moving, waiting for an appointment in an office, etc. Even taking three deep breaths can help reduce feelings of stress I experience. Notice I said *reduce—not completely get rid of* the stress or tension.

I am in a whole different place with this process. When I come back to my breathing, that is the focus. It interrupts the "parade" of thoughts and ideas. A "nothingness" prevails. What a relief! (This is a reflection I had during the most recent bout with cancer—a whole different understanding and experience from the past due to mindfulness.)

Another benefit of mindfulness has been a complete reframing of time. I always thought I had to work on things fast and that I could not quit working on something until I was "all done" or "finished." Fatigue has been a huge issue, as time has moved forward, due to a number of different things. I cannot physically push myself through tasks. I have learned to set smaller goals. If I reach the smaller goal and still have energy, I can move on to another small goal. Because I know myself, I tend to sit down at the computer or sewing machine and lose all track of time. My strategy now is to look at the clock and set an end time for whatever I am doing. That means leaving things only partially done, which is especially hard for me when I am close to finishing a project. I check in with my body physically and mentally, which serves as a barometer that informs or guides me through the day. I need a nap almost every day, and, so, I lie down in the early afternoon. I start with a brief meditation. Sometimes I sleep, sometimes not, but I *always* rest.

The ability to immediately meditate through mindfulness is an invaluable buffer in many situations. I don't feel as threatened; I deflect negativity; I ponder my own experience and reactions to a situation; I can better deal with someone I find annoying, etc. Does this make me immune to discomfort, fear, or a desire to *do* something about a situation? No. It helps me reflect before acting and focus on acceptance and patience with others or situations in which I find myself overwhelmed. I appreciate my own reactions and the dramatic fluctuations I endure.

1.21.2011: I just did a meditation where mindfulness and depression had a conversation. Depression couldn't come up with any good reasons other than making a living [if the depression were not so severe]. When I looked at it more deeply, depression said it has always been there and has nowhere to go. Depression was defenseless yet wouldn't let go. I am calm and not anxious. I am stumped. I need to continue the dialogue between mindfulness and depression. I will turn it into compost for emotion, experiencing pleasure, connection with the "Divine," and inspiration.

9.13.2015: This past week I have been practicing MFN (mindfulness) daily, and I've noticed a difference. I am calmer and less anxious; I sleep better and am better able to roll with the punches of the day-to-day.

In mindfulness, I am an unbiased observer whose sole job is to keep track of the constantly passing show of the universe within. It is not intellectual or analytical. It is just consciousness. Mindfulness is extremely difficult to define in words—not because it is complex, but because it is so simple. Mindfulness is nonjudgmental observation. It is the ability of my mind to observe without criticism. I don't have to examine and judge my own irritation, agitation, frustration, and all those other uncomfortable emotional states. Whatever experience I have, mindfulness just accepts it. The moment is simply another of life's occurrences, just another thing to be aware of. No pride, no shame, nothing personal at stake—what is there, is there.

Mindfulness helps me see with greater clarity how I approach the moment-by-moment experience. I take more pleasure in good things that often go unnoticed or unappreciated. I deal more effectively with difficulties I encounter, both real and imagined. My experience is that, over time, it is easier and easier to enter a state of meditation at any time.

TAKING MY "SPIRITUAL" PULSE

There were gaps of time when I could not practice meditation because of the overwhelming challenges of physical health, including surgeries, DBS, cancer, and other serious health problems. Despite all of this, I was able to return to my practice intermittently, as I tried to refocus the lens on the bigger picture of life, if only for a second. *Daily Word* and *Guideposts* provided readings of inspiration and prayers for contemplation. Intellectually, I knew the importance of my practice, but my energy had to be used in other ways for periods of time. When I was most consumed by depression, just getting out of bed and taking care of my basic physical needs were all I could do.

1.31.2017: Going back in my journals, to a time right before my last surgery, the themes remain the same: patience; take it slow; "BE"; when I can just "BE," time is limitless; I have whatever amount of time I need; listen to my body; stay with my heart; don't let my head get in the way. Discomfort can be the catalyst for change and growth, in ways I probably have not imagined.

Key elements are represented in this passage, to maximize coping, success, and growth. It is interesting that the "Aha!" that seemed so profound in one moment disappeared in the blink of an eye. My musings have similar and repetitive themes:

I feel I am in a battle I know I will not win, in the sense of banishing depression from my life. Is my searching and writing a stall tactic? A means of surviving? Part of the endless struggle to try to understand? Somehow, I think it keeps me going and lets me feel I am "doing something" about my state.

Through "*staying present in the moment*," I am more likely to connect with "Spirit." The presence or lack of presence of "Spirit" permeates my journey. I could not necessarily describe what was missing or how I would even know if it existed. I am certain that it is an integral element of my life and "Being," and I wanted it to be there, and for me to be aware of it! The contemplation, meditation, and mindfulness practices help me stay in touch with "Spirit" because they drown out the difficult, swirling chaos, at least briefly.

Maybe the many challenges I have faced have been my ticket to the life of contemplation and "Spirituality." Perhaps it is only the depths of despair that could open my "Soul" to the very rich discovery of "Spirit." Would I continue to pursue and contemplate the life of "Spirit"? Perhaps the gift is the deep despair, the thing that drives the search for what seems so elusive.

I realized practices that kept me in the present moment increased my appreciation of "Spirit." They affected how I realized or experienced support, security, guidance, and the potential for enrichment of my life, which felt like a disaster. A sense of hope for the future was missing—or at least out of my reach. I conjured up many things it might feel like or look like if "Spirit" were more apparent, but I had no confidence or belief in myself.

4.22.2005: Spiritual pulse—it does not seem to be there. Once again, I believe that if it were there, this time would be easier to endure or pass through. Remain open. Just observe; attend; be open; be receptive; know that expectations will not make things happen any quicker. Letting Go—yes, I have marched this road before!

The main gift of this challenge over time has been my connection with "God Within," an understanding that I am part of "God" and that "God" is *within*. Especially as I release into that notion, there is great relief, because guilt and personal responsibility vanish. The "knowing" that comes with these experiences serves as a salve to relieve the pain of the challenge of the moment. Unfortunately, I am rarely able to *sustain* that "knowing." However, I am able to fall into it, to trust that "God" is within and that my "Spirit" is growing richer with each life encounter that raises questions.

LETTING GO TO MOVE ON

Letting Go was a further extension of the notion of staying present in the moment. Letting Go is a way to create more space to be open to the present. While I had the image of thoughts dancing through the sky without fixating on them, I was still stuck with the idea that depression would always be part of my life. The notion that I was somehow going to be able to control it was a futile effort. The struggle became to acknowledge the presence of depression and not allow it to consume my thinking and carry me into a deeper hole. Over time, when I was present in the moment, there was no point in trying to lasso the depression or attempt to do something about it. Letting Go of a need to *control* my mind freed up lots of energy and released elements of frustration. This was a challenge of my "Soul," and the release of these ideas required trust in myself and, ultimately, in the belief that "Spirit" would keep me safe. What I feared was useless perseveration on the need for control that pulled me down into the muck and mire.

> *6.17.2011: Yet, we must all, at some moment, "hit bottom" and vow to change our lives. We must learn differently and think differently. Maybe I am trying to control the depression and the outcomes of breast cancer and my broken toe. Maybe I truly have to let go and let "God" lead the way. Let go of the need to control and just be with the situations in my life that I simply want to go away. The reality is that it is an illusion that I have control over any of these issues.*

A vital element of staying present in the moment was letting go of whatever I was thinking. As I struggled over and over again with the idea of "Letting Go," I found myself trapped in my own thinking. My "Perspective Angel" reminded me one day that I needed to forget the depression and zoom in on visualizing the containment of the tumor in my breast as well as my overall health. I wanted to *improve* the state of my mind—not *control* it.

*Letting Go means . . . experiencing a great spaciousness that
simply lets everything come and lets everything go.*

*[This means not closing doors on each thought but letting it
pass into the spaciousness.]*

I DON'T HAVE TO "DO" IN ORDER TO "BE"

The constant presence of depression left me always looking for
additional meaning, understanding, or insight into life. I seemed
to believe that if I could find answers in that realm, I would get
better. A constant illusion with which I lived was "*Do* something,
and things can't help but get better." This dilemma between
doing and being was both my ally and my enemy. It emerged
over time, ultimately leading me to realize that there was not
anything I could *do* to tackle or get rid of the depression. It was
hard to *Just Be* when I was struck by an urgency to change my
thinking. If I was not *doing* or *being productive, Just Being* was
a waste of time. This was a barrier to understanding the idea
of being present in the moment. As I released into the realm of
Just Being, I discovered it could be anything from experiencing
nature, to prayer, to meditation, to simply being mindful of
where I was and how I was feeling. Sometimes being present in
the moment also meant being with the chaos of my thinking
and living. To *Just Be* allows my attention to be totally engaged
in the present moment. There are no expectations or demands
for any kind of performance or accomplishment.

Another way of understanding *Doing vs. Being* was to accept a
big shift in the idea of *Doing vs. Being*, moving from the conceptual
understanding in my head to the emotional and physical experience in my gut. The shift let me engage in simple "attention" to

sensations in my body and of my breath. There is much less effort in staying in the intimacy of the moment. There are no demands, have-to's, to-do's—just *being*. Awareness is void of polarities that have to be attended to; they just *are*. Simple focus helped me realize I could not predict what was going to happen next. By losing that expectation, I could be present to whatever was happening, without judgment, to accept what I was experiencing. That *is* what it means *to Be*. The vastness of simple acknowledgment has room for so much—most of it beyond my imagination. Not *paying attention to* but *recognition of* doesn't require any engagement unless I choose to do so! This is a non-conceptual experience—there is only attentiveness to thoughts and sensations.

This theme of *just being present* repeats itself in many places in the writing in my journals, but it *is* such an important idea. I have at times driven myself crazy on a never-ending journey of researching, reading, searching for insights, understanding, and information about my health—especially depression and cancer. I *knew* that, if I learned enough, there were answers I could put together to come up with a solution. You see, I was *in my head*. I have a Doctorate. I attained that by doing all of the things I just mentioned. I learned a tremendous amount and truly felt wiser. Depression required a whole different kind of wisdom, obtainable only through patiently waiting over an unknown period of time. I had to *just be in the present moment*. For me, the idea of a concept or lesson out there that explained everything seemed like the only way to get answers, ideas, or directions to "get rid of" the depression. All of them were *external*! Actually, the real wisdom lay in my internal experience and the degree of my ability to *stay engrossed in the moment! Being* does not really require understanding, physical energy, or description in words.

When I stay open to awareness, I frequently experience wisdom without words.

*I can feel and **be** enough, anywhere, anytime, with anyone. How do I thank you, "God," for depression?*

Being Instead of Doing has been one of the greatest and hardest lessons of this whole journey. My penchant for always *doing* became my enemy in this process because it left me with expectations of what I "*should be able to do.*" This led to flogging myself for not making headway. One of the things I had to confront was that my thinking was reduced to mechanically handling the activities of daily living to survive. After all, if I entered the space of contemplation, I should have feelings, and become one with "God." Even beginning to think about *Being vs. Doing* felt like an overwhelming task. But it was something I could write extensively about because it was an everyday element of my process of attempting to move along. The insight and glimpses of possibility were always there; I just did not seem able to hold on to them without persistent vigilance.

I cannot just be like a production-line robot, because there is an inner growth and metamorphosis that continues in spite of me and to that which I want to and will attend [to]. I want to return to nature and to find a place or places where I can experience peace and serenity. Alone with nature and thought. I noticed that such an environment is important for me.

During a period of more than forty years, I learned and understood how vital it is for me to *Be* first and then maybe *Do* something.

ARE "SPIRIT" AND "GOD" PRESENT?

Part of staying present in the moment is prayer, meditation, contemplation, mindfulness, or, in what follows, a dialogue with "God":

A Week-Long Conversation with the "Divine"

6.3.2011: "God"—I didn't choose depression. It came into my life and doesn't seem to want to leave. I could certainly do without it. Help me out of this deep, dark place that has and continues to rob me of so much. I choose life with meaning, purpose, and direction if only for the next few minutes, though I would love to see the bigger picture. I think there are enough things going on that there has to be insight or sunlight somewhere. Where is the learning in all of these experiences?

6.5.2011: I went to church today. Ken [Reverend Ken Heintzelman] talked about waiting and that the quiet space of waiting is filled with the Grace of God. He talked about patience. I had "Yes, buts" for everything. "Spirit" fails me! I doubt that I will heal from the depression until I have Spirit, positive emotion, some self-confidence, sense of passion, less fatigue, and the ability to stay focused on something besides reading a book. I needed to check out this afternoon and took hydrocodone and Klonopin.

6.6.2011: Dear "God": I do not fear solitude; rather, I seek it out. I come with the hope that I will reconnect with you. That I will reunite with you believing that your presence in my life is healing and that your absence, from my perception and feeling, leaves me in a wilderness. As I continue to struggle with depression, your absence seems even starker. I await your healing, your guidance, and your gifts of direction and sense of the future. I await the return of faith.

6.11.2011: "God": Bless me as I face BC (breast cancer). Let me see the probability of health. Let me feel your warmth and direction. Let me know that, with you, all is possible. Help quell my fears of cancer and depression. Open my eyes to possibilities for my life, and open my ears to hear your guidance. I know there is wisdom within me that I don't seem to be able to reap. Help me know that wisdom and harvest it for my own best well-being.

6.12.2011: "God": I beg of you that you guide me forth. Help me find work that is intellectually demanding, that is meaningful to me, and that lets me be of service to others. I open my heart and "Soul" to Your Presence, your Guidance. I pray for an island of peacefulness in the violent storm I am in. There have been many challenges, and I have trudged my way thru them. The depression feels like a weight around my neck that has dragged me down. I believe that, if I could only feel your presence, I would know that you are ever guiding me. I come in prayer and mindfulness with an open mind and "Soul" to receive whatever Guidance you have for me. I know the answers are within, but I have been unable to tap into them. Help me recognize your messages, no matter how small they are. Help me as I face the surgery for BC, and guide the surgeon's hands to excise all of the cancer in the breast and the lymph nodes. Spare me from further surgery and chemo.

I am aware that my writing seems to be all over the place and that it lacks coherency. My life has felt all over the place, and insight and understanding have been sorely missing. While I could relay a litany of experiences I have had *staying present in the moment*, the greater insights are the many, many things I gained over time. There are definite touchpoints that are evidence of my evolving life of "Spirit." These times are not something I planned for, rather, my ability to stay present in the moment increased the chances of realizing my growth. I want to share an experience that provides a glimpse of one of the fortunes I have been gifted.

One of the most wonderful and profound events occurred during a private retreat I took to Payson, Arizona, at the Merritt Center. It was near the end of winter, so it was cold. There was snow on the ground that had not fully melted, yet the day was crystal clear. The sky was the most amazing blue and the sun warm and refreshing. I was hiking among the majestic pine trees and felt attracted to a specific tree. When I reached the tree, I literally bared my chest and breasts to the tree. A bolt of lightning (on a truly clear day) came down through the tree and into me. I briefly felt lifted off my feet, into the air, but I also felt cleansed. To me, it was a sign of healing to come, hope for the future. I was afraid to share the experience with anyone because of how I might be judged. But I took the risk and shared it with the wise Betty Merritt, who just smiled at me, shook her head affirming what I'd shared, and bowed to me, saying, *Namaste*.

Such experiences are few and far between in life, but they cannot be dismissed or denied. I gave myself the gift of time and space to optimize "being present in the moment." The feeling of being consumed with wisdom, resolve, warmth, vitality, and resolve totally enveloped me. "Spirit" was so alive within me at that moment. And when I visited the Merritt Center again, I knew exactly which tree had been my companion during those precious moments years before.

Part of such experiences is immense gratitude for something that comes out of nowhere. It is not a time to ask questions, rather, to bathe in the energy, light, and affirmation of the moment. As I mingled with the tree, appreciating it in the moment, I unsealed a door that I did not even realize was there until I reflected on the whole experience later.

I have heard about the "search" for "God," as if there is something that is hidden—without or within me—that I somehow need to catch and join. You see, we try to explain "God" using the language we have, but it defies definition. My host father in Germany, an evangelical minister, Hans Dieter, once raised the question of whether there was a "virgin birth." He suggested that the words "virgin birth" were all that people had in their vocabulary at the time to describe something extraordinary that, once again, defied definition. In other words, we imposed a mold, based on our limited experience and knowledge of something unusual that happened. Hans Dieter, who studied the Bible back to its original language of Sanskrit, eloquently explained that meaning is lost in the translation of anything! So, if we have people of diverse backgrounds, beliefs, disciplines, experiences, traditions, hard-and-fast meanings, cultural biases, etc., it makes sense that we end up with such variation in translations. Even those who subscribe to atheism find fascination with the notion of something greater than themselves, but obviously, they don't buy the definitions and interpretations of the traditions.

I wish I were well in body and mind. I am so very aware of this.
I can pray this, but how can I live this when it simply isn't true?

Everyone says "God" is within me. I am not experiencing it. My not experiencing "God" is a fact, not just a negative thought that I have. It feels like breast cancer has brought my life to a halt. There is so much unknown.

In summary, it seems to me that we are all talking about the same thing or entity. I believe that, whatever we call it, we are also talking about something that defies definition with words. My own experience of "Spirit" has morphed over the course of my life. I was raised in the Methodist tradition (as were both of my parents), and "God" and Jesus were what I was taught. Over time, I found myself shift to "Soul" and "Spirit." To me, that has a greater meaning that feels more all-encompassing. It is also a way to refer to that which is present but not evident. There are all kinds of efforts to define "Spirit," but, ultimately, there seems to be some unspoken shared meaning that cannot be pinned down.

I moved away from pleading prayers to something greater, to something of which I am actually a part. It is present within me at all times whether I can identify, name, or appreciate its presence. The journey of life takes us down different paths to explore, discover, and gradually build an understanding of something larger than ourselves. It means I am never alone, though I have felt that way many times.

Staying present in the moment has been a key to moments of respite in my life. There is always more to learn, and the present moment continues to be a prize to cherish. While I ask, *Is "God" there or not?* I have rediscovered the presence within me. So many avenues have helped pave the way for my return to "God Within."

◆　◆　◆

DARK NIGHTS OF THE "SOUL"

Depression ebbed and flowed in my daily life, and, along the way, I encountered what are known as "Dark Nights of the 'Soul'" (DNS). My understanding of the DNS evolved along the bumpy road I traversed. Agony is an integral element, infused in the experience. Many thoughts march through my mind, as always, but, during the DNS, they seemed particularly troubling. Obviously, I endured these times alone, which required attention to what was taking place in my "Soul" and demanded focus on caring for my personal needs. A few others with experiences and thoughts about the DNS have shared their insights and hope. For me, a reframing of the ideas of *darkness* and *depression* happened during the journey. Ultimately, I emerged from each DNS with gratitude. I discuss examples of ways DNS impacted my thinking on this journey. The structure of a DNS may have not always made sense, but, every time, I found it worthwhile to endure. These historical descriptions may help illustrate and exemplify the meaning of the DNS.

WHAT IS THE DNS "DARK NIGHT OF THE SOUL"?

Julia Cameron provides the following brief description of the "Dark Night of the Soul": "I believe that the 'Dark Night of the Soul' is a common spiritual experience. I believe, too, that the answer is continued seeking and perseverance. It helps to know that others have endured a loss of faith."

There are volumes of works, from a variety of sources and traditions, filled with a wide range of interpretations and accounts of the "Dark Night of the Soul." The term "Dark Night of the Soul" can be traced back to medieval Christianity, especially the words and work of St. John of the Cross. He describes a journey toward union with "God." Specifically, he says, "*God has to work in the 'Soul' in secret and in darkness, because, if we fully knew what was happening, and what mystery, transformation, 'God' and grace will eventually ask of us, we would either try to take charge or stop the whole process.*" (Wikipedia)

The "Dark Night of the Soul" is a very personal experience and matures over time to move toward union with "God." In the process of a DNS, one's belief system becomes undone. The "Soul" seems to be melting away.

The descriptions from the teachings of St. Teresa of Avila and St. John of the Cross identify "Soul" as part of each of us, to be joined with "God" over time; these best describe *my* experience and learning. "Spirit" is the experience of "God," which is always present and not within my control—even in those moments of feeling detached from "God/Spirit." During those turning points, I do not have access to the presence of "God."

I imagine that an open vessel for "Spirit" resides within. During the DNS, the most current vessel of the "Soul" is emptied so that "Spirit," the light of the "Divine," can swell within me. The inflow of "Spirit" into the "Soul" can be triggered unexpectedly at any time. The "Soul" can mistake "God" as hostile, because the most recent notion of "Spirit" has been shattered and purged to make room for the unexpected expansion of the "Soul." That may not make any sense. No matter what anyone says about the DNS, you are unable to believe them. These activities are part of a design to join the "Divine" with the human as part of a growing and emerging foundation of "Faith."

> *"The dark night of the soul is when you have lost the flavor of life but have not yet gained the fullness of divinity. So it is that we must weather that dark time, the period of transformation, when what is familiar has been taken away and the new richness is not yet ours."*
>
> —*Ram Dass*

From the tradition of Islam come the words of the Sufi teacher Hazrat Inayat Khan, who notes:

"There can be no rebirth without a dark night of the 'Soul,' a total annihilation of all that you believed in and thought that you were." (Vibrations Quotes Website)

WHAT DOES DNS MEAN TO ME?

I've come to understand that, for me, the meaning of DNS will forever evolve. As I reflect on my history with the DNS, I realized over time that I needed to learn about it. The evolutionary story of my experience of DNS feels disordered. How I felt about the episodes and how I emerged from them varied. Sometimes, I traveled a previous experience, and others felt like I was regressing in my understanding of the DNS. This unpredictable, nonlinear trajectory felt jumbled to me. It involved pain, confusion, and endurance, and yet, eventually, I saw the light in my "Soul" even in the midst of darkness.

The *person of "God"* was central to my religious beliefs growing up. My Protestant background did not talk about any such experience as the DNS. The Catholic association with DNS was somewhat off-putting, due to my limited view of the practice of Catholicism. As I learned and experienced more, I noticed that the DNS created a connection not only to "Spirit" and the presence of "God" but to the deeper expansion of my interior "Soul."

The most perilous challenge of the "Dark Night" impacted my "Soul," during which it demanded *trials* of my "Soul." To endure these encounters with the "Dark Night" did not test my beliefs or spiritual practices. Instead, they offered me chances to explore, experiment, and enhance my spiritual life. Surrender of my "Soul" to "God" did not erase my "Soul" but opened up the vulnerability of my "Soul" to something greater and better. Even though I did not *feel* the presence of "God" in those times, I knew I was in a safe, potentially growth-filled situation. The "Dark Night" did not bury me; in truth, it created a vast universe for consideration and further expeditions into my "Soul" and awareness of the presence of the "Spirit" and "God." There is no way to predict when a DNS will happen or how to avoid it. It is a very private matter and feels embarrassing at times, because it is so abstract and impossible to share.

When I entered an episode of the "Dark Night of the Soul," I felt completely stranded. In the fullness of the "Dark Night," I did not know where I was "Spiritually," except that I felt persistent separation from "God." I did not know where to turn or what I was supposed to learn. I found each "Dark Night" was a journey worth taking, with the offer of something unexpected and richer in my "Soul" and my relationship with "Spirit."

Over time, I appreciated that the storms of the DNS not only disrupted my life but also came to clear a path for new directions for spiritual development. Even in the "Dark Night," I performed activities of daily living despite my inner suffering. The familiar parade of an army of *negative* thoughts ensued. I lost all hope. *I couldn't resurrect the skills I had in the past. Nothing will ever change. I am worthless. I am unlovable. I do not have a future worth living.* These thoughts reverberated throughout me. The potential to revive insights from previous instances of the "Dark Night" was inaccessible. Still, there were the infrequent flashes that there must be more to learn, to feel, to see, but I could not grasp them. Eventually, I would recall that, indeed, I needed to indulge in silence to emerge from this hell.

The "Dark Nights of the Soul" also produced more endless questions and mixed messages. However, I learned that I could observe, acknowledge them, and let them peacefully pass by without question or judgment of myself. My thoughts were random expressions of my meandering understanding of life. In one sitting, I could cover the gamut of despair to the recollection of wisdom I received.

6.3.2011: I am a victim of many circumstances. I don't trust myself. I am a worthless person because I don't work. Depression won't go away. I have no sense of direction in life. I have a fractured image of myself. I see myself as broken, helpless, and hopeless, without merit—all images that come from me (and from no one else).

Woven in between . . .

I am loved by my family, especially my mom. Work is just a necessary part of life. The birds are singing without cares/worries. I am intelligent. I can overcome the challenges life throws at me. "God" is present. Breast cancer is a passing affliction. I can focus energy on healing.

Finally, there is so much negativity present, and I don't know how to combat it. Maybe it isn't about combat, rather, about letting go.

Agony. In the fullness of the "Dark Night," I didn't know where I was "Spiritually," except I felt persistent separation from "God." I did not know where to turn. Amidst suffering, "Spirit" can be obliterated, but "Soul" is still there. My loving friends and family wished me well, but my condition did not improve. I deeply wanted to feel joy and fulfillment, and to manifest prosperity, but nothing from others had an impact. I sensed a difference, something was awry, and my meditations failed to console me. At these times, the agony in my mind and heart briefly rested from turbulence, and even these fleeting times of calm were deeply appreciated.

I just dragged through the motions of day-to-day survival during the "Dark Night." Negativity and despair seemed amplified by the depression; I had no concept of whether things might get better for me. There were no signs my life would improve.

I turned to activities, like reading specific books or listening to special pieces of music that previously had created insight or comfort, but nothing touched me deep inside. I returned to previous enriched *words of wisdom* collected from so many sources, yet now they were useless. I was struck that there was nothing I could do! I tried to stay receptive to randomly occurring options, but despite any efforts I made, nothing soothed my anguish. My separation from "God" widened and penetrated sharply within my bones. This only reinforced my assumption that I could not get better.

Depression constantly left me gripped in hopelessness and helplessness, without a motive to go on living. My animated celebration of life was gone, and through the DNS, I trudged onward, in what seemed a devastated and barren land, abandoned by "God." Despite this, I learned there was an inkling in the back of my mind that connection with "Spirit" was forecast with the experience of the "Dark Night." Pieces of art, my means for the expression of periodic insights, were typified by the inclusion of light during these times.

> *3.3.2011: It is being with the "Divine" that will let me hear the messages and guidance that I know comes from within. It is the union with you, "God," that I seek to feel and experience peace and to gain some clarity about the direction of my life. I don't need to know it all, but I need some first steps. Help me be non judgmental and not "should" on myself. I know you accept me unconditionally, but I don't "feel" it.*

Waves of agony constantly swept me into oblivion, with occasional glimpses of possibilities.

WHAT IS THE RELATIONSHIP
BETWEEN DNS AND DEPRESSION?

Learning about the "Dark Night of the Soul" brought me to explore a possible relationship with depression. There are those who believe that the DNS and depression co-exist. In the traditions of "Faith" and "Spirituality," the "Dark Night of the Soul" is sometimes associated with depression, though not always. Could I integrate the two? Was the experience of the "Dark Night of the Soul" an essential element of the journey through depression?

> *6.23.2016: Interesting to note that I am having trouble seeing the relationship between the "Dark Night" and depression. I have long thought they were linked. What strikes me is whether depression can happen **without** a "Dark Night."*

Ironically, the unpredictable course of my depression delivered to me prospects for change and improvement. Amidst the repeated excursions through the "Dark Night," I embraced them as an integral part of my life, even in the face of depression. This change in perception helped me further cradle and accept depression. I started to believe that depression did not have to cripple love, kill friendship, or silence my courage. Despite shattered hopes, corroded "Faith," destroyed self-confidence, separation from my emotions and the future, and memories erased—my "Soul" sucked dry—I survived!

In fact, many others and I pass through multiple excursions of DNS during life. Depression and "Dark Nights of the Soul" defy description through words and are difficult to separate. I struggled to communicate the mystery encountered in these eventualities to very important family, friends, and mentors with little success. Eventually, I had to accept that what I expected of myself was unrealistic. I did not have to have words. I just needed to be open to the supports that surrounded me, without any expectations. In the long run, the DNS provided a metaphor for depression that moved it from an affliction to an experience of life to appreciate. The notion of whether depression and the DNS are related does not have a specific answer. I came to realize they were unique events but not necessarily related. In my life, they frequently coincided.

CAN I RETHINK *DARKNESS* AND *DEPRESSION*?

By virtue of the use of *dark*, there may be a foregone conclusion that the "Dark Night of the Soul" is negative. Historically, *darkness* is characterized as a negative attribute. We use simplistic, manufactured dichotomies to attempt to make sense of the world around us. We somehow need to categorize things, organize them, and put them into neat little boxes that we think will somehow help us better understand and translate what transpires around us. I know, as do many mystics over the eternity of time, that darkness generates seeds for new ideas, enriches me, provides new insights, introduces new options to explore, and precipitates eternal growth. The "Dark Night" sets the scene for learning, a reason for me to have optimism. There will never be enough time in my life to acquire all of the enlightenment available to pursue and consume. I choose topics or aspects of life to explore and find myself on the receiving end of a continuous string of options to reflect on and absorb. Maybe the darkness is just about a resting time, to prepare my mind and "Soul" for whatever is next to come.

My mind drives me crazy sometimes, and I just wish I could turn it off! Too much bombards me. I step out of the *time frame* that I have put on the world to allow a different context to emerge. Sometimes the new time frame is necessary to remind me to regroup, back off, and return to the present moment, where reality lives. Maybe my feeling that things are bad is because they are different, something I cannot explain or convey to others yet are very real to me. Does that make me wrong or crazy? No, in fact, it might mean that my perception of life events from a different point of view provides new ideas, insights, and direction to myself. OMG—I feel like I am completely reframing my experience of the "Dark Night" and depression as an opportunity to see the world differently and share possibilities with others who might be stuck in paralyzing ruts that they don't even realize they're in.

Being in a rut is often viewed as dreadful because it means one is *stuck*. But the rut-dwellers should not be judged as *bad*; rather, languishing in a rut may close off access to other possibilities, explanations, and directions. The rut can become *safe* and feel *positive*, though it may actually be *stunting growth* in many different ways. I can share my perceptions and thoughts, but I don't have to proselytize. I can just lift up food for thought. Some will be refreshed, some will be overwhelmed, some will find it a bunch of BS, and some will welcome another view/opportunity. If one is a lifelong learner, there are no borders, limitations, or restrictions to the evolution of change, because there is always another route that can lead to abundance. Just as the old trees of centuries past tell us, the paths and possibilities are actually infinite. That can be scary because it can potentially open doors that I don't like or want to explore. If I am not receptive to the range of options, then I am truly at a dead end. In a sense, *it's a problem of my own making*, because I have put limits on the potential realities.

Due to depression's debilitating power, my deeper dive during "Dark Night" episodes was less apparent to others. My "Perspective Mentors" saw evidence of a difficult time though did not discern me as any better or worse off from the palpable, pervasive presence of depression. Those who recognized something was up had no idea how to help or support me. My loving friends and family wished me well, but my depression did not improve with DNS. I deeply wanted to feel joy and fulfillment, and to manifest prosperity, but nothing I got from others had an impact. I sensed a difference; something was awry, and my meditations failed to console me during the DNS. My previous sensitivity to and awareness of the suffering of others—even when I was depressed—was nonexistent during DNS, and that runs contrary to my history of compassion and care for others.

Some others thought they understood what I was going through because they claimed they'd had a similar experience. From them came a message of encouragement to keep on going. They knew me well enough to know that, if I quit attempts to move through my despair, I would beat myself up and only intensify my depressed state. My "Perspective Mentors" were sure I had inner potential that was yet to be realized. I tried the advice that came from wise people around me, but for naught. My "Perspective Angel" knew I was ready to take on a new challenge even if I did not believe it myself. I needed to step out of my comfort zone and explore new directions in my life. This led to moments of self-alienation and doubt. I felt inadequate, and my sense of bewilderment seemed endless. When I was buried in the depths of the "Dark Night" and depression, I didn't grasp or understand what was going on. I felt isolated because I was sure no one else could possibly imagine or appreciate how I thought or comprehend the degree of my misery. I would do *anything* to get out of the state of depression or the DNS, yet I was stuck.

3.9.1997: I have talked to my sister and a friend about the process I am in, and both are concerned about my depression. I knew it was a "Dark Night of the Soul." Even at my worst with depression, I knew I should not make a judgment about myself or anyone or anything else because of my skewed view. This was not a time to set expectations for myself, which would only add to my frustration. I needed to give up the need to know why things happened as they did. I tried to remind myself that the unscheduled events of my life were a form of spiritual direction I could trust. I needed the courage to make necessary choices and to realize I simply could not change something. I needed to stop driving myself to "be better." I needed constant reminding that my life could come back to being meaningful if I was patient and took whatever amount of time was necessary to resurface and move on.

BENEFITS OF ENDURING THE "DARK NIGHT OF THE SOUL"

DNS sets the scene for hope and brings forth a richer love of "Soul," life, and "God." There have been innumerable gifts from the experiences of the "Dark Night." Key aspects of my life that have been impacted include the maturation of patience, an evolving and deepening sense of responsibility for my spiritual life, and chances to explore, experiment, and expand my "Soul" and "Spirit."

Patience has always been a challenge for me, which I discuss in a previous chapter devoted wholly to the development of patience. I discovered that enduring the "Dark Night" challenged my patience. But I also learned that the ability to stay with the experience of the "Dark Night" provided intense lessons in the practice of patience. The stripping that occurred during the "Dark Night" laid bare aspects of my character at times and required a closer look at my transformation with patience. This required ongoing consideration of ways that I misunderstood and even dismissed the benefits of practicing patience. The intense encounters with the "Dark Night" did not allow me to ignore patience. These times became a womb for me to shelter from the demands of the day-to-day and contributed to the maturation of my understanding of the importance of patience. I attended to possibilities perhaps otherwise inaccessible if I had not taken time away to reflect.

My sense and understanding of responsibility also grew. A key realization was that taking responsibility for the needs and wishes of *others* detracted from taking responsibility for *myself.* Part of the challenge for me was not wanting to appear selfish or self-centered. Episodes of the "Dark Night" taught me that I could build personal strength and stamina through attention to my needs and self-care. Over time, that sense of responsibility grew, and I realized that no one else would take responsibility for my specific needs. I needed to exercise my self-responsibility to open avenues for further growth.

Unexpectedly, these times became incubators for me to practice patience. With the passage of time, my hindsight of the "Dark Night" experience showed "Dark Nights" as *spiritual trials*, not a psychological illness. Inspiration filled the emptiness of depression temporarily. I often questioned if I should willingly revisit the road of the "Dark Night." Was I ready to learn, or did I have to experience something more in order to be ready?

As I emerged from occasions of the "Dark Night," I was filled with wonder, reflection, a chance to learn, signs of growth, fresh insights, inspired meaning, and new directions for my life. I saw my existence through a novel set of lenses. Sometimes it took me to a deeper level of contemplation, perhaps more confusion. This shifted my rigid, logical linear thought into something much broader and far more interesting. Easy . . . No . . . Pleasant . . . No . . . Amazing . . . Yes!

The process of the emergence of "Soul" and "Spirit" and the presence of "God" is just that. I never *arrive*. I am on a voyage or trek to investigate life. There are many twists and turns; the ability to remain open to them—not anticipate or expect particular outcomes—kept my eyes and heart exposed to a boundless spectrum of prospects. I discovered that challenges became opportunities. I may have been blunted by depression and left to believe there was no future. I understood that I could remain in the "Dark Night" as a way to shut out the rest of the world. It extended my receptiveness to whatever came from outside of myself or from within. Frequently, I sold myself short. I didn't give myself credit for what I knew. Often, I would not respect my insatiable thirst for the unknown. I suspected there was always something more to seek that was not even on my radar screen yet. Instead of over-scrutinizing myself as damaged for life by depression and the "Dark Nights of the Soul," I emerged with a view of myself as renewed, enriched, and privileged, with unlimited chances to deepen my "Soul."

What were some of the things that made the "Dark Night" amazing? My view of creation expanded infinitely. My broadened sphere incited a thirst for more learning. I was reminded of the importance of spending time in nature. I gained a renewed commitment to regular time for meditation and contemplation. I, at least temporarily, banished the expectations of how "Spirit" should or should not be in my life. A few times, this led to further study of multiple spiritual traditions. I wanted to read about the lives, shared lessons, reflections, musings, wisdom, and experiences of figures like Buddha and Gandhi. I also expanded my meditation practice through the integration of messages from more current teachers, like Sharon Salzberg, Jon Kabat-Zinn, and Jack Kornfield. I learned, once again, that there were not any easy answers, but there **were** unlimited potential options.

I love how Caroline Myss, a modern mystic, characterizes the "Dark Night of the Soul."

The dark night of the "Soul" is a journey into light, a journey from your darkness into the strength and hidden resources of your "Soul."

✦ ✦ ✦

LIVED EXPERIENCES AFFECT
MY THOUGHTS

The good news is that—over time—a stunning metamorphosis took place, and in the end, I found lessons hidden behind relentless, overwhelming doubt and negativity. My life has been one of constant change, which has impacted my thoughts, insights, questions, and perspectives. These challenges were also present in the unfolding of my "Spirit." They have not been static; they've continued to evolve, yet I vigorously maintain core principles and values about life that have always nourished me.

Many, many times, I have felt like my thinking had gone astray, *but* I discovered I have a powerful brain that explores many ideas, with results that can help me or hinder me. For example, I gained numerous illuminations as I sought to *be with my views*. I realized I could not change things by "speeding up" my thinking. The impact of the rumination traps I fell into could be either helpful or not helpful. I needed a shift in the classification of my thoughts from negative to positive.

Above all, I needed some self-compassion, which could act as a life preserver from my interpretation of lived experiences. It is not pathological to think differently from others. Even changes in my notions of "Spirit" could be healthy. These ideas encompassed ways that I think about myself, through self-appraisal and awareness of positive/negative characterizations. Examination of the contrasts led me to realize I needed to figure out how to be gentler with myself.

The downside of my powerful brain? My days were filled with unlimited questions without answers and left me like a dog in an incessant chase after my own tail. Was I at war with myself? Was I caught in a world of "yes, but," "if only," and "why can't it be"?

I eventually concluded that my thoughts had not really *gone astray*. Rather, they reflected the influence of my lived experience, how I often felt, and how I saw my life in a particular instant. I could not paint in words how I felt or what I needed. Depression colored, clouded, and created further turmoil in my head and heart; it reflected ongoing struggles and lack of insight into what was happening to me. The questioning continued.

TOO MUCH THINKING WILL
NOT SPEED THINGS UP

I had unknowingly created one of my greatest challenges. I presumed I would get crystal-clear clarity if I thought long, hard, and fast enough. Maybe an analysis of my ideas could explain what was going on with my approach and perspective. For example, I fantasized how these efforts would result in insight or direction to lead me to *Just get to it and do it!* I thought this

106

would speed up the process of finding a treatment to relieve my anguish. I wanted to flip a switch in my thinking that would suddenly change my assumptions of the situation for the better.

The clarion call of my misery screamed from the kinds of books I chose to read and the copious number of journals I filled. My rambling thoughts in many different colors of ink in my journals frequently led to voracious "thinking" and searching. Naively, I believed that all of these efforts would gain the upper hand for good. Instead, I felt more confused and incompetent. Failure seemed certain. I *really* needed help with perspective and insight to adjust my perceptions.

I consistently felt disadvantaged by my intelligence because I could not turn off my constant drive to *do something* through thinking I was convinced that improvement of my thoughts would shift my perspective in a better direction. In truth, if I stayed present in the moment and indulged in what I experienced in the here and now, I might experience some relief. Inadvertently, I put myself on an endless hamster wheel of divergent thinking, whisking me away into infinite clouds filled with how I could make myself feel better.

5.20.2011: Our upsetting emotions and maladaptive behavior are caused by distortions in thinking and irrational beliefs. I must have positive feelings to know that the depression is fading, and I am moving toward health.

The relentless presence of depression perpetually incited me to look for scholarly information to provide meaning, understanding, and insight into my life. If I could find answers in those professional realms that told me what to do, I would get better.

Again, it was the old mistaken notion that, if I *do* something, things can't help but get better. Despite my efforts and mistaken hopes, I continued to feel overwhelmed. Interestingly, I always seemed to experience an affirmation from somewhere. *I will be okay!!!* (Was that "God"?)

Cognitive-Behavior Therapy (CBT) was currently held in high regard as a very effective treatment for depression at the height of my most severe episode, but it complicated my assessment of my thinking and beliefs. CBT is a therapy that is supposed to adjust thought patterns related to stressful life events in order to change moods and behaviors. Negative feelings are viewed as the result of twisted beliefs or thoughts that need to be altered.

My conclusion about CBT was, in theory, *if I just hurried up and changed my thinking, I would feel better faster.* Naively, I thought my intense reasoning should be able to move my difficult treatment process along. Instead, I beat my already-bruised and -aching head against wall after wall. Nothing changed except the size of the wound. If my thoughts were irrational, why couldn't I rationalize my way out of them? I could see the premise intellectually: My inability to disengage from my thinking-head thoughts left me isolated in my head, divorced from reality. My intellect had detached from my "Soul."

Even this intellectual analysis of what was happening to me did not help in the midst of despair. I continued to repeatedly ask questions; sometimes I hoped "Spirit" ("God") would have answers or recommendations I could pursue to help me stop just flapping in the wind, consumed by misery. Yet, in the midst of despair, I discovered insights into what was taking place and what I thought I needed. Here is a vivid image of my experience of despair:

6.26.2011: As a dragonfly, I feel tied down, unable to move. There are millions of threads weighed down by the depression. I don't know what those weights are. Are they fears of moving on with my life? Of being so depressed the rest of my life? Of not succeeding in wherever and whatever I move on to? What would flying free feel like? Will it take the death of my parents to set me free? Would flying free mean the return of self-confidence, self-esteem, opening doors, and making new friends? Of being and feeling independent?

Fortunately, or unfortunately, I experienced feeling like a spinning yo-yo, because my mood fluctuated wildly from one extreme to another within brief periods of time. There were remnants of hope that seemed just out of immediate reach. I felt instances of inescapable despair, and then, out of nowhere, I would be filled and overflowing with possibilities of how "God" could help me.

5.20.2011: Are the depressive episodes harming systems, such as the cardiac, in my body? I feel like there is a screen over my mind that muddies it, makes it feel inaccessible, and doesn't let good things in. Can I analyze the depression? I think I have, and it has gotten me nowhere. How could my reasoning affect the depression? It seems like meditation should be helping the depression, but I'm not seeing any results. I see my life as burdened by depression, which has cut me off from my emotions, the future, and my connection with God. I do see myself as "mentally defective." I don't see myself as undesirable, though sometimes I feel I am needy. I don't see a future, so how can I judge it?

Less than one month later, I wrote:

6.12.2011: "God"—I beg of you that you guide me forth. Help me find work that is intellectually demanding, that is meaningful to me, and that lets me be of service to others. I open my heart and "Soul" to Your Presence, your Guidance. I pray for an island of peacefulness in the violent storm I am in. I come in prayer and mindfulness, with an open mind and "Soul," to receive whatever Guidance you have for me. I know the answers are within, but I have been unable to tap into them. Help me recognize your messages, no matter how small they are.

These real and pervasive thoughts of misery flooded my mind and "Soul." They would not beat me down, nor would I surrender; so, I thrashed through the image of darkness, determined to conquer the pall. Despite this battle I waged with myself, I eventually came to comprehend that accepting depression as part of me would be essential to give myself permission just *to be*. Wherever I landed in my own process, I would respect the authenticity of my ideas, based on lived experience, even when it felt bad. I didn't have complete control over change. I still bludgeoned myself for my thoughts. Even though there were no answers in my mind, heart, "Soul," or "Spirit," I had come to understand that I was often hard on myself for not changing my thinking.

RUMINATION ON HELPFUL AND NOT-SO-HELPFUL THOUGHTS

Rumination was a trap that often captured me and carried me deeper into the bottomless pit. I went around and around with considerations that did not take me anywhere but only spiraled me into greater pain. In those moments, thoughts generated by my lived experience did not redirect me—they actually exacerbated my state. At the same time, they triggered strong emotions that were real and needed to be validated—not labeled or judged.

Like anything, the many definitions of rumination hoist its complexity to the surface. Rumination is not always a bad thing. The aspects of rumination most present in my life included contemplation, meditation, worry, a variety of considerations, and deep thoughts. My worry focused on possible causes for why things happened to me. How could I have prevented excursions that I assumed led me into vicious circles? In the repeated searches to uncover reasons for my misery and strategies to ameliorate my despair, I missed the importance and benefits of staying present in the here and now.

Rumination, a definite component of depression, quite often frustrated me because I could not break what I perceived as running in circles, which led nowhere. I recognized this process when I noted that my journals held the same repetitive descriptions day after day, especially at times of my deepest depression. No sense of future, one of the most persistent and agonizing topics that circled my mind, took me down. I kept wondering how I could take care of myself in the future. Thoughts of suicide accompanied this preoccupation because I could not come up with any solutions to these troubling ideas. Despite reassurance from those around me, these concerns persisted.

2.19.2010: I worry that any form of motivation will return, that I will not have any idea about how to live my life, and that I will *be permanently financially dependent on my family and unable to live independently. I wish I could turn the rumination in my mind off. I have been in negative-thinking mode for more than two years. If it were only thoughts, I would have changed them by now, but I feel trapped, unable to reframe my despair or to see any hope of any kind. How **does** this get turned around? I don't trust my own thoughts. I feel they are jaded and seen through a lens of negativity. I don't trust myself because I feel like a failure.*

I felt an element of shame. "Why can't I take care of myself?" Without a second thought, I had cared for others for years. Now, it was time to attend to *my own* personal health and needs. I asked many times how to get myself out of this conundrum. On some level, I knew I was stewing in my own toxic and rancid juices, but I could not break out of the tortuous progression. Another distraction that consumed me was "When does the depression get better? *Or, does it get better?*" If it was not going to get better—if there was *no* potential for that—then why go on?

For a period of time, my rumination focused on questions related to my future: Should I leave the field of psychology? "Give it up"? Was I competent? Is there enough knowledge left in me to do the work I loved? Do I have anything left to give? Will I be throwing away the years of higher education and the associated expenses? How could I handle the pressures of private practice? How would I keep up with a full-time job that required stamina to function during the week? There were no guarantees for me; it was clear that I never knew from day to day how I would/would not be able to function. Fatigue also contributed and was present, no matter what I did (e.g., exercise, meditate, eat healthier, take vitamins, volunteer, read positive or entertaining things, etc.).

From a positive perspective, rumination can be a way to solve problems. By keeping a goal in the forefront of my mind, I was open to means of solving problems. That was interesting, as I had solved many problems over the course of my life! For example, my dad was not a handyman, but I always tried to fix things or figure them out. The chair I am sitting on right now had a broken caster, and I had the piece that had fallen off. I just kept at it until I got it on firmly. This took thinking of multiple possible solutions to the problem, and I figured it out!

When it came to addressing depression, immobilization, hopelessness, helplessness despair, none of my problem-solving skills was available. I was told by my "Perspective Mentors" that my cognitive abilities, including problem-solving, were still there, that I never suffered from cognitive impairment. So, why couldn't I come up with ways to stop the progression of depression?

SHIFTING THOUGHTS FROM
NEGATIVE TO *POSITIVE*

Most people would characterize my expressed thoughts as *toxic*. The fluctuations of my disease pushed me into unknown forests of darkness that blinded me, jolted my "Soul," and pulled me away from any hint of optimism

There is a familiar theme throughout my journals. When I had an upbeat experience or thought of something I knew was positive, I continued to feel depressed and/or unable to respond in an emotionally optimistic manner or see any inherent worth or value in me.

I considered depression *negative*. How could I possibly express the experience of depression to reset the negative connotation I associated with it? Logic would say that if you were in a beautiful, restful, healthy, nurturing place, there would be no reason to be depressed. I had such qualities, but I still lived depressed. I strived to stay afloat uneasily. I became disenchanted with my journal writing and the overall feeling of being *down*. How could I lasso those rogue thoughts that seemed to take me down? Rein them in and maybe *think* my way out of them? My clueless brain would not let go of *thinking* as a powerful approach to change my mindset.

The underlying thread of depression I lived with made shifts in my thinking and feeling from a *negative* perception to a *positive* one utterly impossible. Writers in professional literature, non-fiction works, and novels regularly associate depression with darkness, and in doing so, frame depression as negative. I view darkness versus light as a manufactured dichotomy people use to try to make sense of the world around us. Without a sense of future for myself, it did not matter whether an event was on one side or the other. As I rode the roller coaster of up-and-down moods over so many years, I never felt I really ever landed in a place where I felt self-confident or believed in my own recovery. I could not even find any peeks into my future or discover anything positive I could grab to hold on to for an extended period of time.

My perception and labeling of the *positive* and *negative* experiences in life remained relative to what was happening on a given day. I craved continuity and stability. I guess I also wanted the predictability of the next steps, which proved non-existent. Chronically *going to war with myself* wreaked collateral damage to my body, mind, and "Spirit." I once viewed "going to war" as a strong, admirable representation of the intensity of my determination to get better. While the process drained me, it gave me *something I could do*, which was better than sitting with my ruminating thoughts.

Those around me put in tons of effort to try to shift the valence of my perspective from bad to constructive or to help me find some beneficial insight. Many times, the extraordinary bids from others did not seem to make any difference, though, in hindsight, they planted seeds of hope I did not recognize at the time. I independently discovered an important contribution to a shift in my thinking. When I paid attention to myself, my strengths, my productive thoughts, and my legitimate needs, I could grasp some positive perspective.

GRABBING THE LIFE PRESERVER OF SELF-COMPASSION

The notion of self-compassion raised many questions in my mind, however, as my insight expanded, I came to better comprehend its importance. I learned that self-compassion opened space in which to flourish. Raised by my parents to be thoughtful about others, I worried that self-compassion could be interpreted as selfish or self-serving. I now appreciate that, unless I practice self-compassion, I personally cheat myself of opportunities. I found it difficult to put myself first; it took time and concerted effort. In the long run, this action signaled self-respect, and, sooner or later, it would benefit others. Self-compassion made me treat myself with kindness and acceptance. The realization that everyone is imperfect in some ways eased my ever-present feelings of personal degradation.

Permanently available self-compassion, regardless of mood or situation or location provides reliable support. I can implement it at any moment. In theory, the more I engage in self-compassion, the less the chance I would exacerbate my depression. Key forms of kindness I used to nurture "Me" include self-awareness and patience. When I stopped the worthless comparison of my life with others, I saved energy. I realized self-compassion's importance over self-improvement. To have compassion for myself meant acceptance of life for where it is in any given moment, and I viewed it as a springboard for the future. Use of self-compassion reduced my search for someone to reinforce, affirm, appreciate, or praise me. When I embraced self-compassion, it freed up energy for other actions.

My epitome of self-compassion occurred as I cared for my aging Mother, as her needs continued to increase with time and grew more intense. I waited a long time to cry "Help!" to my sisters. Insight from my circle of "Perspective Mentors" thought I waited too long to express my needs. I came to realize exhaustion and lack of patience affected both me and my mother. I needed to climb over the barriers of shame and achieve a sense of responsibility before I could express my needs. I had discounted the fact that my reactions and feelings *were* warranted. It also meant I had to voice the irrational fear that, somehow, I would become estranged from them. Self-compassion helped "Me" recognize that and strengthened my ability to speak my truth. To feel whole, I needed to practice several forms of self-compassion to move forward with my life.

THINKING DIFFERENTLY IS *NOT* PATHOLOGICAL

The insinuation that accompanies thoughts viewed as *pathological* or *negative* implies that something needs to be fixed or a person needs to be *treated* and changed. If someone saw my frame of mind as pathological, that meant that I was, somehow, responsible for the "strange" or different thoughts I expressed. Alternatively, those thoughts expressed my own experiences at that moment in time, my sense of vulnerability, or my willingness to risk and to reach out for understanding. These efforts need to be respected and not judged. To share such emotions with another person or therapist requires bravery of you and of me, because we must expose our vulnerability. I know most people do not want to talk about emotions for many reasons. To find the help I required, I wanted to be heard and held with care and concern. That didn't require "Me" to change my thinking, rather, I preferred someone to listen carefully and provide a reflection. I longed for someone to compassionately encourage me to accept and explore the present, not feel blamed or admonished.

A specific example of a human characteristic sometimes viewed as pathological is the notion of an introvert as opposed to extrovert. I am an introvert. Our society views extroverts as generally more ambitious, driven, goal-oriented, and outspoken than introverts. As an introvert, I find my preference to sit back, listen, and watch interactions more beneficial than to jump into the fray of conversation and debate. As my close friend and I thought about and discussed introversion, we learned about the benefits and contributions of people who identify as introverts. We delved into consideration of other ways to characterize intro version. Were there other possible labels with a more positive connotation, as well as affirmations of our own lived experiences that we viewed as positive *because* we were introverts? I wondered if anyone ever saw my actions as foolish or inappropriate at the same time I actually found myself pleased with what happened.

It's a timeless question: What's better? To be an introvert or to be an extrovert? We base our perspectives on what we have heard, lessons taught, experiences, and what other people have defined. This dichotomy has been the subject of a number of books that, largely, have come from the business world. Interesting research has identified advantages for each orientation to the world and assumed that introverts were somehow too quiet for their own good, or depressed, or shy or unable to engage in whatever activity. Negative assumptions about introverts focused on how internal beliefs, experiences, and thoughts of the individual interfered with their ability to step outside of themselves. Such negative frames rarely addressed the context of a person's thinking or lived experiences. They were probably unaware of the possibilities that may explain a position. These alternatives might include a person's health preferences or situations in which a person could be struggling with grief, mental illness, or threats to daily life functioning. Without knowledge of the context of an individual's life experience, thoughts labeled as "pathological" may actually be important, healthy, and meaningful.

Here's an "Aha!" moment: For me as an introvert, my pondering repeatedly proved beneficial and led to surprising and rich wisdom. Time for reflection and a surrounding where I slowed down, opened "Me" up to receive unexpected visions that proved fruitful. You see, I recognized the "Aha!" moments as reconnections to the presence of "Spirit," with the "Greater Being Within." I sometimes lost touch with and even dismissed these ideas as unimportant or "off the wall." Time for reflection allowed "Me" to delve into my genuine ability, no matter what form it took. I embraced these sentiments and did not label them good/bad, right/wrong, unrealistic/realistic, or something new/

something everyone else already knows. If everyone else knows it, what was wrong with me? Nothing.

My life now unfolds as it is, without requirements for certain attainments. The awakenings may seem odd or inexplicable when looked at from the outside, but I trust who I am and acknowledge my gifts. I have so much more to gain. The thread of "Faith" helps "Me" hold on to possibility, optimism, and interest in whatever arises. I need not question the messages that appear because they always carry goodness within them (despite my first reaction).

Once again, my "Perspective Mentors" came to the rescue. They appreciated and valued my way of thinking, which others might label as pathological. They took the time and listened with interest to understand what I was expressing, not judge me.

CHANGING THOUGHTS ABOUT "SPIRIT"

One moment, the presence of "Spirit" seemed certain, but if I "felt something missing," I thought I lacked a connection to "God." In part, I relied on ideas about what "God" should do to help "Me" as long as I prayed. Of course, if I prayed to "God," she would make everything better. On the flip side, I experienced the presence of "God" multiple times in my life— without fervent prayer—which expanded my understanding of the presence of "God." My changes in thoughts about "Soul" and "Spirit" were unpredictable and even stressful at times. My ambivalence about separation from "Spirit" is woven throughout this journey.

Among my explorations of "Spirit," I learned about the "Dark Night of the Soul" (previously discussed), an actual experience of any number of spiritual icons. I kept this in mind, to avoid dismissal of my experience, and to cultivate my awareness of something greater in my life.

Another vital change in perception emerged as I learned that the "Dark Night of the Soul" was shared knowledge of highly revered individuals and that such times carried many important insights and lessons. Sometimes we need to experience the disconnection from "God" to recognize when we are connected. The "Dark Night" is not a pleasant experience; however, it *is* an experience of growth. Questions about the "Dark Night" and the presence of "God" are a necessary part of the experience. There may be multiple times of the "Dark Night" in anyone's life; perhaps, most important of all, they ultimately lead to an even stronger relationship with "God." The evolution of my understanding from walks through "Dark Nights of the Soul" meant I realized they were not to be eradicated from my life— they were to be endured and appreciated.

The profound wisdom gained from "Dark Nights of the Soul" had the most dramatic impact on a change in my thoughts related to "God." My deep knowing did not require words or explanations—it became ingrained. It permeated my thoughts in such a way that I could no longer say "God" was not present. I knew I was part of "Spirit," and when I acknowledged that, I experienced peacefulness. These experiences did not "cure" or wipe out my gloomy thoughts, rather, they injected possibilities for the future and opened up opportunities. This stark series of events shifted my thoughts from negative to positive. I realized the difference in my thoughts reflected my "Spiritual" evolution. I understood in general that my thoughts were not deviant—they were, in fact, formative, regardless of how I perceived them.

SUMMARY

The presence or absence of "Spirit" was always on my mind, and I so wanted to feel that reconnection. I knew that my relationship with "God" had already made a huge difference in my life many times before. It also took me down, as I lacked an understanding of the presence of "God." I lived in a world of *if only* . . . a belief that feeling the integration of "God" in my life most certainly would make a difference.

In the end, I understood that my thoughts had not gone astray. I did not need to change my thinking or shift its value from negative to positive. I needed to practice self-compassion to appreciate my perspective and understand how I arrived at a given point. What I interpreted as *different* or *negative* was actually based on meaningful personal interpretations of lived experiences. I guess my *negativity* signaled not giving in or giving up and affirmed that other possibilities existed. I realized something was wrong and felt powerless to change the unwelcome drift of my thoughts. Of course, the unuseful [sic] question of "why" endlessly reared its ugly head. In reality, there are common interpretations or understandings of ideas, but that does not make everything else problematic. Our thoughts should not be judged dichotomously. The value of thoughts is in the eye of the beholder and changes with time to expand and enrich understandings.

◆　◆　◆

RESPONSIBILITY—A GIFT WITH A DOUBLE-EDGED SWORD

Even in my weakest times, I knew that, on some level, I had responsibility for my own well-being. It might mean revealing my vulnerability by asking for help with perspective. When I was confused, unsure, and afraid, I was on a downslide. I knew I needed help to relieve the pain in my gut, keep my chin above water, and reduce my anguish, at least a little. Taking a deep healing breath seemed to ease the knots of tension in my body. Other times, I simply made sure I ate a meal or got enough sleep. I tuned into the moment and realized there literally was something I could *do*, an action I could take in my own best interest. Such mundane, simple daily self-care was often difficult, yet essential to my ability to survive. The bigger aspect of responsibility was how I participated in my own mental and "Spiritual" healthcare.

ACCURATE DOCUMENTATION OF SYMPTOMS

The slog down the pothole-ridden trail of depression was ever-present. The ups and downs of the disease took me into uncharted waters, a constant quest. Part of getting the correct treatment and diagnosis required exact documentation of my symptoms. I was the most critical reporter of what was going on in my body (aches, pains, weakness, churning insides) and mind (anger, doubt, fear, self-beating, despair).

I felt an obligation to educate myself to be sure I was not missing some important symptom or factor that might be part of the puzzle. There was fatigue, no appetite, abdominal pain, lightheadedness, trouble sleeping, overall weakness, dull headache, profuse sweating, anxiety, and the list went on. Exasperating intellectual analysis madness kicked into gear when I started to worry. I took out my tools to dig some more, read, and research to figure something out even if it might seem far-fetched. One question arose for me: *"Are there additional characteristics of depression to consider? Just because we have the* DSM (Diagnostic and Statistical Manual of the American Psychiatric Association) *does not mean we have all of the answers or understand symptoms specific to depression."*

I used numerous strategies to document and follow my experiences. Charts abounded of my blood pressure, pain level, water consumption, amount of sleep, and when medications were taken. I recorded differences I noticed after taking medications or having medical treatment or a therapy session. I feared I was a hypochondriac who tried to get all of the attention I could get! But who would *want* to be fussed over in the manners required to figure out what was wrong and what I needed? The same symptom was typically related to multiple physical issues. Providers had to convince me that I needed to trust my experiences, not question them. They wanted me to objectively report what was going on. This was another place where I had to learn self-confidence and trust my observations. An accurate report of my well-being might help my providers decide the direction of treatment. Repeatedly, I had to be reminded of the stupendous number of factors I was coping with physically, emotionally, and mentally.

FOLLOW THROUGH

Diagnosis was an initial step in the convoluted system required to treat me. The therapist's experience and skill as a sleuth led to a quite in-depth probing and gentle exploration. In the big scheme of things, it was just a tiny step to determine the beginning of a course of treatment. As a child psychologist diagnosing toddlers with autism, I always have a conversation with families about the reason for a diagnosis. The bottom line is that a diagnosis does not really tell us what the individual needs or a specific treatment modality, but it does get the ball rolling.

In order for me to harvest maximum benefit from treatment, my responsibility was to accept and implement particular suggestions offered during therapy sessions and medical appointments. At times, I was so desperate I would have done anything to help myself! Typically, there was an endless wait for me to notice differences in how I felt. Most medications used to treat depression take four to six or more weeks to build up in my system and take effect. I had to document, chronicle, and report subjective symptom changes and side effects. Without information from me, the prescriber was unable to do her magic to determine the most effective doses. Despite my frequent reservations about medication, over time, I learned that my brain chemically needed them to help me be the most functional and successful person. At times, my duty was to record what was going on in my head in my journal to help chronicle troubling thoughts. Other times, it was literally documenting what I did to take care of myself.

I required constant reassurance that what I felt in my body was not my imagination and that meandering thoughts were part of my disease. I had to share embarrassment and humiliation if I wanted help. At times, I blindly trusted the insight and support of my "Perspective Mentors" and let go of whether I would be judged in a demeaning manner. This was all despite the ceaseless devotion, understanding, wisdom, patience, and respect of my "Perspective Mentors." They worked hard to maintain a protective safety net, to keep me from self-destruction.

Sooner or later, I listened to the guidance from that team which was so invested in my well-being. I began to endeavor to find ways to rise out of the ashes of the ruin to survive. My terror consisted of lopsided perceptions, questionable symptoms (my own questioning), and fears. I provided my team with copious details. I accepted whatever members of the team offered to guide me on a different trajectory.

Responsibility took on numerous forms and, over time, had a powerful impact on the treatment of my depression. Accounts of the "Faith" aspect of my journey were vital. I had to accept where I was at a given moment with the knowledge that depression and "Faith" were intertwined.

PERSONAL ADVOCACY

An extremely critical role I played in my own care was making sure that all of my key providers were in communication with each other. I also stayed current on the conglomeration of various treatments I was receiving, as well as daily life experiences that might figure into the big picture and state what I needed. It seems incredibly simple to listen to what the doctor says, fill the prescription, and take the medicine. But there is so much more than medication for the treatment of my depression. I wanted to stay informed and educated about options, because, in many cases, I often did not *fit the mold* or anticipate the effects of a particular treatment. I frequently endured rarely seen side effects of medication.

Psychiatric medications have a wide variety of side effects, as well as problems interacting with other drugs. At one point, there was a discussion about whether I should take one of the post-breast-cancer drugs (Aromatase Inhibitors, AIs) that impact hormone levels for prophylaxis to reduce the chances of cancer recurrence. I had horrible side effects that were intolerable and included deep pain in my bones, feeling more depressed, diminished concentration, and weight gain. There were not many drug options in this category, but another one was prescribed. When I got to the pharmacy, they told me that one of my antidepressants was contraindicated with the drug. I faced a complicated choice that I knew I had to make sooner or later on my own. I previously tried to take two different AIs that had side effects I could not tolerate.

I went back to my amazing oncologist, who had an in-depth conversation with me about my options and the possible amount of risk of recurrence affected by taking/not taking the AIs. He is a partner in my care who respects what I feel and think. He encourages me to make choices based on facts and consideration of my overall quality of life and personal preferences. Taking the AI would reduce my chances of recurrence by only three percent (so, again, the manipulation of hormones was raising its ugly head). He said that the risk of taking me off of my antidepressant was worse than not taking an AI. He gave me permission to make my choice. I *am* a whole person, and my wellness needed to encompass *all* aspects of my medical and psychiatric care.

One of the best examples of taking responsibility for my own care came when I decided I wanted a double mastectomy. There were different opinions about whether that most dramatic, drastic treatment was necessary. I was *truly* clear that I had already had an earlier bout with breast cancer and endured surgery and chemotherapy. My frustration was further fueled by the process of determination of the new diagnosis (multiple mammograms, biopsies, and the waiting and other tests to get to the most recent diagnosis). The new tumors were in both breasts, and one was a different kind of breast cancer from my first diagnosis. My breasts were quite large, in fact, the tissue they removed was almost 10 pounds. There were suggestions about possible targeted-radiation therapy. There are many different ways to deliver targeted radiation, and decisions required input from physicists, technicians, radiation oncologists, *et al*. *But* I had a Deep Brain Stimulator (DBS) generator at the top of my left breast. The DBS became a tremendous source of controversy. I was more than ten years removed from the DBS surgery, and I experienced more enjoyment, increased personal independence, and more. It was quite important to keep the DBS (Deep Brain Stimulator). I was faced with a choice between surgical removal of the stimulator if I wanted the mastectomy or just lumpectomies with the knowledge that cancer would probably recur.

I consulted several surgeons. One of them read an article about how the electrodes in my brain could fry brain tissue and do brain damage if cautery were to be used. Again, the size of my breasts was going to require cautery. This led me back to the doctors on the team in Atlanta, who constantly monitor my DBS treatment, and they assured me there should not be a significant risk. They had not seen an example of such a thing among the current study participants. I facilitated communication between the Phoenix and Atlanta doctors in an attempt to determine the safest treatment. In the end, the neurosurgeon from Atlanta wrote an incredible letter and explained the mechanics of how the DBS would/would not affect or damage my brain if they used cautery for the proposed surgery. Finally, I took his letter to a third surgeon, who read it and said he did not see any problem going forward with the surgery. I cannot begin to describe the effects of bouncing around with nothing to hold on to because there was so much to consider. Fortunately, there was no time for a depression episode.

This is one of the starkest illustrations of the importance and necessity for me to advocate, coordinate, and manage my own care. If someone is treated by an integrated team via an institution like Mayo Clinic, the patient is told when and where to show up and what to do. On the other hand, I had to coordinate lab work, x-rays, make appointments with specialists, make sure my insurance would cover the procedures and treatment, ensure medications were not contraindicated, and confirm who would physically help me during my recovery. When faced by such an overwhelming condition, to have to worry about all of the logistics and specifics, the accumulation of stressful factors continued to mount. There must be healthcare systems that value and implement coordination of care, so patients don't have to carry this burden. I found myself wandering in a maze that swallowed me up and left me dangling in the air. Given my multiple health problems, I wanted comprehensive and compassionate healthcare. Such care demands coordination and integration of care among multiple providers, to orchestrate healing. Ideally, the availability of a professional familiar with the different facets of my care could coordinate the care, keep me informed, support me through decision-making, and gift me a centralized contact.

INDISPENSABLE RISKS

The notion of risk was important in the evolution of my responsibility to myself. I discovered it was essential to be willing to risk trying or doing new and different things. The risk could be about: when I would do something; how I would do something; why I would do something; what belief might affect where I took a risk; what my motivation was for taking the risk. I was careful because all of these incessant questions could also be great stall tactics for a necessary move.

One of the biggest risks I took was when I went to the German ICYE (International Christian Youth Exchange Program, which landed me in Germany for one year). I went to the committee and told them about how one of their top people was *abusing* applicants who wanted to go on an exchange year. There were weekend gatherings where those of us who were in Germany from other countries and individuals from Germany who wanted to go on an exchange year came together. At these events, Germans were being interviewed and evaluated as potential exchangees. This person was extremely negative. He repeatedly found a vulnerability in an individual and manipulated that, taking the rug right from underneath them. One consistent observation was that, if a person said they wanted to go to America, he knocked that down, and it seemed to hamper the chances for that person. I was not the only student who felt that way, but I was angry. Other exchangees and I warned new applicants not to answer the question of where they wanted to go with "America" because he would take them out, and pull them under. I don't know where the gumption came from, but I actually contacted the committee, shared the numerous situations I had experienced with this person, and, in the end, I understand he was removed from the organization. In this instance, I acted on a belief in the value of every human being and doing no harm. I was willing to bring this situation to light because I did not want anyone else affected. I felt confident enough in my perceptions and decided to act.

An early struggle that is pervasive in my journals was needing "friends." With reflection and hindsight, I discovered this was triggered by an experience with my Dad. When I was around 20 years of age, he and I had an interaction that blew me away. He commented on how I brought many things of honor to him and my mother to be proud of, but I was socially a failure. As I have described, I always valued my solitude. My Dad was a social butterfly and could strike up conversations and interact with total strangers in any setting. While I heard "social failure,"

I think it was his frustration at me for not stepping out more socially. He sorely wanted me to have friends, engage in more social interactions, and find a husband. He thought I would be so much happier if I had friends and a husband. What is clear in my writing is that I then thought I *had to* have more friends. If I didn't have friends, that was bad for me. But it was also hard for me, something I had to *work on*. I actually had something *new* to worry about—the risk of making friends. So, I started to explore what I had to offer to friendships. What would make me appealing to others?

SOLITUDE—ESSENTIAL FOR HEALING

I am responsible for myself and drawing support for my healing. Another concern about an aspect of depression expressed by people on the outside is the tendency to self-isolate. I learned there are distinctive differences between isolation, loneliness, and a legitimate and healthy need for solitude. The benefits of isolation exist for many reasons: inability to carry on a conversation; fear of what someone might ask me or tell me; frightened that I was not physically up to doing something; worry about mistakes in my compromised state; and creation of a safe zone, where I would not be disturbed. Sometimes I simply did not have the physical energy to engage with anyone.

> 11.8.2008: Isolation prevails. I can't talk about what is going on. I can't do so many things because of the immobilization, physically, emotionally, and mentally. This removes me from professional friendships, and, while I feel quite sure I can rekindle them, I am separated for now. It is just more of this incredibly low place I am in.

It is interesting I rarely find references to loneliness in my writing. I think that is because "loneliness" meant a lack of anyone or anything to support me, based on my unworthiness. I *relished* the solitude. Solitude provided a time to experience the internal pandemonium, confusion, and chaos in my mind and heart; solitude meant a silent space to quiet the storm and listen to or talk with myself. Self-care meant a focus on breathing, stretching out the breaths, and evening the inhalation and exhalation, which created time to renew my energy, rejuvenate myself, or experience mindboggling insights. Over time, I discovered I could have solitude, anytime, anywhere, by taking some deep breaths and a personal reminder to stay present in the moment. Solitude opens the possibility of communion with "God." Patient waiting in silence allowed presence in solitude. There were times when solitude signaled acceptance of something I was unable to change and an incentive to move on.

8.15.1999: Silence is always available. I must choose to enter it. It is warm, enveloping arms, full of endless embrace. Silence is both empty and full. Thoughts, problems, and ideas may all step aside for these moments of total silence.

Solitude is a time that is effortless, fulfilling, healing, grounding, and growing. In the "hurry-up" world where I try to squeeze all I can out of 24 hours, silence is a warm, safe spot. One of the greatest things I found in solitude was the presence of "Spirit." It was not always there when I wanted it, but, on another level, *I knew it was always there.* At any moment, in solitude, I might be swept up in a net of shelter and security that served as an elixir and weakened the claws of depression.

6.6.2011: Dear "God": I do not fear solitude, rather, I see it as an opportunity. I come with the hope that I will reconnect with you. That I will reunite with you, believing that your presence in my life is healing, and that your absence from my perception and feeling leaves me in a wilderness. As I continue to struggle with depression, your absence seems even starker. I await your healing, your guidance, and your gifts of direction and a sense of the future. I await the return of faith.

One of the most marvelous experiences of healing solitude came during a weeklong retreat to Sedona, Arizona. I rented a *casita* up on a hill, with a flowing fountain, cool breezes, and the rich sounds and smells of nature. I was completely surrounded by vegetation, but also the Red Rocks of Sedona enveloped me. I also created one of my favorite pieces of multimedia art. I believe I was inspired by my surroundings and the solitude, which gifted me peacefulness and receptiveness to "Spirit." I felt like I was floating on a cloud that lifted me above the heavy pall of mental illness. Depression was still there, but I experienced relief, a smile on my face, and a creative flow of inspiration and imagination that I missed.

4.27.1997: I give up my order: I indulge in alone time, which is necessary. I am here, I deserve it, oblivion is okay! "God," I will do whatever you want. Okay, it's interesting: I talk about surrender to God, though I don't believe "God" tells me what to do or how to live my life. I have a responsibility for myself and the implementation of whatever guidance I receive, in whatever form it is in! This is not blind faith.

Sometimes solitude is about merely quieting my mind and "Soul," not emptying them but, rather, becoming aware of what is racing through them. I may talk to myself, and, other times, I simply wait and listen without an agenda for problem-solving or action. I discovered panic as many thoughts darted through me. But when I stepped back and listened to the fear, it melted away. Ram Dass has said, "The quieter you become, the more you can hear." It is truly a place of tranquility and refreshment, which can even strengthen me. Deepak Chopra says, "Silence isn't a blank. It's the pregnant possibility of what is about to be born" (*Jesus*, p. 10). The quiet time holds a precious wealth of calm and clears the confusion and bedlam to make room for visions of potential avenues and direction when I emerge from silence. Solitude is a responsibility I take for myself.

PERSISTENCE: REMINDER OF MY RESPONSIBILITY TO KEEP GOING

Persistence can be a gift, but, sometimes, it is a barrier. My persistence has saved my sanity many times. Even in my most devastating moments, on some level, I *knew* I would survive. But I did not feel it or believe it. How could I know "God" was there when I did not feel or experience my connection with "Spirit"? That was only one of many mysteries I encountered. My persistence was always present, but sometimes what I was persisting at was not taking me anywhere or benefiting me in any way. I knew I had to break out of the cycles of rumination, but . . . I didn't seem to be able to.

What kept my persistence alive? Why should I keep going, searching, pursuing an unknown solution to my grief? Fortunately, I had enough earlier positive, uplifting experiences to know that life could be better. The supports around me persisted in their belief in me and my capacity to come out of the darkness. I also recognized that the core gifts of who I am were still present and held the potential to enrich my life. My mother claims I was persistent from the time I was two years old, which made her feel crazy sometimes.

*6.20.2016: For three days now, the pall has been heavy again! As I try to take inventory and understand what is happening, all I can identify is the overload of the past few months. Yet I feel like I have handled it effectively on a day-to-day basis. Mom sees it and reminds me of it. There have been a number of environmental variables, however, the biological seems paramount right now. This I cannot change or undo, but I **can** take care of myself. Do yoga, walk, meditate. Right now, when I meditate, I fall asleep. I have to be okay with that for now. What other brain avenues can be explored regarding different types of depression? I **am** an explorer, and, while I believe that the problems/puzzles are never totally solved, there are **always** more avenues, pathways, explanations, new insights, and understandings to shed further light on depression.*

Finally, I had to change to be able to recoup my life and well-being. I am unable to explain *what* sustained me, pushed me, or served as a safety net. I feel blessed that whatever "it" was, it was strong enough to overcome my desire to end my life at different times.

TRANSCENDING EXPERIENCES BY
ACCEPTING RESPONSIBILITY

My sense of self-respect and responsibility for my own well-being urged me to acknowledge what I had accomplished and to experience an improved level of belief in myself and "God." Part of transcending the state of depression was accepting the mystery of my existence and to stop asking, *Why me?* I often wondered—when I would get to the point that I didn't want to live under the aura of depression so badly—if I would find a way out. I wanted to emerge from the darkness to a world where darkness comingled with light. I knew the eradication of darkness was not realistic, but I believed I did not have to live consumed by gloom and doom forever. My responsibility included acceptance of where I was in any given moment, no matter what anyone else saw or thought about me. Even more important was that I did not feel like I had to take so much responsibility that it bordered on unrealistic expectations.

4.19.2007: I just need to embrace my biology in a warm blanket of forgiveness, love, and acceptance. I don't have to like what is happening, but I can accept that it is there and quit "working" so hard to push away the adversity that it leaves me with.

A balance between how I could realistically change and my expectations and desires for a particular outcome needed careful consideration. I realized no one else was going to make the changes in my life or "make it better." I *had* to be an active participant, advocate, and willing partner in my healing. I did not have to do it all alone! I informed others that I wanted and needed help. I was willing to listen and implement recommendations, and I quit being so hard on myself.

What could "Spirit" do? I was quite cognizant of the actuality of a connection to "God," but there was some kind of obstacle blocking my passage. Of course, there was the constant fantasy of a magic wand, which, with one stroke, could eliminate the pessimism and boundless agony. I perpetually created energy and space for prayer, reflection, meditation, and silence to clear the way for access to "God." "Spirit" did not need an invitation to my "Soul." I had an urgent responsibility to make my "Soul" approachable and reachable.

◆　◆　◆

HOLISTIC EXPLORATION OF TREATMENT OPTIONS

Despite the presence and gifts of multiple support systems, a roof over my head, adequate meeting of my basic physical needs, money to pay the bills, and a job I found meaningful, gaping craters in my heart and "Soul" remained. I constantly felt I lacked quality of life, even with all of the help I received. I felt no emotions or feelings, and I lost awareness of the presence of "God." This deficit overshadowed whatever relief or satisfaction providers expected with any given treatment. An integral aspect of my healing was a broad base of support that created a safety net. In this chapter, I provide personal experiences with various types of treatment. It is an overview of some of my treatment options, medications, including antidepressants and anti-anxiety medicines, and additional drugs that impacted the bigger picture. I explain weaving in approaches beyond Western medicine, such as gifts from the Middle and Far East, Traditional Chinese Medicine, and massage. Finally, I explore how to bring them together to maximize their collective impressions on body, mind, "Soul," and "Spirit." Subsequent chapters will also address *talk therapy* approaches, meditation/mindfulness, and my evolution of "Spirit."

My abundant curiosity moved me through the world of science to understand and seek treatment options for my lifelong, persistent depression. I found out about countless medications, different propositions for therapy, and a wealth of methods of meditation. Through infinite internet resources, I discovered facts, research articles, Facebook pages, private Facebook groups, online support groups, referral resources, and personal stories. As a discerning seeker, I stayed objective and open to possibilities, and I constantly remained aware of how my personal state of depression affected what I heard. When I felt most desperate, I willingly tried anything! I scoured the internet long and hard to find personal stories about the positive outcomes of helpful treatment methods. There are not many. Usually dramatic and frequently even exaggerated, the "negative" or unfortunate stories tend to draw us as human beings, and these flourish in today's multi-media environment. This can leave an adverse experience in the reader who might, for personal reasons, be significantly affected, whether patient or family member. I was disappointed.

HOW IS DEPRESSION TREATED?

It became clear that I needed healing of body, mind, "Soul," and "Spirit" to move toward wholeness. Though a medical lens should begin the evaluation and treatment of depression, a multidisciplinary approach remains necessary for the effective evaluation and selection of the most appropriate therapies.

There is great complexity to depression, and many factors may trigger it; biological vulnerability may be present; religious and philosophical beliefs, and life-altering crossroads may contribute to the bigger picture. Consequently, meeting the individual needs of each person usually requires a wide range of combined methods.

Like most people, I wanted the "magic wand" that would make me feel better. "Me" being "me," I needed to investigate any practical options that might support my efforts. I wondered what additional avenues, pathways, explanations, or understandings might shed light on aspects of different ways to treat my depression.

I knew, from the beginning of my exploration through treatment options, that I needed a comprehensive medical exam to rule out other medical problems that might be contributing to my depression. I cannot emphasize this enough. Depression can co-occur with many different medical problems. There are obvious terminal illnesses, like cancer, ALS, and other degenerative disorders. But not-so-obvious contributors include hormonal problems, diabetes, thyroid problems, stress, nutrition, weight, undiagnosed heart conditions, and many more that, when treated, can reduce depression.

MEDICATION

Today, as in the more distant past, psychiatrists, primary-care physicians, psychologists, and nurse practitioners consider medication the first-line treatment of depression. The use of medications, usually in the form of antidepressants, has dominated research into depression and patient treatment since their inception.

Medication has emerged as an essential part of my treatment since around my age of nineteen. Here I describe *my* experiences in hopes that these stories may help someone else. Because my focus is a personal one, I will not provide technical descriptions of the drugs I have taken or include an exhaustive list of side effects and concerns associated with them. The reader can refer to the appendix in this book for links to resources for more complete information on psychotropic medications. As I took various medications over time, I endlessly wondered, *Is it possible to have a drug alter my thinking and behaviors to such a degree that what I thought I believed does not exist anymore?*

I cannot even recall the specifics of all of the medications that my providers prescribed for me over the years. On my own journey through the maze of medications, I learned that to prescribe medication effectively is an *art*. Knowledge of both brand names and generic names, primary targets, various dosages, potential side effects, etc., is not enough. There are so many variables that influence the effectiveness of medication, with individual metabolism one of the biggest complicating factors. To reach the artist level requires that the prescriber be quite experienced with psychotropic medications and how other drugs can interact with and influence these medicines. All of the medications recommend no alcohol use. Though infrequent, I chose to drink a glass of wine, but always at least three hours before or after I took any medications (my own rule). I always discussed this with my prescriber.

Antidepressants

Selective Serotonin Reuptake Inhibitors (SSRIs) increase levels of *serotonin*, a neurotransmitter that affects mood, sexual desire, appetite, sleep, and memory. SSRIs are started at a low dose and gradually increased over time. My experience includes generic versions of Lexapro (escitalopram), Zoloft (sertraline), and Prozac (fluoxetine). Lexapro had no effect on my depression, except sedation. A new drug could not be introduced before I came off the drug Lexapro. To come off of it *was horrible!* As I dealt with its withdrawal symptoms, the typical protocol for coming down proved too fast, not unusual for me. To end this medication, I needed to split tiny tablets into one-quarter of the original size. My provider told me that they rarely had seen withdrawals from this med as treacherous as mine. Zoloft, one medication I have used off and on, required *vacations* from it and then slow reintroduction. Prozac proved tricky because the set doses available from the manufacturer made the gradual increase difficult. For example, it comes in 10 mg, 20 mg, and 40 mg capsules. I ended up needing 60 mg, which meant I needed to take two different capsules of 20 mg and 40 mg. There are insurance challenges and pharmacist cautions because it requires two different capsules to establish 60 mgs. Ultimately, it proved very helpful.

Serotonin-Norepinephrine Reuptake Inhibitors (SNRIs) help improve serotonin and norepinephrine levels in the brain, which may reduce depression symptoms. The only medication I took in this category was Effexor. If I remember correctly, the main side effect was severe fatigue. This was difficult to tease out, because of my constant fatigue due to ongoing medical conditions. Finally, coming off of it proved a good thing.

Tricyclic Antidepressants (TCAs) were the primary drugs of choice early on in my treatment before SSRIs or other antidepressants came onto the market. It isn't fully understood how these drugs work to treat depression. I tried a myriad of these drugs, including Elavil (amitriptyline), Tofranil (imipramine), Pamelor (nortriptyline), Ludiomil (maprotiline), and Asendin (amoxapine). Side effects were quite difficult and included dry mouth, weight gain, constipation, and dry eyes. In addition, I needed higher and higher doses, which meant more intense side effects, finally the medication became prohibitive to take.

Monoamine Oxidase Inhibitors (MAOIs) were one of the first classes of antidepressants developed in the 1950s. This class was designed to free up neurotransmitters for mood regulation. These were used early in my treatment but are not used widely today. One of the specific meds I took was Nardil. Since many of the MAOIs have been taken off of the market, I know there were others I received, but I cannot recall their specific names. MAOIs fell out of favor because of the "cheese effect," which caused life-threatening headaches in people on MAOIs who ate products that contained cheese. People who take MAOIs are advised not to eat aged cheese (cottage cheese, cream cheese, and farmer's cheese are allowed), fava, or broad beans, sauerkraut, pickles, olives, soy sauce, teriyaki sauce, tap beer, vermouth, or red wine and to limit their intake of chocolate, caffeinated beverages, yogurt, sour cream, avocados, and raspberries. As I recall, the medications were not effective. Also, it was a hassle due to the many food restrictions.

Norepinephrine-Dopamine Reuptake Inhibitors (NDRIs) are considered Atypical Antidepressants. The full impact on the brain is not totally clear, however, they enhance the effects of other antidepressants. I was prescribed Wellbutrin (bupropion), the specific drug I have taken for many years. Dosage increases and decreases are required due primarily to insomnia, but when I take it in the morning, it does not have this effect. Anticonvulsants (aka seizure medications) are sometimes used as mood stabilizers, especially in Bipolar Disorders. The drug that is prescribed for me is Lamictal (lamotrigine), and it is part of a cocktail that I take. My current prescribed depression cocktail includes Wellbutrin (bupropion), Prozac (fluoxetine), and Lamictal (lamotrigine). I take additional supplements, including fish oil, zinc, and Vitamin D. These each have contributing factors to treatment, though these can be difficult to tease out and determine which specific role each substance plays.

The *waiting* is the greatest challenge of these different medications, because, when I am depressed or have some other illness to grapple with, I want immediate relief. Most psychotropic medications do not begin to start to be effective until six weeks or more after starting them! Even after I waited the magical six weeks, the drug might not start to affect me and required more waiting.

Anxiety and Sleep Medications

Anxiety can accompany depression. My anxiety takes the form of physical symptoms as opposed to intellectual worries. I describe repeatedly a sensation of my finger in an electrical socket that travels up my arm and fills my body. It's very uncomfortable and distracts me from the current moment. Efforts to treat my anxiety with medications varied over time. Sometimes we circled back around to medication (e.g., Benzodiazepines: Xanax, Ativan, Librium, Klonopin, Soma, and Valium). Soma is a drug used to relax muscles related to pain and should only be taken short-term. These medications helped relax muscles and calmed my racing mind. I experienced dizziness, drowsiness, and balance problems. These side effects restricted my ability to drive! They can be addictive as well, and doses were adjusted up and down, and monitored for the total length of time I took them. Coming off of any of these medications too fast could lead to withdrawal symptoms, which I actually experienced one time. Fortunately, I learned how to use Ativan, for instance, on an "as needed" basis for spikes in anxiety or trouble sleeping, although it has potential long-term effects on memory.

I needed treatment for sleep problems periodically. Sleeping medications such as Halcion and Ambien were prescribed for brief periods of time. There are a few meds that impact sleep and are considered antidepressants (e.g., Amitriptyline, Trazadone). Side effects that I experienced included those noted under anxiety medications as well as lightheadedness, prolonged drowsiness, dry mouth, daytime effects on memory, and performance problems. Such medications affected my alertness for work, not to mention weight gain and constipation, which required over-the-counter remedies and led to a proliferation of experimentation with weight-loss approaches. I also took Ramelteon to help with sleep, which does not have the addictive quality of medications previously listed. However, short-term use is recommended.

Other Medications Impacting Treatment

Early on, treatment for endometriosis involved birth-control pills and Danocrine (to suppress hormones related to menstrual problems). The doses were incrementally increased to completely suppress reproductive hormones like Estrogen. Numerous surgical procedures required alteration of depression medications so I could undergo anesthesia. There were periodic pain medications (Tylenol 3, prescription-strength Ibuprofen, Oxycodone, Percodan, Anaprox, Tramadol), following surgery, many of which can be addictive if taken too long, which I avoided.

Additional medication challenges impacted the mix. Chemotherapy for breast cancer involved chemo drugs, anti-nausea, and steroids. After breast-cancer chemotherapy and surgery, an Aromatase Inhibitor (AI) is routinely prescribed as preventive for cancer recurrence. These drugs have dramatic side effects. I tried different versions after each occurrence of breast cancer: Arimidex (anastrozole) and then Aromasin (exemestane), after my double mastectomy. I experienced deep-muscle, joint, and bone pain that could not be relieved, trouble with concentration, increased depression, and weight gain, which were intolerable. Night sweats and hot flashes are a given in menopause but are magnified with the AI due to the manipulation of hormones. Again, the manipulation of hormones was raising its ugly head. I chose quality of life over potentially reduced quantity of life and did not take the new AI.

In general, I was prone to upper-respiratory problems, which sometimes required antibiotics (e.g., Cipro, Augmentin, Amoxil, Keflex, Bactrim, Zithromax). I am allergic to the Sulfa class of medications, which caused severe hives! Each medication also has its own set of side effects, perhaps most typically nausea, diarrhea, abdominal pain, loss of appetite, bloating, and indigestion. These medications led to vaginal yeast infections, requiring localized treatment, but sometimes an additional oral antibiotic. Yep, I experienced every one of these at some time. These types of symptoms many times led to additional over-the-counter medications (e.g., Imodium, Benadryl, Dramamine, Kaopectate).

When I had a cold, I tried Vitamin C or Airborne, but, when those did not work, I eventually took Mucinex, Vicks, Claritin, and cough syrups. If the coughing was really bad, my primary-care doctor prescribed cough medicines with a little bit of codeine in them. Once in a while, this further evolved to mild asthma, which required prescription medications such as Montelukast, Advair, or Albuterol, and the primary side effects were feeling jittery or agitated. If it went on for a long time, a steroid like Prednisone was needed for a while. Prednisone has to be taken in gradually increased and then decreased doses. I felt physically wired, jittery despite exhaustion. More recently, after eyelid surgery for ptosis, a prednisone eyedrop was prescribed to reduce inflammation. Within approximately ten days, I felt anxious, out of control, panicked, unable to concentrate, more depressed, and scared about how I felt. I melted down, in crisis because I could not control the anxiety. The eyedrop affected my whole body and had to be stopped. Within a couple of days, I felt better.

Medications for other medical problems brought additional factors, and, when an antidepressant is added, well, the intricacy grows exponentially. Consequently, I required ready accessibility to my prescriber—that meant at least once a week when meds were started—to monitor the effects. Even more importantly, this person provided me with support, encouragement, and reminders of the critical need for patience. In the world of managed care, the frequency and number of visits per year are limited, and only with in-network providers. Despite mental-health parity recently passed by Congress, the insurance industry still needs to catch up with the legitimate medical needs of patients. The frequency of my visits vacillated, depending on my mental status and/or the need to adjust medications, so weekly sessions were not always "necessary."

So, my experiences with medication management make it clear that there is truly an art to prescribing meds. While individual meds have *specific purposes* or *targets*, everyone can have a different response. I remember one of my psychiatrists (who was extremely vigilant) prescribing Thorazine (antipsychotic), generally reserved for individuals who are hospitalized for mental-health treatment. He did it with reservations and candidness that this was viewed as a drastic, highly controversial step to take, but he felt it worth a try. It didn't work, but I survived and was no worse for the wear. But he took the time to explain why he prescribed it and its potential side effects or reactions, and he monitored me very carefully, with sometimes daily check-ins for a period of time.

From the world of alternative medicine, various herbal supplements and formulas are prescribed to treat depression, anxiety, and sleep. Individuals may turn to these when told they can be helpful. The problem with these substances is that they are not federally regulated, and, therefore, doses may be inexact. In addition, some common formulas such as Sam-E actually negatively collide with other medications or cause other potentially dangerous side effects. My personal situation contraindicated these formulas.

It is critical that I stay aware of how any substance I ingest can interact with others. Prescribers of *any* medication or supplement need to be in the loop of the medication portion of my treatment plan. To monitor the effectiveness of medication regimens, as well as to avoid issues, requires great care. That said, medication is an essential part of my holistic care, but it cannot take care of all aspects of my depression symptoms.

INTEGRATION OF TREATMENT
BEYOND WESTERN MEDICINE

The National Center for Complementary and Integrative Health is a division of the US Department of Health and Human Services. On their website, they clarify these two approaches. Both Complementary and Alternative medicine use methodologies developed outside of mainstream Western medicine, or so-called "conventional medicine." If the approach is combined with Western medicine, it is considered Complementary. However, if the method is used *in place of* "conventional medicine," it is considered Alternative. Ideally, nonconventional services would be combined with conventional Western medicine to provide Integrated Medicine. Most of the methods I chose are considered Complementary.

Practitioners in the medical field talk about holistic propositions to integrate a variety of treatments. The focus of traditional Western medicine is pathology and *curing* illnesses. Invariably, this omits the individual human experience, as well as emotional and "Spiritual" aspects of the patient's life. By contrast, Complementary and Alternative approaches maximize health as means to avoid or treat pathology. A broader picture of personal overall wellness develops with these approaches. The Western medical doctor's oath to "heal" and make better can preclude broader consideration of "health" for individuals with untreatable progressive and degenerative illnesses. These patients prefer to try alternatives, incorporate nontraditional treatment, stop treatment, and/or make a choice about when to end their life in a meaningful way (*not* suicide; some view these choices as "assisted suicide"). Newer physicians have led efforts to change this, to stop conventional treatment or look at alternative methods, which may insult some doctors.

A large number of Complementary and Alternative treatments are available. The greatest challenge of combining multiple therapies is assessment of the alternative nature of regimens, as well as any contraindications. Development of such a formulated plan requires providers to respect each other's practices and show an interest or inclination to coordinate care. Realistically, as the patient, I became my own advocate of any form of these therapeutics. I gathered resources, asked questions, investigated, scrutinized pros and cons, and made conscientious choices. I keep all providers informed and aware of the bigger picture of my care. Also, a trial-and-error process to safely integrate and include additional therapies has motivated me over the years. When my illness progressed to a place where I became nonfunctional and unable to care for myself, I needed an advocate who knew me, kept my best interests uppermost in the process, and helped me realistically consider choices. My "Perspective Angel" became my primary source, with input from "Perspective Mentors" as well. I present a few helpful nontraditional experiences I integrated into my personal holistic plan.

I was privileged to receive a Native American Healing Ceremony (4.23.2005). During my work on the Navajo Reservation, I gained a close friend whose father is a Medicine Man. She wanted me to "try" his healing. Gifted a crystal, we engaged in crystal gazing, prayer, and smudging (sage is burned and is waved over my body). I dressed in a full skirt, required rest during the day as part of preparation, and arrived in the late afternoon to where the *hogan* for the ceremony was located. My friend wanted me to wrap myself in a special handmade

Navajo blanket. The Medicine Man talked with me, wanting to know what was on my "Soul," and explained what we would do. As dusk unfolded, he guided me through blessing the four directions of the Earth, and a fire was lit.

4.6.2005: "Spirit" pulsed literally through me. The crystal shone hints of light in varying degrees of brightness. As the crystal turned, there was much darkness drawn to the fire, at times pointed and focused, at times darker than others with some somberness. An emptiness, a despair, darkness. The form of a dark growing ball/ magnet moved up my spine, creating a soft gray tunnel, pushing along the dark growing ball/magnet, drowning out the fear, anger, cobwebs, weeds, and debris. The blockage moved upward into my heart chakra. Intermittently I felt opening and closing. A choking (not life-threatening) block is present as the march continues.

The Medicine Man: "You think and worry too much. You need to let go, cleanse, make room for other things. You forget because there is too much in your head." He has . . . a sense of humor, personalization, caring, teaching, a man of integrity and values, confident in his healing, generous. I felt very blessed that my "sister" arranged this for me.

I was not to shower for 24 hours after the ceremony. I slept well that night, and, while I definitely felt drained the following day, I felt lighter.

I practiced light therapy off and on for years as complementary to my medical treatment. I spent time outside in sunlight and even used an Ott Lamp. These lamps have properties similar to sunlight and are used especially in individuals with seasonal depression. Sun exposure always comes with the precautions of spending too much time in direct sunlight. But there is natural healing energy from the sun even in the shade. I knew that the research was clear about the importance of sunlight for my overall health. My sister and her family live near Portland, Oregon, and the darkness due to weather and much shorter days can contribute to depression. I could not stay there for more than ten days in the winter, to avoid increased aggravated depression; so, sunlight does make a difference for me!

TREATMENTS FROM THE MIDDLE AND FAR EAST

Many recommendations to augment wellness from the Middle and Far East offer Complementary and Alternative approaches based on varied understandings of *health*. This includes actual physical treatments, spiritual approaches, and movement practices. Common complementary-health approaches include Natural Products; Deep Breathing; Yoga, Tai chi or Qi Gong; Chiropractic or Osteopathic Manipulation; Massage; Special Diets; Homeopathy; Progressive Relaxation; and Guided Imagery. These supports are often labeled "Mind and Body Practices."

Traditional Chinese Medicine (TCM)
Traditional Chinese Medicine (TCM), perhaps the widest category of Complementary and Alternative therapeutics, includes Acupuncture, Chinese Herbal Medicine, Cupping, Acupressure, and Moxibustion. Practice of any of these approaches requires specialized training and licensure. These treatments are based on the ancient anatomy of the physical body. In Traditional Chinese Medicine, each organ is part of an integrated system throughout the body that regulates *meridians*, which are energy paths in the

body. Meridians pertain to certain attributes of health related to five elements, including water, metal, fire, earth, and wood. Diagnosis looks at which body/organ systems are involved and how they compromise the function of not only the identified system but also other systems in the body.

I've clearly oversimplified this quite elaborate and amazing system and recommend a deeper look. (Here's a little secret: local schools that train individuals as TCM providers continually look for willing patients for practice, and the rates are quite reduced. All trainees are supervised by very experienced practitioners.)

The best-known example of TCM is acupuncture. Very thin needles are inserted in specific points on the body, at varying depths, based on problems presented and the meridian system diagnosed as the probable source of the problem. Overall, the process is rarely painful. I don't even feel the needles going in, unless a *blocked* point is treated, and energy (known as *Qi*) is released. This is a unique sensation; it's brief, and I can feel the impact throughout a meridian (e.g., I had an acupuncture needle placed, and a sensation went from my big toe to my shoulder).

As one example, I personally experienced acupuncture treatments when I could not move my head because the muscles in my neck were so locked up. I sought acupuncture after an emergency-room visit, where I received muscle relaxants and pain medication that really did not provide any relief. Acupuncture seemed magical in the reduction of this pain and release of some of the muscle spasms.

At times, infrared light is used over the acupuncture needles to generate more energy. Massage and cupping can be incorporated. An ancient remedy, *cupping* involves cups made of any number of materials (e.g., glass, silicone, bamboo, earthenware).

The practitioner puts cups on the skin to create suction in a particular area. The suction draws blood into the area, with a variety of effects. The varied length of time it is left in place determines whether a mild redness or a significant bruise remains. Initially, it can be painful until the best placement is reached. Otherwise, it was really not that painful; it relieved pain and increased mobility in my joints.

Examples of physical approaches of TCM include yoga, Qi Gong, and Tai Chi. These methods also reflect the meridian system and generate stimulation and healing through specific forms of movement, poses, and breathing. Deep breathing also enhances the process of all of these treatments by oxygenation of the blood, reduced heart rate, and relaxation of muscles.

I integrate the very beneficial practice of yoga formally and informally. The beauty of this approach is that it does not require any specific skills or abilities to get started. The focus is on individual abilities and needs. There are no expectations about what you are supposed to be able to do. You are guided to become more aware of sensations in your body so that you can gauge your own limitations. Instructors remind you the two sides of your body are likely to feel different, and your body can even feel different from day to day. At some of my most challenging times, a session of yoga boosted my energy incredibly. My mother even commented on how different I looked—more relaxed, brighter, and more peaceful—after a yoga session. I am always impressed with the range of body sizes, weights, ages, flexibility, commitment, and determination of the participants in yoga classes. Anyone can benefit. Yoga emphasizes breathing with inhalation and exhalation, coordinated with specific movements and parts of poses. No matter the pose taught, instructions offer alternatives to meet individual needs. Classes are typically ninety minutes long and feel amazing. I can be in pain, exhausted, or feeling down; but if I drag myself to yoga, I am always grateful.

Reiki is a spinoff from Japan, based on the energy system described above under Traditional Chinese Medicine. *Reiki* focuses on the body's natural ability to balance and heal itself. Physical-, mental-, emotional-, and spiritual-energy levels are affected. Not tied to a specific belief system, it focuses on the energy of the treated individual. The practitioner senses where there is energy imbalance, which usually involves blockages. The *Reiki* practitioner uses her hands to detect probable blockages, as well as placement over specific parts of the body to send energy for healing. There are twenty targeted areas of the body where the practitioner focuses on energy flow and then transmits energy as needed, until they experience a stop in the flow of the energy. The practitioner may also include *chakra*-healing crystals to help concentrate the energy. During sessions, I remained clothed, typically on a massage table, face up. My body was supported by various pillows and bolsters to help me relax. Breathing again stands out as a vital component. I knew to release my thoughts and feelings into the hands of the practitioner. I experienced warmth and increased energy flow in places I did not even realize were blocked. While some may label *Reiki* as kind of "woo-woo," my experience belies this characterization. When I released into the hands of the practitioner, I left with a definite positive effect. Sometimes I cried, which was an important release. I did not have expectations going into treatments, but knew I would feel better.

Craniosacral therapy is another version of Complementary therapy I found helpful. This therapy involves the manipulation of the head and neck to support the increased flow of cerebral spinal fluid. The feet are pressed at various times to enhance flow. I noticed I was calmer, relaxed, and free of physical pain. The therapist intuitively knew how I was feeling on any given day and asked me if she was accurate. She was!! She then customized her therapy on that issue.

Massage

Massage is one of the oldest forms of treatment documented in ancient civilizations, as early as BC 2330. The obvious evolution of massage methods occurred over centuries, but all forms of massage are rooted in ancient civilizations. Personally, I experienced the following methods of massage: acupressure, lymphatic drainage, myofascial release, reflexology, Swedish massage, and Thai massage. The differences from one kind to another depend on the skills and background of the therapist. Providers include nurses, occupational therapists, specifically trained massage therapists of different orientations, acupuncturists, physical therapists, chiropractic practitioners, and some trained in bodywork. Every single form feels good in some way! The particular part of the body targeted varies. For example, reflexology involves manipulation of the feet and hands, which have zones related to other parts of the body. I did this only a couple of times. Myofascial release channels more on the fibers of the muscles to help increase range of motion, help release knots, and is usually part of other methods.

Lymphatic draining massage has been critical for me. It involves massage to stimulate the movement of lymphatic fluid to help reduce swelling and decrease inflammation. In my case, it was vital to my healing after my mastectomy. It helped keep tissue from becoming adhered and helped increase blood flow to distinct parts of my body.

Other factors that vary among providers include what lotion, cream, or oil is used. Most emphasize a naturally occurring oil in whatever form. Coconut oil is a common base and does not end up making me feel "oily." Scented oils are also selected based on the medicinal characteristics expressed in the scent of the oil. Lavender is one of the most common oils for relaxation and stress reduction. I have also experienced scents of lemongrass, peppermint, bergamot, eucalyptus, and rose infused in various lotions, oils, and crèmes. One therapist mixed her own concoction of a crème that used all-natural substances, smelled really bad, and was quite messy, but it was soothing.

The depth of pressure into muscles during massage differs from therapist to therapist. I prefer massage that goes deeper into my muscles. My massage therapists *always* find places I did not even know hurt, were in spasms, or had knots. Fortunately, I got referrals from friends who used a particular therapist they liked. I had a couple of "long-term" therapists. As my needs changed, I switched therapists. After my mastectomy, I needed someone who would work on my chest. My longtime therapist was uncomfortable and unwilling to do any work that even bordered on what could be interpreted as *sexual*. I have had male and female therapists and am so pleased to see male therapists be so meticulous in draping to be sure private places on my body were covered.

There are any number of other items combined as part of a massage. There may be an aromatherapy candle burning; a heating pad might keep the table warm, but the therapist usually applies it to a specific location on the body. Heated Himalayan salt balls may be rubbed and pressed into particular places on the body. Moist towels may be applied to warm an area or to soothe an area after treatment. One time I had a massage tool that looked like a jackhammer and provided deep pressure and massage especially to the back. I view massage as an essential part of my health and well-being. It feels good but is restorative. Relaxation that puts me to sleep can be a great escape!

Our eastern neighbors are more aware, intentional, and practiced in the integration of body, mind, "Soul," and "Spirit." Expansion of our understanding in the Western world may embrace this broader notion of wellness. Such integration includes some manner of belief system, religious practice, and/ or attention to our "Spirit."

BODY, MIND, "SOUL," AND "SPIRIT" COME TOGETHER

Clearly, there are no actual cut-and-dried therapeutics that apply to only one specific part of my body. We are only beginning to understand the interrelatedness and greater awareness of physical sensations. I have discovered the blended nature, remarkable influence, and benefits of combined methods that support overall wellness. Anything I do with my body affects multiple systems as well as specific parts of my body. Fortunately, our society's mindset is shifting into a direction of a more integrated and broader view of overall health. I've experienced ongoing results and would argue for the exceptional benefits from awareness and application of combinations of approaches to depression.

By now it should be apparent that depression reverberates through all aspects of my life. The degree of desperation also contributes to the likelihood of feeling suicidal. That being said, it is obvious to me that I want to attend to the big picture. This goes well beyond technical, therapeutic, and spiritual practices, and encompasses, diet, sleep, exercise, surroundings, personal care, friends, and support systems.

I can be overwhelmed in an attempt to integrate so many different ideas. Or it can be an invitation to reflect on further possibilities that might maximize feeling better. Of course, there are myriad recommendations, and that can feel unwieldy at times. When I step back and evaluate the bigger picture of my life, I focus my energy to ensure my maximum benefit and health.

"Talk Therapy" has taken on many shapes and forms of treatment over the course of my life. It is interesting to realize I have benefited from every provider and approach. Talk therapy includes a variety of methods, which we will visit in the coming chapters.

COMING BACK TO "SPIRIT"

For me, my "Spiritual" life is the foundation and core of my overall wellness. When I feel "spiritually healthy," other annoyances fade into the background. Hence the quest for the broadest spiritual development is essential for me. I know that I want to be healthy in body, mind, "Soul," and "Spirit," which is no small undertaking.

◆ ◆ ◆

MY DESPERATE CHOICES: ECT AND DBS TREATMENTS

Medicine offers many alternatives for treating depression. During my absolutely worst episode of depression, I searched for *any* potential new approaches. Through research, I found out about a study of Deep Brain Stimulation (DBS) for depression at Emory University in Atlanta, Georgia. However, I needed to undergo Electroconvulsive Treatment (ECT) before researchers could decide on my eligibility to join this study. I did not seek out or receive other available electronic interventions for depression, including Vagal Nerve Stimulation (VNS) and Transdermal Magnetic Stimulation (TMS). I soon learned that DBS and ECT are unique technical treatments, with many different facets. Each modality took me on roller-coaster rides with endless peaks, valleys, and unexpected sudden turns.

ELECTROCONVULSIVE THERAPY (ECT)

ECT is highly specialized. Many professionals and the average citizen remain ignorant of the situations in which ECT can make a difference and of its possible benefits. Historically, negative depictions and social stigma have characterized the field, as they did when I needed it. Unfortunately, this characterization remains today and needs to updated and reconceptualized. The multiple negative connotations associated with ECT complicate the perceptions that potential patients develop as they consider it (e.g., what it involves and what happens; long-term implications of receiving treatments may become distorted based on what they read or hear about it). A recent study in *Experimental and Therapeutic Medicine* discussed the efficacy of ECT.

Based on the initial ECT information presented to me, even the thought of the treatment scared me. Like that of so many people, my antiquated image, which depicted someone's body in severe convulsions, is no longer an accurate representation of ECT. Currently, seizures are induced, however, the patient is medicated to reduce the chances of any severe physical injury. I reviewed copious amounts of information from a variety of sources that contributed to my decision to pursue ECT. Given my limited responsiveness to many medication regimens, my longtime treating professionals wondered if ECT might help me. Many thoughts raced through my mind as I made my decision to go forward with ECT. This journal entry illustrates some of them.

9.30.2008: Preparing for discussion of ECT with the psychiatrist who would administer the treatment; it seemed like it is a forgone conclusion. But my history with treatment in the past couple of years did not support something working now after all we have done. I was scared and, as usual, hit the internet. My sister accompanied me to the first meeting with the doctor. I requested that we start with one side only, rather than both sides of the brain. I was concerned about the fact that they had to use a paralytic medication to prevent any bodily injury during the seizure induced by the treatment.

How Did I Experience ECT?

ECT involves administration of electric shocks to the brain to potentially change brain chemistry. That, in turn, may help a variety of mental illnesses, including treatment-resistant depression. Under current ECT procedures, the patient receives general anesthesia. This reduces the potential for dramatic physical injury such as broken bones. In turn, the use of anesthesia with ECT has rendered previous images of people in severe convulsive seizures grossly inaccurate as they relate to present-day practice. Today, electrodes are carefully placed in specific locations on the head. An anesthesiologist administers the anesthesia, monitors heart rate, blood pressure, and respiration, while a psychiatrist administers the carefully determined shocks to each patient via paddles. Side effects include confusion, memory loss, physical side effects, and medical complications related to the effects of anesthesia. Multiple treatments are given over a period, with consideration of the unique needs of a given person. Sometimes shocks will be given on one side of the brain and, in other cases, on both sides. Some individuals receive one series of treatments, while others require a periodic or ongoing series of treatments.

Description of an actual treatment session:

11.02.2008: There is a small area for about three gurneys. You get on the gurney, and the anesthesiologist asks you a whole bunch of questions, like how much you weigh (which I always hate). You have to be honest, because that is how they decide how much medication they need to give you. He starts an IV in my hand, (ouch, but he is pretty good). They have me on oxygen because this doc apparently wants high oxygen saturations. They make sure that I'm nice and warm (those places are always cold). There were a total of four people in the treatment room: the anesthesiologist, the psychiatrists, and two male nurses ("Big Mike" and "Minime"). Big Mike explained step by step what is happening and then what is going to happen once I was anesthetized. The anesthesiologist rattled off a lengthy list of meds he is going to put into my IV (I guess the doctor would know what he is using). There are electrodes on my chest in three places. I guess there are also a couple of monitoring electrodes attached to my head for an ongoing EEG. I think there are two electrodes that get attached to one side of the head (therefore, unilateral ECT). I don't even remember all of the electrodes going on. Of course, I am hooked up to a blood-pressure cuff. They started "blow-by" oxygen, and then they give me the stuff to put me to sleep. So, I am actually completely out when they give the shocks. I wake up in the same area, to a perky little nurse, who is dressed in a skeleton shirt (it is Halloween, after all, so I don't think I am hallucinating). I wake up with a really bad headache, so they gave me some medicine for that in the IV. I think they give me medication for nausea in the cocktail as part of putting me out. As I wake up, I noticed pain in my

*jaw, my neck, my shoulders, up and down my spine, and in my
back in general. I felt brain-dead. Not really thinking, numb,
dead to the world around me. Not able to read or concentrate.
I am just wiped out. Home we went, and I headed for the bed.
That's about it.*

The actual routine from treatment to treatment stayed the
same. I went to an outpatient treatment area in a hospital. Due
to the sedation from the anesthesia, my mother transported me
to the treatments, patiently waited for me, and drove me home.
She met family members of other patients waiting for their
loved ones during their treatment. Many of the other family
members shared the positive effects of ECT that their relatives
had received. I chronicled my treatments.

*11.4.2008: 2nd treatment. Don't remember much after entering
the ECT room. Headache and neck ache were far worse than on
Friday (the day of the actual treatment). Slept excessively. I don't
see any difference in memory or mood—that elusive change.
Starting ECT feels like "doing" something, but it is a hurry-up-
and-wait time.*

The effects I experienced from one session to the next were
similar. I went every three to four days, and the doctor increased
the treatments to both sides of my brain after four treatments had
no apparent impact on the depression. Before each treatment,
the team assessed what benefits I'd gained over the course of
the treatment. Nothing—again and again. The frequency of
treatments eventually varied from weekly to every couple of
weeks. With increased signs of suicide, the frequency increased

briefly. Overall, reflection and questions occupied my mind for several months.

> *11.12.2008: An awareness of the last couple of days is concern about whether I am stagnating in this state of my own volition, but if that was truly the case, I would have used that volition to have avoided and certainly to have gotten myself out of this mess of isolation, poverty of social contact and emotion, and unemployment, the results of this insidious disease.*

> *12.03.08: OMG—the process is interminable. I want to feel and know things are getting better, but no. I am left to the observations and musings of those around me.*

> *02.25.09: There is also being in my 50s as an element of the whole picture. Today sucks. I am not rolling with the punches. Every little thing is leading to tears. Anxiety is through the roof. Confidence is blown, which has accentuated the dysfunction and the immobilization. How close to suicidal ideation? It feels really close right now because I feel trapped in a bad space. I want a way to escape and don't see alternatives.*

Still Pondering What I Wanted and Needed

Of course, I ceaselessly reflected on ECT treatments and their effects. At one point, I felt compelled to write a letter to the psychiatrist giving me the treatments. I needed to write this letter, which provides some insight into my overall experience of ECT and what else I thought could help my experience—but I decided not to send it.

Dear Dr. _____,

The work you do is lifesaving, but I feel compelled to share my observations and experience with you. Deciding to undergo ECT was a big step, and part of that, for me, was putting my private practice on hold for two months. There is financial hardship, but, more importantly, there is the challenge of maintaining self-respect, self-acceptance, and self-competence. Even though I am under treatment for a disabling condition regarding my emotional well-being, that does not make me any less of a valuable human being, a competent professional, and a respected person. I have not felt those things in the process of my treatment. From my perspective, severe depression does not render me incompetent or incapable of being an active participant in my care—part of the team. Research has demonstrated that the more active the patient is in their care and treatment, the greater the progress and success.

What would have made it different for me in the ECT process? More respect for the psychiatric nurse practitioner who has coordinated my care for more than fifteen years—attending to the ups and downs and methodically making changes in medications. She is the ongoing thread and therapist who will be there even after ECT. You have important decisions to make in the lives of your patients—be their partners. Many may not want or choose to be active partners, but the option should be there. Not every patient wants or needs the same thing, but individualizing care requires some level of sensitivity to differing needs. There were not any arrangements for someone to talk to if something came up between treatments.

I felt there were many aspects of ECT treatment that were not well explained up front. Many questions came up about this process. How am I to know what number of treatments is enough? What is the yardstick? Will my memory be affected long-term? I would have preferred to have been told it would be at least twelve treatments instead of being strung along and intermittently told some different number of treatments I still had to undergo. I requested unilateral, which you did not seem to agree with, and you did not make it clear that, if the unilateral did not work, there would be at least twelve sessions of bilateral. I had some thoughts about how ECT is presented when it is being considered as a viable option for treatment. I also think your delivery could benefit from a little consideration of the impact in a more integrated manner. Some form of literature that provides the historical context of ECT that has changed dramatically over time. More complete information up front!

Informing family members about treatment numbers, etc., knowing patients are very likely not to recall things that were said when being put under—the family member should be present until the patient actually goes under. The attendant said you told me one thing, yet what was written was different (five to seven vs. twelve treatments). You told my mother a couple of months into treatments that it could take six months to a year for ECT to work. I had not been told that. In the waiting area, my mother and I spoke with relatives of other patients. These individuals praised the success of ECT for their loved ones and noted that they continued to come back when needed for additional treatments. There had not been any discussion about the possibility that this might have to continue throughout my life. This would have entailed a discussion of the cycling nature of depression and the consequent need for repeated treatments.

It might have helped to have asked me to rate my depression at each visit. Family and close friends were providing feedback regarding change—despite a major dive.

I continued to process the ECT experience in the next entry.

I want to move out of the space I am in but can't. Would the "ongoing ECT" make a difference? What/how will I know when I am better? I feel like I have succumbed to depression and its disabling nature. It's like I can't see things any differently—maybe because things are not any different!

*The adverse effects of ECT may be more long-term than readily apparent. I am in a downward spiral and don't know why. Time to be patient. Time to look at a candle and appreciate the flame, the beauty thereof. The psychiatrist wants me to consider VNS (Vagal Nerve Stimulation) since the ECT did not seem to be working. Insurance doesn't pay for it—$27,000—and there is a very low hit rate as far as effectiveness goes. I kept telling myself to just **trust** that all of the pieces would fall into place.*

My series of ECT treatments finally ended. I don't think I received any permanent damage from the treatments, but like so many other treatments, ECT dashed my hopes for improvement. I wondered if that meant something else might be wrong with me. There are no *one size fits all* methods to treat depression. With one more failed treatment added to my history, I needed to work to stay open to additional options! After I endured the twenty-six ECT treatments, I contacted the DBS Study to see if I qualified to be a participant.

DEEP BRAIN STIMULATION (DBS) TREATMENT

As previously described, in my tireless search for help with my depression, I came across the Deep Brain Stimulation (DBS) study underway at Emory University in Atlanta, Georgia. After I notified the study administrators that I had completed twenty-six ECT treatments, I learned I met the criteria for diagnosis and the study: an episode of depression at least one year long, failure to respond to a minimum of four different antidepressant treatments, and, finally, ECT treatments. My eligibility launched a lengthy entrance saga. They obtained medical records of all the treatments I'd received for depression as far back as possible. I completed a long and very detailed medical history. I participated in a long phone interview. The study required travel to Atlanta, Georgia, for evaluation and video interviews with the doctors involved in the study. They used all this data to determine whether they would finalize my participation in the study. Even after that, I made another trip for testing, and my mother traveled with me for interviews and videotape sessions required by the study. For the science nerd, there is a reference for ways to read an article called "A Depression Switch," which describes the neuroscience behind the treatment and how it was developed. I was filled with doubts, fears, and an enormous number of questions. When I got to Emory for my initial in-person interviews and evaluations, I still waited for a day or so to get started.

8.23.2009: I am skeptical because the profound depression has made me cynical about anything. "I am preoccupied with Emory and scared to death that it (DBS) won't work out for any number of reasons: not enough distinct types of meds tried, no hospitalizations, depression episodes not lasting long enough, even though I am totally disabled at this point. The "what if" game is draining and scary. I keep thinking of other things to fill the time, to distract myself and even brought things with me to do, but I have no stamina, motivation, or interest.

Reluctance and reservations about the whole thing continued to envelop me. One doctor in Atlanta gave me a diagnosis of Bipolar Disorder Type II, which identified an emphasis on depression. Distortions in thought included:

8.23.2009: I just want to be bad enough to qualify for the study. I worry about coloring my responses. I think I am trying to figure out how I should be, how I should respond, how I should present myself. I am very skeptical about the DBS, but, then again, I have no reason to believe it will work because nothing else has worked.

One of the doctors in Atlanta noted that my major depressions seemed to coincide with transition times. Is he implying that I don't respond well to change?

8.25.2009: Interview with a consulting psychiatrist. I broke down at the end of the session; I was not impressed with him. I then underwent neuropsychological testing. I am so frustrated because I am cognitively intact, which I feel overshadows the severity of my depression.

I met these specific requirements for acceptance into the study: failure to respond to a minimum of four different antidepressant treatments (actually many more than that over the course of my life) and a psychiatrist to work with me in Phoenix. Luckily, they accepted the psychiatric nurse practitioner who'd worked with me for many years (provided ongoing psychotherapy and medication management). Atlanta periodically consulted with my psychiatric nurse practitioner. I agreed to relocate to Atlanta for three to four months to prepare for the implantation surgery. I also agreed to return to Atlanta on a specified basis for follow-up. The study paid for the surgery, various tests, and ongoing evaluation. On the other hand, I paid for my lodging and travel. Even once accepted to the study, my meandering, doubt-filled thoughts continued.

> *8.25.2009: I find myself with many reservations and doubting whether I should go thru with the DBS. I can't even articulate everything. What are the risk factors and travel costs? What will the ongoing treatment involve? What will it be like telling my own very personal story? Will there be support in Atlanta? Will I get invited for the interviews? Should I even do this? Is it better to just do med changes and let time take its course?*

> *9.24.2009: I am anxious. I know I need the DBS but still wonder if it is the right thing to do. Why can't anything be simple and clear? Even writing is a strain just to keep it legible.*

> *9.26.2009: Today I read a couple of articles about DBS and it made me realize how lucky I am to have the chance to get a DBS. If only it will work—even a little relief will be welcomed. Oh, my God!*

I chose to go forward with the DBS study participation.

Right before I left Phoenix, I was blessed. A close family friend led a "ceremony" with more than twenty-five of my friends to send me off to Atlanta. I would be gone for a few months. The hearts of those closest to me held hope that my treatment with DBS would make a difference in the future of my life.

Description of the DBS Process and Experience

Given my responsibility for my own lodging and travel, I needed to find somewhere to live in Atlanta during the months around the surgery. Thank goodness I learned about the Atlanta Hospital Hospitality House (AHHH), an old mansion converted into a place for family members of individuals in the hospital from more than forty miles away. The rate to stay was $10 a night. This included dormitory-style sleeping. They provided dinner and made self-serve food available for other times during the day. AHHH became my Atlanta home away from home—then and for years to follow.

I arrived in Atlanta almost one month before the scheduled surgery. I participated in meetings with the doctors involved in the study. I completed many questionnaires about depression. This became part of my weekly routine at this time and whenever I visited Atlanta afterward. Additional tests administered included: MRIs, CAT scans, EEGs, cognitive testing, neuropsychological assessment, and perceptual testing—a very full schedule!

10.8.2009: Visual testing w/ EEG was awful. I had 36 electrodes attached to my head and face. They could not get me in a comfortable position because of my height. It was four hours of watching a computer screen and responding to it. My eyes showed I saw double images. I got a headache.

The doctors in Atlanta explored ways to change how I thought about and talked about my depression. That experience socked me in the gut and left me feeling dismissed, misunderstood, and frustrated. I wanted *concrete* directions for what to do to make the changes I needed. *What effect did my thoughts have on my well-being?*

> 10.11.2009: One of the other doctors on the team told me that patients need to want to be better and feel some optimism related to the surgery and the effects of the implant. I don't.

> 10.8.2009: I talked with Dr. Mayberg* about the study. (*Helen Mayberg, MD, a neurologist and lead investigator). Dr. Mayberg is a dedicated scientist with millions of dollars to do research to "prove" or document the efficacy of DBS procedures on depression. Despite this essential backbone of her work, she became an ally and a friend, interested in me as a human being. She genuinely wanted to know how I felt each time we met. She explored my thinking, perceptions, thoughts, and concerns with great curiosity. She made herself remarkably available whether by phone or email. She always responded to me within hours unless she was out of the country to present her work. I am convinced that my relationship with her contributed to the improvement I experienced over time. Patricio Riva-Posse, MD (Neurologist/Psychiatrist), also affiliated with the Emory study, gave me extremely supportive, helpful, and responsive care as well.

Early on, Dr. Mayberg asked how I would know when things were better. I told her I had no hope about the DBS working, and she articulated that *something* must have driven me to pursue the study. My family repeatedly talked about how I impressed them with my pursuit of the study and how

I jumped through the necessary hoops despite my otherwise shut-down state.

10.29.2009: My surgery Day. My Mother and one of my sisters had traveled to Atlanta to be with me during the surgery, which took more than twelve hours. The nature of the surgery required admission to the hospital. They placed me into a "halo," which is a contraption that goes on your head and is supported by your shoulders. Heavy and necessary, it helped during the surgery and with the placement of electrodes in the specified part of the brain. After surgery, every couple of hours, a different neurologist (Emory is a teaching hospital) checked on me. I received excellent care. Pain proved quite minimal, despite the holes drilled into my skull and electrical leads placed under my scalp, down the side of my neck, into my clavicle, where the actual battery was implanted, similar to the placement of a pacemaker. One wonderful thing I found out after the surgery was that they did not shave my whole head—just areas where there had to be stitches or entry into my skull.

In an appointment with Dr. Mayberg two weeks after the surgery, I did not feel any different. Actually, the depression seemed worse. Dr. Mayberg reminded me I was only two weeks post brain surgery. She felt like the increase in the severity of my depression meant, at least, that this evidenced some variability in the depression. (*Patience is a never-ending, recurring theme in my journey.*) Distortions in my expectations persisted. I continued to go into the office every week, and then every two weeks, every three weeks, and then once a month, every three months, and then every six months since approximately the year after the surgery. I continued annual visits even after the original five-year participation commitment.

> *10.23.2011: I was operating under the assumption that the DBS was going to miraculously heal the whole depression. I should have known better. Now I realize it is the biological that the DBS is addressing, but the psychic pain still remains. That is what I must be patient about.*

The multiple aspects of treatment that coincided with the surgical implantation kept me on my toes and in constant self-assessment, even though I was cognitively aware that my perceptions and perspective were off.

> *12.09.2009: I found myself angry with one of the doctors for saying my ratings were better when there were absolutely no signs of getting or feeling better from my standpoint. Every time I was seen, I was given the Hamilton Depression Inventory, which is completed as an interview. It was the primary determinant of improvement or decrease in depression. As a result of this encounter, I had a bunch of questions for my therapist in Phoenix, trying to understand the difference.*

I had weekly phone sessions with Dr. Kieffer-Andrews in Phoenix (a requirement of the study as part of my treatment). Of course, I knew I needed to process my reactions to "getting better." Many questions remained:

- Is my reaction about resistance?
- Why can't I get into getting better?

- ❧ Is this a lack of trust that I am getting better?
- ❧ What do I lose by getting better?
- ❧ What do I gain by staying depressed?
- ❧ Is this about getting attention?
- ❧ What does "getting better" mean?
- ❧ Am I worried about resisting a return to a more productive life?
- ❧ Is this fear about expectations of my getting better?
- ❧ I have worked so hard at accepting the depression and now—"*poof*"—it's supposed to be over?
- ❧ Even if I get better, I fear that the depression will return and make me incapacitated again.

As a vigilant reader of this story, these thoughts sound familiar! These endless questions also continued in my conversations with the Atlanta doctors. I endured emotionless, interminable, immeasurable pursuits that persistently haunted me.

After a brief trip to Phoenix for the holidays, disappointment filled me, since I had hoped I would *feel* enjoyment or happiness. But *no*. It was not meant to be. Instead, numbness and emptiness consumed me. Once I returned to Atlanta, I processed more with the doctors.

12.30.2009: Dr. Mayberg kept looking for changes and pointed out that I seemed to be expressing negative emotions, which she views as an improvement. I feel nothing. We talked about suicide, and Dr. H. gave me the option of going into the hospital for a couple of days; I said "No." He said to be sure to call him if the feelings returned or persisted. He is having me come in next week because he says, I am worse this week, and I feel worse. It

*is about wanting the pain (depression, not physical) to go away.
If only I could fall asleep and not wake up feels like a solution
on days like today. What do I have to live for? Not even family
seems motivating. It was such an awful trip to Phoenix. (Could it
have been that I had expectations of "feeling a difference" more
quickly after the implant?)*

I survived this period. Ongoing visits to Atlanta required
the completion of questionnaires, interviews with doctors,
assessment, and sometimes adjustment of my device settings.
In January 2010, I struggled with the feedback I got from one
of the doctors. My general nature is to first look at myself to try
to determine what I need to do, what I am not doing, and to
attend to my own feelings.

*01.17.2010: I want to remain calm and open to my time with
Dr. H and Dr. Mayberg, who are there to help me. I go without
expectations, and the only question was whether my stimulator
settings would remain the same. I would report no change in
emotion or connection with the "Divine" and the med changes,
although they stopped last month because of my suicidal episodes.*

*01.7.2010: Meeting with Dr. H. He feels I am turning things in
on myself and using too much self-blame. He drew a distinction
between "can't" and "choosing" not to change. If the stimulator
is working, change will happen. He noted that I am caught in
metacognitive spiraling circles. (That was a real kick in the butt!)*

*01.17.2010: If the stimulator is changing my brain, why am I not
changing how I feel, my perspective on life, my self-blame?*

Another interpretation and approach to my condition at the time:

01.17.2010: I saw Dr. Mayberg today. She is concerned about the backslide and tried to figure out if there was a trigger. She said it could be we need to adjust the stimulator or my meds. I might be on too much med. It's like I am glad to be in this bad space. Like I am proving the stimulator doesn't work, or that I still have depression. I can't see my way out of depression. I can't see it ending. I feel like I can't be helped. Dr. Mayberg pointed out that I may be missing something that is affecting me. I don't know what I want. I am scared about being able to get back on my feet financially—this weighs very heavily on me.

Contradictions in thought and process continued.

01.19.2010: Dr. H told MKA that I would get better, even with resistance. He later told me he knew I had a strong will to get better, as evidenced by just getting to Atlanta and jumping through all of the hoops. Dr. Mayberg had previously been involved in a DBS study in Canada, and so there were some previous positive results to work with. Previous results shared with MKA by Dr. H included:

- One patient went one year without any improvement and had the device removed.
- The six-month point was seen as a progress point for some.
- He feels my progress will be very up and down because of the significance of the losses I have experienced and my own cognitive processes related to depression.
- He emphasized I needed a "half-full" view.

Contact with Dr. Mayberg always helped. She reminded me again I would not have come to Atlanta if I did not have hope that DBS would work on some level.

03.9.2010: I finally talked to Dr. H. He thinks my recent melt-down is a positive sign of variation in mood—a sign that I have affect. I didn't understand what he said about how I need more positive experiences to increase the chances of having positive affect. He thinks anger is an underlying issue that is aside from the depression. Why am I now so much calmer? Because I think I can be helped. Dr. H said he thinks MKA is a good therapist and that a little guidance from them can help me.

Difficult, ongoing conversations with the psychiatrist continued. He told me I was very angry. I turned that into self-blame. He felt anger pertained to the disease. I decided I needed to move toward acceptance of depression. I also learned not to react personally or try to change things said to me. At that time, I couldn't change anything. The doctor articulated concern that my cognitive rumination works against "Me" and slows my progress. He noted they don't really know how my brain is different, and they don't know the implications for the recovery process. At the same time, he said I could not cognitively work my way out of my situation.

Not surprisingly, I ruminated about being identified as "angry." I wanted to know what specific signs the psychiatrist observed. Was it even possible to deal with issues in treatment when I lacked affect? Is it a combination of anger, cognitive awareness, and loss issues that is the obstacle? Or is my lack of affect about making any progress the real barrier? The endless questions in my mind seemed to set me in motion against myself. The central question became,

> *03.9.2010: Ultimately, am I looking for something that cannot be at this point? I believed Dr. H and Dr. Mayberg concur on this question.*

BREAST CANCER ALONG THE WAY?

In February 2011, I traveled to Atlanta for another visit to determine if I needed a battery replacement in my DBS. It had to be done annually until an anticipated rechargeable battery became available. Even two years after my initial surgery, I continued to express doubts as I recorded in the journal passage below.

> *02.02.2011: I feel like I am at a turning point with the depression. I was assuming expectations of my being well, to go back to work. Was I standing in my own way of recovery? I shouldn't feel sorry for myself being hard on myself. Keep looking for little positive sparks.*

My battery needed replacement, and I would require a return visit for surgery in May. Two days before I headed to Atlanta for surgery, I had a biopsy for possible breast cancer.

> *05.08.2011: I am in Atlanta, preparing for surgery to replace my battery for my DBS. There were concerns about my insurance covering the surgery, and I received a call with a phone number I recognized as being from my insurance company. I took the call only to find out I have breast cancer. I have a bunch of questions for Dr. Mayberg:*

- It's okay to feel some anxiety, isn't it?
- Could the dip in depression in the previous month be accounted for by the battery dying out?
- Does that mean I am that dependent on the stimulator?
- Why am I not feeling more positive things?
- How do I handle breast cancer when depression still feels so present and overwhelming? Will I ever get better to a point where I will be enjoying life?

*05.09.2011: Surgery to replace battery. It will help me. It **is** something to be thankful for. It will make me better.*

05.10.2011: I got through the surgery okay. I am having some pain. The doctors in Atlanta noted there is an outside chance that my stimulator generator may have to be moved, depending on the decisions around the treatment of the breast cancer, which is in the same breast on the same side where the stimulator is implanted. We'll cross that bridge when we come to it. The doctors were all very understanding and supportive . . . I must trust the "Spirit" within me to heal me, to see me through breast cancer and depression. I am worried about the depression affecting the treatment and healing from breast cancer. I just want to get that cancer out of me! My diagnosis of breast cancer in May of that year added another wrinkle to the complexity of it all. My cancer required surgery and then chemotherapy. The chemo is still kicking my butt. And the fatigue is unbearable. [I share more thoughts about cancer later.]

10.23.2011: Today is the two-year anniversary of my DBS surgery. I am clearly better than where I was but still lack emotion and physical sensations; I feel hopeless and desperate. I am best when

*I meditate and stay present in the moment. I am more relaxed
and better able to handle what happens to me and how I "feel."*

The above journal entries tell the story of the process of
receiving, adapting to, getting revisions, and surviving DBS.
My participation continued. For four more years, the battery
in my clavicle had to be replaced annually in outpatient procedures in Atlanta. Then the team announced, with excitement,
a ten-year rechargeable battery could be implanted. It required
weekly charging for three to four hours with no surgery needed
until the battery had to be replaced! Annual visits to Atlanta
continued to monitor my ongoing progress and check the device.
I filled out the questionnaires (which it seems like I should have
memorized by now!).

A second diagnosis of breast cancer in 2018 raised more
questions about the location of my implanted DBS. I decided
to have a bilateral mastectomy. Because cautery was required
for my mastectomy, surgeons in Phoenix were concerned about
the DBS. They had read an article that suggested that the use of
cautery might cause brain damage. In the end, the neurosurgeon
in Atlanta advised the surgeons in Phoenix that the electrodes
in my brain were sheathed in such a manner that rendered such
damage highly unlikely.

The only ongoing obstacle of having the DBS is that it pro-
hibits MRIs, except of the brain. The concern is that hardware
in my DBS and in my ankles could convert electricity and
lead to potentially *permanent* brain damage. The neurosurgeon
confirmed use of cautery alone did not present this risk. But the
potential for this interaction with the DBS necessitated vigilance
and that I apprise providers of this risk. It repeatedly surprised

me that a variety of doctors (e.g., cardiologist, sleep specialist, surgeon, eye doctor, etc.) had never heard of such a thing. They expressed curiosity about it and how it worked.

SUMMARY

I survived the ECT and DBS treatments, drastic decisions for me. I had to put my trust in my accomplished doctors. Both required a willingness to risk procedures that I hoped would improve my depression. I am grateful for the scientific advancements that resulted in these treatments. Each of our brains is different, and our responses to the treatments are individual. Significant improvement in my depression did not appear for months following DBS implantation; the study identified me as a "late responder." Ongoing psychotherapy and medication management were carefully monitored and modified by my trusted therapist in Phoenix. The depression gradually improved, and I felt better.

✦ ✦ ✦

TALK THERAPY

Treating me was not necessarily an easy task for providers, due to the multiple physical problems, such as my hormone imbalances and cancer, which challenged and contributed to my overall well-being. Did a physical problem trigger an episode? Maybe a memory or thought disturbed or confused me. The process required careful assessment of the bigger picture and my history of both physical and emotional problems. Treatment for significant mental illness should always be a combination of approaches that include talk therapy. The evolution of therapy and treatment during my life is complex. Often people are curious about how "Talk Therapy" is defined, what I talk about during therapy, my experience of therapy, and various approaches to psychotherapy (theoretical and participative). I share a snapshot overview of some of the who, what, when, and where of types of therapy I received.

Psychotherapy is one type of treatment for mental illness, but it is also used for a variety of other challenges faced in life.

The incorporation of spiritual themes varies from therapist to therapist, as well as from one approach to another. Sometimes it is just personal growth. One overarching issue is relationships, and the communication associated with them. Each individual does better with some forms of therapy. There is not a "one-size-fits-all" therapy, though proponents of a particular approach or theory may claim that. Different approaches recommend or require a certain number of sessions. Some types from the psychodynamic field can end up being daily, for many, many years of a person's life.

Typically, a person goes in and out of therapy, dependent on life's challenges or the status of their mental illness, referred to as "maintenance therapy." There are categories of types of therapy, with sub-methods included within most of them. I use broader categories to provide their general flavor and orientation. The reader is encouraged to explore approaches to see what feels the most comfortable or useful personally.

WHAT DO I TALK ABOUT DURING THERAPY?

A close friend recently posed this question. We talked about it briefly, and decided to think and write about it. My initial reaction was that it is difficult to describe a "therapy session" or what goes on in therapy, but I gave it a try. First, themes and common patterns of the structure of sessions:

Sometimes therapy is like "show and tell," because I just relay what transpired in my life in the past week. A response to "What's going on?" or "How are you doing?" often led to exploration and discussion of a specific issue. Other times, I walked in bursting with something that happened such as insight gained, an event that rocked me in some manner (positively or negatively), a mounting frustration, or something I anticipated with angst. The therapist immediately read my body language, my facial expressions, posture, tone of voice, and eye contact. What felt like just "reporting in" typically triggered the emergence of a more-specific issue unrelated to my initial eruption. Themes related to my beliefs, thoughts, and "Spirituality" weave in periodically.

Therapy is a time to share, question, examine, dissect, reveal, contemplate, quiet, revel, cry, and use bad words that come out of my mouth or as expression of frustrations. On some occasions, we made plans to "investigate" something related to an arising issue.

02.24.2009: Therapy is a place to go to hard places and then go back out and function. Let what I want to be float by, allowing myself to be human. Depression is not the whole of me.

I learned about the benefits of meditation, visualization, journal writing, exercise, "Spirituality," healthy eating, hypnosis, EMDR, and creating balance in my life, as vital elements for functioning and coping daily. Resources for learning, better understanding, and growing were provided. Balance of work, personal-care activities, including body, mind, "Soul," and "Spirit" rolled in and out of discussion. Sometimes the conversation led to realization of pieces of life I needed to revisit—especially those on which I overfocused and which drained me.

Times of transition opened doors to dialogue (e.g., change of jobs, the beginning of my role of caregiver, return to graduate school, logistics to set up a private practice, move, revisit losses, *normalizing* emotions that I judged as somehow deviant or problematic, the end of relationships, a feeling that "life isn't fair," which interrupted the flow of "Spirit" and "Faith" beliefs, an unending stream of medical problems, and exploration of alternative treatments for depression). At times, I felt like I was in school, because "assignments" were given in response to my question, *What can I do?* Meditate or walk for X minutes daily. Draw a picture of parts of my life in a pie graph. Practice calming, deep breathing at least six times a day, anywhere or anytime. Journal daily experiences of gratitude. A few times, I wrote a letter to someone, which I never intended to send but needed to write to release my feelings. Then I shared it in therapy and felt affirmed by the process as I released thoughts or feelings that were pulling me down. There was no judgment of what I expressed, rather thoughtful further exploration, respect for my expressions of concern, and my eternal gratitude.

Occasionally I wondered if I still *needed* to be in therapy. Inevitably something came up and reminded me of the benefits of therapy. I dealt with a range of issues with threads that continued to weave through my life. I am a *thinker*, and, hence, there is always something to explore. Periodically I felt like I *was done* with a theme, however, somehow, it showed up in another guise, led to discovery of a new aspect of the theme, or I dove deeper into my understanding that enriched me.

WHAT IS MY EXPERIENCE WITH THERAPY?

I chose to talk about therapy experiences working backward, because my current therapist continues as such a huge contributor to my treatment for an extended period of time. Dr. Marilyn

Kieffer-Andrews, RNP, PhD, psychiatric mental-health practitioner, is my previously described "Perspective Angel." To me, she is "Marilyn" or "MKA," because of her long name!

MKA is an historian, aware of my previous patterns of thought, interpretation, and problem-solving. She smiled, nodded her head, and kept listening. Invariably, I learned lessons from each experience, but the lesson did not hold for me over time and required reminders, reviews, or updates. She is a mirror that reflects improvement in experiences and thoughts. There are reminders of themes that I get caught up in, for any number of reasons, and she patiently helps me break free from them. She followed me through the maze of my body, mind, "Soul," and "Spirit." I appreciate how her questions bring me back to an issue or consideration of something I avoided or encouraged me to take the time to closely examine a thought. She creates a safe place and environment (comfortable chairs, a gentle fountain with soothing sounds right outside the sliding patio doors, with her Yorkie coming and giving slobbery kisses), and built a quality relationship with me.

My therapist knows buttons she can push to nudge me along and maybe even *piss me off* to help disrupt my useless thoughts or circles of rumination with a silly chuckle. She understands "Me" well enough to make comments or raise questions that interrupt the craziness of a given moment. She is a person, not a goddess. I do not always agree with her! I probed her sometimes for her opinion, approach to something, or insights. I got angry at times, but I usually realized that showed that I needed to think about and examine an issue on a different level or in an alternative manner.

Friends and family asked whether my therapist was a substitute for a friend. Well, maybe a little bit, but in the realm of questions of the "Soul," someone trained and prepared to help me process or cope with what was going on spiritually was essential. As a skilled therapist, she recognized my questions of the "Soul," and my previous experiences, and supported me in an exploration of my thoughts. She gently urged me to venture into the world to build a broader support system of people. *No one person or therapist* could meet all of my needs. Not because they didn't care or didn't want to listen, but because the issue or our relationship could be adversely affected. Even with my closest friends, I did not want to burden them. *But*, I definitely built friendships that provided a safe place for exploration of some of the issues I encountered in therapy. I often discovered that the other people shared a similar experience or quagmire.

APPROACHES TO PSYCHOTHERAPY

There is not an agreed-upon designation of psychotherapy categories. Much of this is related to the theoretical orientation of the individual professional, associated organization, or related field (e.g., social work, counseling. psychology, "Spirituality"). The following information is an amalgamation of general labels for the most well-known categories and orientations.

Psychodynamic

Psychodynamic—focuses on the meaning of behavior, feelings, and thoughts related to unconscious processes and past experiences. I always had an image of a patient lying on a couch, with the therapist sitting nearby. It is a more traditional form of therapy. Patient and therapist explore the roots of personal depression as part of a much-larger exploration of unique aspects of development over a lifetime. Depression brings to the forefront conversations about the roots of experience and development that require processing to understand them in the larger context of an individual's life. I had little personal interest in psychodynamic therapy. In retrospect, I did not know much about the approach. My misconceptions included the notion that you had to do psychodynamic treatment for an indeterminate period of time! I thought it involved microscopic analysis of one's development and key relationships throughout life. In addition, it is expensive, quite time-consuming, and not practical for me. Psychodynamic analysis has been quite effective for many people over time. I have a highly respected friend and colleague who had a very positive experience with the approach and helped me better understand the developmental nature and emphasis of the approach and process.

Trauma can be a specific focus of psychotherapy, viewed as a significant contributor to depression and a primary focus of treatment. I explored possible traumas in my childhood and the history of depression in my family with therapists. As part of the much broader process of therapy, these small pieces did not provide me much information or insight. But my friend and colleague shared the profound personal impact of the method.

Cognitive or Cognitive Behavioral Therapy (CBT)

Cognitive or Cognitive Behavioral Therapy (CBT) explores the relationship between thoughts and actions and includes strategies such as Dialectical Behavior Therapy. The focus is on new ways to react to situations to help reduce the impact of depression and challenge preconceptions of issues that compound depression. These techniques usually involve some form of homework to address one's thoughts and ways to practice shifts in them. Therapist and client select specific thoughts as targets or goals to help change one's view of the contributions of depression. CBT is considered "evidence-based" therapy, which speaks to scientific research done to determine the effectiveness of a therapy or treatment, usually conducted with college students. Conceptually, CBT may help alter thoughts that may contribute to feelings of depression.

There was an ongoing discussion with the doctors in the DBS Study in Atlanta about whether CBT was part of my therapy. For the most part, my reaction to CBT was negative, because I felt that such a mind shift was unattainable. Targeting changing my thoughts had already proved unhelpful to me as I explored various types, and I admonished myself for lack of change. Some aspects of profound depression preclude improvement via CBT. The doctors in Atlanta told me repeatedly that, if I could "think" or "learn" my way out of the depression, it would have happened a long time ago. How confusing! Think about your thoughts, ideas, and. . . . But no, if you could have a thought and learned a way out, such disruptive thoughts would have already changed.

02.11.2015: I want to believe in the plasticity of my brain, but, from my perspective, crucial influential features and factors have not revived. My logic-driven left brain is passing lots of judgment, hindering the creative, intuitive, holistic goodness of my right hemisphere to shine.

Humanistic/Experiential Therapy
Humanistic/Experiential Therapy—focuses on an individual's human nature. Gestalt, Person-Centered, Narrative,

Emotion-Focused, and Transpersonal methods help individuals reach their greatest personal potential. These are viewed as secular (non-religious) approaches. Unique personal experiences are the central target, and ways to grow and heal are addressed. Specific psychological or physiological aspects of problems are not necessarily addressed; complicated daily experiences take the spotlight. A vital element is the "whole person" nature, which centers on personal acceptance and, hopefully, "self-actualization." To Abraham Maslow, self-actualization is the ability to become the best version of oneself. Maslow stated,

> *"This tendency might be phrased as the desire to become more and more what one is, to become everything that one is capable of becoming." Of course, we all hold different values, desires, and capacities.*

Maslow's hierarchy of needs addresses levels of meeting basic needs, starting with physiological needs (food, water, sleep, and warmth), followed by safety needs (financial, health, personal safety), a sense of relationships (love, friendship, intimacy), self-esteem, and, ultimately, "self-actualization." This shift in psychology moved from *abnormal* behavior, development, and problems, to *healthy* growth or "humanistic" psychological development as the focus. Elements of these ideas presented in a variety of ways over my years in therapy. In particular, this approach addressed my self-esteem and character.

Behavior Therapy
Behavior Therapy—is applied in the treatment of mental-health disorders, with a focus on the idea that *all* behaviors are learned

and can be "unlearned" or modified. The goal is the promotion of "good" behavior and the reduction of problematic behavior. Specific forms considered under this category include applied behavioral analysis, social learning, cognitive behavioral therapy, dialectical behavior therapy, and desensitization-and-exposure therapy. It is apparent there is overlap among various categories. Biting fingernails is a great example, with methods such as the use of a bad-tasting substance on the hands and fingers or snapping a rubber band on one's wrist when there is a thought of biting fingernails. There are limited circumstances and behaviors responsive to narrow attention to a problem. Certainly, change of specific behaviors can be beneficial, though it will not necessarily help larger, more-pervasive problems or needs.

The targeted approach of this type of therapy restricts the intervention to a single behavior, such as taking medications as prescribed. It is simple to just record whether the medicines are taken at a certain time, a given number of times daily. An individual may even feel better if they take their medication consistently, but medication is unlikely to address the more-complex issues of depression that affect thoughts, feelings, and actions on a deeper level.

FORMATS OF TREATMENT: WHO IS IN THE ROOM?

Individual Counseling

Individual Counseling is a one-on-one session with a professional therapist—who might be a PhD, EdD, PsyD, MD, DO, DSci, LCSW, NP, MFC, or PA with experience in treatment of depression and other mood disorders. The therapist aims to teach more about depression and help you understand the diagnosis. New strategies to manage stress and to prevent further worsening or return of depression are shared. One-on-one sessions help identify specific stressors and triggers that aggravate depression. A therapist helps work through issues at home or at work and encourages the preservation of healthy connections with family and friends. Encouragement is expressed for the patient to sustain good life habits (e.g., taking your medications, regular doctor visits, exercise, and getting enough sleep). Optimally, a combination of approaches is provided. Individual therapy dominated my treatment for years.

Family Counseling

Family Counseling treats the entire family—because an individual diagnosis of depression also impacts the family; they feel it, too. Unfortunately, even family members with the best of intentions, without professional guidance, made things worse at times. Family therapy is a great way for family members to learn about depression and the early warning signs of serious trouble. Studies suggest that family sessions also help with treatment through the improvement of a person's lifestyle, compliance with medication, and sleep habits. Family meetings also offer an opportunity for everyone—you and your family members—to talk about the stressors of life with depression. Everyone feels more comfortable with open discussion, as a therapist thoughtfully guides the conversation and ensures each person is heard.

I had only one session where my parents and my three sisters participated. I was pretty much unresponsive to treatment and other people at the time, and my therapist wanted to help the family understand what was going on with me. It was hard to hear her present my status to family members, even though what she said was accurate to me. In a slumped-over position, I stared at the carpet. The ongoing struggle of self-acceptance and appreciation of the efforts I made were heightened, as my *secrets* were revealed with my permission. My family wanted to know how to help me. The session affirmed the seriousness of my problems and informed them that I was doing everything I could at that time to help myself. I was relieved of the need to personally describe what I could not explain, and this helped put my family on a similar page. This opportunity helped them with their frustration as well.

My parents also met with my therapists periodically. You see, *they* needed support in their efforts to nurture and care for me. The more a family understands, the easier it is to deal with day-to-day living.

Group-Counseling/Support-Group

Group-Counseling/Support-Group sessions provide a chance to meet other people who struggle with depression or other similar problems. Personal experiences and strategies for coping are shared. The give-and-take at group sessions is often a productive way to learn different ways to think about my illness. I participated in only a couple of formal group-counseling sessions. My frustration was that I felt so different from the other members and did not relate to them. In hindsight, I realized my inability to take advantage of that process. Many years later, I participated in a group of individuals who had cancer. Though quite unusual and diverse, we morphed into a group that supported each other even many years later. The emphasis on the group made a difference as well as the background and experience of individual participants.

"Spiritual" Direction

Though not typically viewed as "therapy," it supports consideration of various issues in life. There are individuals trained specifically in spiritual direction, and religious leaders provide this as well. The spiritual director knows how to be with someone as they explore and deepen their relationship with "God/ Divine." The process helps a person learn and grow their personal "Spirituality." The spiritual director listens and asks questions, may pray with you, may suggest readings to explore, and assists an individual with reflection and spiritual growth.

On a journey like mine, spiritual direction proved vital. Fortunately, my therapists integrated "Faith" and "Spirituality" as indispensable aspects of my journey. Critical to my journey, I needed a therapist who acknowledged "God" as an integral part of my life, especially as my perceived image of "Soul" and "God" vacillated.

CHRONOLOGY OF MY CARE

At age ten, I regularly saw my school counselor. She was marvelous, with red hair and glasses, and she listened carefully. Made me feel important. I sat in my classroom and watched excitedly out the window for her car to pull up in front of the school. She became a trusted friend. When we moved to Phoenix, I wrote her letters, but my parents intercepted them and told me, "*We live in Phoenix now.*" What a blow! The one thing I recalled from that therapy was a request for me to draw a picture of a person. The main thing? She asked me to tell her about the shoelaces in the picture. Funny focus to remember. I have no clue why she asked or why I remember. I later discovered, in graduate school,

SPIRIT RISING

that the Draw-A-Person Test is a key tool for those working with children to gain insights into the child's nonverbal intelligence, behavior, and emotions.

Formal therapy began when I returned from Germany. In the meantime, I participated in church activities, which included deep conversations with the youth-group leaders about beliefs, "Faith," and the relationship with the Bible. These experiences nurtured my "Soul," a form of *informal therapy*, for sure.

When I started junior college, I was referred to a counselor on campus to talk with and help me. It felt awkward because I would often run into the therapist, also a professor on campus, who had a distinctive posture and gait that stood out. But here again, as my therapist, he created a lifeline. I waited with antic- ipation to see him or run into him! He introduced his *magic bullet* to me: Albert Ellis' *The Guide to Rational Living*. The ideas addressed my thoughts. I learned to recognize how I thought and the possible flaws in the way I thought about life. I asked myself the question, *"Can a thinking process alter it all?"* which really opened a can of worms. The thoughts it triggered carried me down crazy pursuits in my journal.

> I want to believe one can self-talk from the negative or depres- sion. I have always thought that and tried that, but I was not always effective. I told myself, "Do the best that you **know** how, not **think** how."

I learned a lot about myself from the work of Dr. Ellis. His ideas seemed to fit me at that time. Among other things, I didn't know how to relax. Always *doing*, I didn't create space for enjoyment, savoring, and appreciation of the good parts of my life (aka *being*). I now understand religion, "Faith," meditation, and "Spirituality" as tools to *be*. I found challenges with relationships with others, did not have any friends, and did not realize how vital this missing element could be in my life. I asked questions: "How do I love someone without being consumed by them? How do I maintain my creativity without feeling obliged to be part of others'?" I distanced myself and substituted *philosophizing* for enjoying others and exploring ideas with them. I wondered if my wandering thoughts worked against me.

During this time, I tried to *move away from depression.* I thought I needed to build social skills. I seemed preoccupied with the notion that I felt *special* in some way, and I needed to get rid of that idea, because it seemed to get in my way. Was I a prisoner of my own introspectiveness? Did I just come up with a litany of reasons for my inadequacy to do social things? I ruminated on who I thought *I should be.*

11.20.1973: My therapist asked me how I would look back on this time in my life. Would I think it was wasted? What would I have accomplished during this time? He went on to say he always felt I would become an extraordinary person. Different, but that involved challenges, stepping out on a limb. He told me to quit being so hard on myself. "Let your Being *be." A line still with me to this day, essential to my journey of "Spirit" through depression!*

During my university years, classes, part-time work, and commuting kept me very busy. Time for thought or contemplation eluded me. Still living with my parents when I finished college and started my first job, I wanted someone to talk to. I wanted "help." I crept up the stairs to a room at a community clinic for a group session, and that completely overwhelmed me! I was shy, intimidated, anxious, and I felt out of place. They referred me to an individual counselor. It felt very nice that he naturally included "Faith" in my counseling. This clinic, a church-based program, offered services to members of the community. I did not "connect" with the counselor. I did not have friends, though I was busy at my home and church, where I played my flute on Sundays.

Eventually some friends and colleagues saw my distress and unhappiness, *as well as* my incredible potential as a teacher. They expressed concern and felt I could use help. They referred me to a clinical psychologist, who became a lifesaver over the course of many years. In fact, Matty, Dr. Mathilda Canter, became the first female licensed psychologist in Arizona. Though she is no longer with us, "Matty's" presence remains with me. I find few words to describe "Matty" but *incredible*. She listened, nurtured, reinforced my skills as a teacher, and worked hard to help me see my self-worth. Dr. Canter's background in therapy was psychodynamic. She was not a traditional psychoanalyst. She engaged me in a variety of therapeutic approaches that she tailored to my most immediate concerns or needs. She did not believe my depression was just about my thoughts. She also initiated a process to help me understand the biochemical aspects of depression. She explained that medication might help us work together in therapy. She protected and respected my dignity and showed sensitivity to how I felt about pursuing psychiatric medication and care. She reassured me she would remain my therapist.

Dr. Harris Murley, MD, a psychiatrist, became a member of my treatment team. He appreciated my intelligence, insights, and intense desire to feel better. As he walked me out after the first appointment, he said, "*If you were my daughter, you would be in medical school right now!*" Whether he believed it or not, it uplifted me. He taught me so much about the biological/ neurological basis of depression and constructively pointed out where he thought my biology was off. Dr. Murley saw me as a whole person and integrated my biological needs with my overall well-being. He recognized the intermittent anxiety I experienced physically and figured that into my treatment. In addition, he taught me the importance of adequate sleep and how to check that. He provided his personal phone number if I needed to contact him. I felt I had another safety net. A lot of our contact included his reassurances that I would be okay. He clearly communicated that the medications would not solve all my problems but rather figured into a whole plan of treatment. Dr. Murley's *therapy* included education about my illness and treatment, which empowered me. He also collaborated with Dr. Canter.

> *11.20.1978: Dr. Murley reminded me once again of my unique patience with my kids [in my classroom]. I need to reflect that patience back on myself. Remember, Dr. Murley said, There is growth." I know there is, but I lose sight of that every so often! Maybe I need to try harder to give those strokes to myself as I so capably give my kids.*

In the meantime, the work with Matty continued. She met with my parents (I was in my 20s), and they wondered if I was a "homosexual" because I didn't date at all, nor did I seem interested in dating. She cleared that up quickly. They wanted to know how to help me. Matty reassured them that their consideration and careful listening were important.

I continued to try to figure out what I wanted to be *when I grew up*. I eventually decided I wanted to go back to graduate school and become a school psychologist. My work as a teacher of children with learning disabilities and emotional problems fueled my desire to help more children and families in bigger and better ways. Matty put me at ease and helped me stay in touch with my gifts as a teacher. She never pushed or told me *what to do*. I continued on medication as well. She encouraged me to investigate and pursue graduate school. She provided a broad range of support across various aspects of my life. All of these ideas contributed to my growth and provided me with improved personal perspective. Even though I carried many self-doubts, I hoped my efforts would diminish the effects of the depression.

> 02.01.1979: I do not understand what has happened. I could not accept any of Matty's alternatives. I do not think I can yet accept positive comments about myself or my growth and change. I want to learn to relax and—more than that—to trust my ability to use this effectively. I was seeing many of Matty's comments as threats to me and finger-pointing, even though, intellectually, I understood the intent of what was said. Matty really believes in me and in my fortitude, courage, and ability to get through this thing.

Once in graduate school at the U of A in Tucson, I continued follow-up with another psychiatrist to manage my medications for depression. The presence of a medical school where I was doing my graduate work was fortuitous. I was convinced by then that the antidepressants were important and helpful; at least, I did not *ignore* the depression. "Spiritual" desolation enveloped me during this time. During my fourth semester at the U of A, professors informed me the day before Thanksgiving that I was *not Doctoral material* and was not accepted into the Doctoral program. I drove home from Tucson in tears. *But* something inside me said it was going to be okay and that it was a good thing!!! ("God"? "Spirit"?) Dr. Canter provided support. I planned to wait to check out other options, but she urged me to pursue a program I discovered at Northern Arizona University in Flagstaff, Arizona. A new program in Early Childhood School Psychology was in development. Within a couple of weeks, I visited NAU, learned about the new program, and decided it was for me.

Within six weeks, I moved from Tucson to Flagstaff without any guarantees about admission to the Doctoral program. It looked like a good possibility that I could pursue a doctorate, with a specialization in early-childhood school psychology. Fortuitous for me, the chairwoman of the department, Suzanna Maxwell, PhD, selected me to assist and help develop the new program.

Dr. Matty Canter proved an awesome resource *again*. She connected me with the director of the counseling center at NAU. He was no longer seeing students as a therapist, but he took me on!!! He embraced me in so many ways. Among other things, he hooked me up with his church in the community. Dr. James Frederick was a gift. He understood mental illness, and he also recognized my illness as an integral part of who I was. We prayed together. He sponsored me on a special retreat, an incredible opportunity for "Spiritual" growth. He employed many different approaches to treatment, always with consideration of my most immediate frame of mind and mental status.

Upon completion of my doctorate, I returned to Phoenix. Over my years at NAU, Matty and I became friends such that she could no longer ethically be a therapist to me. She met me for lunch and congratulated me. She believed in me and my potential, and she constantly instilled hope.

I wanted to work on losing some weight, so I received a referral to a perky dietician who was very easy to talk with. She gave suggestions for working with my eating and encouraged exercise. In the meantime, I suffered an ankle injury at work, in my new job. I eventually required ankle surgery for reconstruction. This drastically limited my activity level. The dietician also wondered about depression and suggested I pursue medication and some therapy. She referred me to another *lifeline*, literally for years to come. So started my relationship with Dr. Marilyn Kieffer-Andrews, RNP, PhD, Psychiatric Mental Health Practitioner, aka "MKA."

As a psychiatric nurse practitioner and a therapist, she referred to herself as a mental health provider. She is all of those things and so much more! Especially at difficult times, she reassured me about the status of my body, mind, "Soul," and "Spirit." She never wavered in her availability and support. She designed her integrated approach to address specific types of problems I faced. She included additional methods such as guided visualization, encouraged my creative hobbies, asked hard questions, listened, and always gave words of hope, even when I did not feel any hope.

At one point, she suggested that I try EMDR (Eye Movement Desensitization and Reprocessing) with a therapist specializing in the technique. EMDR is a psychotherapy treatment designed to examine distress associated with traumatic life events. I was hesitant because MKA and I had tried so many different methods, and I just thought, *Now what?* She viewed it as another strategy I should explore. Unfortunately, in the end, EMDR did not work for me, one more failed therapy. I viewed myself as "damaged goods." I felt a lack of any control over my life and figured I was *different*, and not loveable. Really? After all of the years of therapy?

As talk therapy and medical treatment continued, I relentlessly searched for answers to my depression. I found my way to the DBS (Deep Brain Stimulation) Study. Fortunately, another piece of my treatment fell into place. Therapy with Dr. Kieffer-Andrews continued long-distance and proved essential during my six months in Atlanta. She supported me through continued hopelessness, immobilization, irrational fears, anxiety, and suicidality. I lamented the *lack* of "Spirit" and connection with "God" intensely during this time. Despite all this, I was determined to *get better*. Later, she said she knew I would make it through all of the adversity, and she wanted to see it through with me.

MATCHING YOUR NEEDS WITH A THERAPIST

The individual therapy I received over these many years included a variety of approaches subsumed under different categories of therapy. My relationship with each therapist was tantamount to the process of each therapy modality. Those who treated me *worked with* me as a *partner* in my healing process. They did not present themselves as "experts" with all the answers. We launched explorations together. During my most desperate moments of depression, I talked about daily activities (eat, sleep, exercise) Their reminders about the importance and maintenance of these basic life functions and self-care demanded my persistent attention. Over time, therapists provided tremendous resources and helped me to better understand myself. They asked me to stretch my thoughts and stop self-deprecation. Despite the quite difficult processes, I participated willingly. Sometimes I could not wait to get to therapy, and, other times, I dreaded there would be hard things to talk about. Any therapeutic relationship requires a *fit* between therapist and patient. An initial sense of personal issues and needs is a high priority for determining a good match, as well as personal comfort with the therapist, which may be immediate or, more likely, require time to develop.

IS TALK THERAPY FOR YOU?

What do you want/need from therapy? What has/has not worked for you in the past? Consider what you want out of therapy, and prepare to tell a potential therapist your goal(s). Is there a specific problem you want to delve into? Do you want some practical support? Find out about their approach, personality, availability, willingness to work with other providers, accessibility, etc. You have the right to *interview* therapists to get a feel for your match with that individual. And you must *always* have patience with the process of finding someone. Perhaps more importantly, as a patient, you need to assess the success or failure of therapy along the way. You may find a mismatch. You may initially find connection and success but later find that the therapist and situation no longer meet your needs. The key remains for you and the therapist to frequently assess whether the therapy is working for you.

"SPIRITUAL" INTEGRATION

In my chronology of talk therapy, my "Spirituality" and connection with "Soul", "God", "Spirit" were always on my mind. They wove through all aspects of treatment under boundless personal scrutiny and consideration that ebbed and flowed. Even when I did not *feel* the presence of "God," Talk Therapy provided an essential, dependable cocoon whenever and for whatever my heart, mind, and "Soul" were seeking. Frequently, the cocoon was exactly what I needed as a break for reflection.

✦　✦　✦

PATHS TO UNION WITH "SPIRIT"

In my earlier chapters, I shared my moment-to-moment experiences, and how I lived this personal and intimate journey of "Spirit" through depression. Individuals who live with depression and their caregivers have words and pictures that express the indescribable. More importantly, most attribute meaning and find understanding in those kinds of depictions. Here, I share reflections about my process and the paths I followed to find union with what I call "Spirit." Along the way, I will reveal my "Aha!" moments, insights, and ideas that have helped me find my link to "Spirit." My understandings deepened and expanded over time, which allowed me to incorporate them into my "Being." I hope that sharing my personal paths might help others face fewer obstacles along their travels. And I wish that their relationship with their "Holy Spirit" might be infused with the possibility for more intimacy. Each person's path to union with "God/Spirit" is a personal one. I hope my reflections may open windows for each person to find something that makes sense in their own story. I hope persons from many religions and "Faith" perspectives who struggle with depression and other challenges may find something in my story that will help them cope with feelings of disconnection, betrayal, or a changed relationship with their "God."

These gifts that my course to "Spirit" through depression sowed in me have been woven over many years. Though I've found that these threads cannot be boiled down into simple ideas or specific individual explanations, some major themes about "God," "Spirit," and "Faith" are present. I encourage you to explore them if any of them strike a note with you.

My religion and "Faith" have been shaped by many experiences and people. I frequently asked myself, *Who and what experiences have been lights in my life?* I am fortunate to have a living chronicle in my journals of the emergence and evolution of "God," "Spirit," and "Faith." These writings helped me see what I had gained over time.

I practice daily disciplines such as meditation and contemplation of the meaning of "God," "Spirit," and "Faith." Prayer is an ongoing, personal custom that provides me with an opportunity to consider the meanings of my explorations. In spite of frequent lamentations that I have felt disconnected from "God," I now affirm that "God" is *always* present *within.* "*What I have to live for . . .*" has proven to be a critical, continuous, and sustained consideration.

Ultimately, the threads and themes that comprise my journey to connect with "Spirit" have defied summary or conclusion. But our human universalities and connectedness can, with awareness, buffer our ride. With that in the foreground, I hope you will find something in my words to make your route to "Spirit" or "God" a bit softer, smoother, or kinder than mine has been.

INTRODUCTION

Brought up as a child in the Christian "Faith," I started very early on my journey to the place I am today. I have blossomed from an early Christian understanding of religion and "God" to a more expansive, welcoming sense of "Holy Spirit." Over the course of my quest, I describe how I accessed the "Divine." Because I am a seeker and questioner by nature, I believe I would have made this adventure whether struck with depression or not. However, my journey of "Faith" through depression has proved arduous, with a few welcome-but-fleeting moments of grace and connection. More often, I have felt lost and disconnected. I have yearned for and sometimes pleaded for a sign of "God's" presence during my darkest times.

Religion and religious practices have impacted my pursuit to unite with "Spirit" with depression, but there is so much more to my "Spiritual" transformation. Here, through my retrospective, I reveal what it took to get through each day, and I overview my lifelong quest for the "Divine." These observations mirror my evolution from religion to "Spirituality," and I will use the terms "God," "Spirit," "Holy Spirit," the "Divine," and "Soul" interchangeably. In addition, "Faith," for me, means the religious tenets I learned as a child. These observations reflect my evolution from religion to "Spirituality."

I realized over time that my curiosity and questions continued to open new doors to further develop my relationship with "God." Considerations of how and when "God" had been present in my life reminded me I had experienced far-greater manifestations than I often realized or noticed behind the veil of my depression. I discovered an abundance of expanding memories.

With "Spiritual" maturation, I recognized connections with "God" that I had not noticed at the time they occurred. As my "Spirit" unfolded, I reached a pinnacle in my transformation. New paths emerged for me to explore, including how "Holy Spirit" fit into the picture.

The question *When had I felt Union with "God" along my quest for the "Divine"?* led me to discover how "God" dwelled within me. The idea of "God Within," which is a very personal integration, opened this knowing to me. While the intensity of my process to discover "Spirit" vacillated, each heightened moment proved essential to this integration of "God" and "Spirit" into my overall well-being and "Spirituality." Dr. Kenneth Kendler found in his research that one-third of our "Spirituality" is innate and foundational to our way of being, while the other two-thirds are developed during one's life. This insight into the composition of events and ideas related to "Spirituality" rang true for me.

MY LIFELONG QUEST FOR THE "DIVINE"

My *religious* upbringing was steeped in living a life of "Faith" in the world, with values rooted in the goodness of each human being. My parents seeded my belief in the "Divine" with encouragement to participate in church activities for many different reasons. By the same token, they never *insisted* on absolute belief in anything. This open guidance afforded me opportunities to discover and explore. Little did I know that these explorations also helped me build a foundation for my personal "Faith." I took part in ecumenical groups of high-school students, through which we explored each other's faiths. I enrolled in a contemporary theology course that studied theologians like Nietzsche,

Bonhoeffer, Tillich, and Niebuhr. My church practiced *living "Faith" in the real world versus subscribing to specific tenets.* This worldview left doors open for children and teens to develop a personal "Spirituality" that the church community would embrace and respect. This community support remained vital to my personal "Faith" evolution.

I attribute the birth of my "Spiritual" life and a source of eternal support to Rich and Marie Schreiber, the couple who were my youth-group leaders at my church during my high-school years. They are the first people I remember who held up a mirror to show me, the "Spiritual" me. They encouraged my search for the "Divine." I became able to express my questions and hurts, knowing full well that they would accept me the way I was and that they would respect my feelings. Sometimes they would honestly say they didn't know what to say but affirmed I was *special* to them. Their notes and letters still arrive when I need a lift.

My first placement in the rigid religious commune, as my church's exchange student, in Germany, carried unknown and unrealistic expectations. I faced intense challenges to my beliefs, "Faith," and the presence of "God" in my life. I soon realized the members were inflexible fundamentalists and believed they got everything they needed (including food) through prayer. Daily *"austausch"* provided a time for groups of members to meet, pray together, and share anything they might have said or done *wrong* toward another member. *"I am sorry I was short with you yesterday." "I should have been nicer to you during meal preparation last night."* All these apologies and these acts seemed mundane to me and, at times, contrived. The negative emphasis troubled me. I came from a focus on each person's gifts, not their faults. To fill each day, they also spent considerable time in Bible reading and studies. They labeled my expressed desire to spend time with the couple who hosted me as very selfish and not in line with their idea of the benevolence of Jesus. My rebuttal: "If 'God' wanted me to be a puppet on a string, *She* would have made me that way." I held a whole different view of religion, "Faith," "Spirituality," etc. I was taught to think for myself and not blindly accept anything. In the commune, it felt like there were *rules* to follow (or believe) that determined my worthiness to be a Christian.

Fortunately, during this first half-year, I drew on my childhood foundation of "Faith," built before this time—a "Faith" I had not realized lived within me. The questions that arose from these experiences sparked ideas and ultimately confirmed the *Faith* I, indeed, had at that time. These practices, organizations, and people provide just a peek into the place in which I lived for six months.

Because of my discomfort and discontent that grew over time, the German ICYE (International Christian Youth Exchange Program) committee moved me to Worms, Germany. Fresh air threaded through me in my new placement in Worms. My host family and their community welcomed me. My host father, Hans-Dieter, served as the evangelical minister for the church and neighborhood where we lived. Eva Maria, my host mother, practiced as a teacher. I babysat a few times for their adorable two-year-old daughter. I vacationed with them to different places in Germany and Switzerland. They included me in a variety of activities and experiences in the community as well as conversations that supported, renewed, and further stimulated my journey with "Spirit."

I attended the church where Hans Dieter officiated services. The experience kind of shocked me. Older women dressed all in black, aka *war widows*, lined a section of pews, the only parishioners present. I had spent time with many more people of all ages in my church in Phoenix. The Worms church's organist, their one younger member, became my friend. My conversations with Hans-Dieter brought me back to the broader worldview of my "Faith." We discussed many related topics. One of those times, he shared with me that he felt something unique happened with the birth of Jesus, and the notion of "The Virgin Birth" may have been the only way to explain the occurrence at that time in history. He even shared based on his experiences with the study of the scripture back to Sanskrit, that much of the meaning may have been lost in the centuries of translation, which further inspired me to examine my "Faith" with an open mind.

I felt confused about my "Faith" after the religious-commune experience but always maintained my connection to *Something Greater than Myself.* After my year abroad, I finally recognized and named my depression for the first time. It had surfaced with more persistence. As time unfolded after this seminal year, the perilous course of my ever-present depression, with unpredictable turbulence, scattered me into vast unknown spaces and always left me in a search for meaning. In a couple of my darkest times, Marilyn talked with me about "Spirituality" and guided me toward various resources. Father Thomas Keating had taped a long series in which he talked about the evolution of man, the historic development of the brain (from reptiles on), and an emerging understanding of human beings. One comment struck me. He felt that religion (especially Christianity) lost something when it no longer included the feminine side of "God" and returned to a patriarchal model and hierarchy. He noted how "God" lost distinctively feminine qualities that had brought an emotional aspect to the "Divine." What happened to the Goddesses of history? I internalized this feminine notion that there is supposed to be an emotional aspect to religion and "Faith"—something I so badly wanted. It affirmed my personal insistence that feeling emotions is supposed to be part of "Faith," though I *felt* no emotion!

How did I grow to integrate so much into my perspective of the "Divine" and "Spirit" at the same time an ever-present depression engulfed me? The answer is *with great difficulty*: feelings of loss, abandonment, desperation, absence, and punitive judgments from others blinded me to "Faith" and "Spirit." These left me drained, empty, numb, downtrodden, incompetent, and lifeless. Yet, I repeatedly reached out to regain a fragile hold on my "Faith" and "Spirituality," a precious ribbon interwoven throughout my "Being." The religion in which I grew up provided me with an initial set of beliefs and values, a foundation on which I could draw. In retrospect, I concluded I must wander and discover my own journey to "Spirit."

The journal entries shared below memorialize my struggles.

11.07.2009: This whole "God thing" is not on my radar screen and does not exist for me now. I go to the "People Like Me" blog and don't find it helpful. The "inspiration" thread talks about all of the things "God" does for them. He is absent for me. I posted on People Like Me about my lack of connection to "God," and the response I got was almost punitive with regard to how I have to realize "God" is present and that I am part of God.

The next entry exemplifies the practice of prayer, with which I grew up and turned to repeatedly throughout my life, with varying degrees of *success*.

06.12.2011: God, must I pray without ceasing? Must I pray in a different way? I pray for your will in my life; you guided me down many different roads with many more challenges I have faced. I survived and thrived over and over again.

The journal entry below illustrates one of the many situations where I engaged in prayer to help me cope:

02.22.2017: Open my eyes wide to "healing." Think about small gifts when I look at "renewal." Regain something—but maybe that is not to return to a previous state or place, or regain something I viewed as "lost" or is even "gone."

Unfortunately, the disabling cloud of depression rapidly and repeatedly swept in on the footsteps of such insights. It completely blinded me to the precious ribbon of my "Faith" and "Spirit Within."

As I matured and grew as a person, my "Spirit" grew. "Faith" narrowed in meaning to my word for the initial set of beliefs and values that my childhood experiences had instilled in me. "Spirituality" emerged over the past few decades as a more all-encompassing term with multiple meanings for me. The notion of "God," the "Divine," or whatever one calls that which is greater than each of us is often quite personal. This threaded throughout my life as well, and my understandings of "Spirit" intertwined with those of the "Divine." During my "Spirit" trek through depression, "God" became a source with whom I begged and pleaded because I felt abandoned. I felt "Spiritually" empty.

REFLECTIONS: HOW AND WHEN HAS "GOD" BEEN OR NOT BEEN PRESENT IN MY LIFE?

Despite the variability in my awareness of "God" and "Spirit" in my life, there have been times when I was *certain*, I *knew*—I *felt* that presence. Nevertheless, these deeply ingrained experiences seemed hidden or at least inaccessible at some of my most difficult times. I wondered, as the sleuth in a good mystery, how there could be such drastic contrast in these connections.

Most important, I think, I have held close a sustained and overarching belief present all my adult life: *I have the strength to weather the storm of depression.* I believe that, without this underlying strand of conviction, I might have committed suicide. Some might say that I feared religious retribution if I took my own life. I don't think so. Rather, I have believed that my life matters and that there are reasons to go on living, though not always readily apparent. I identified this *something* as a "feeling," a hunch, an intuition, a hope, though it often seemed weak. At those times, it did not seem strong enough to infiltrate my sense of doom and gloom. When I felt unable to access it at extremely critical times, this *something* proved strong enough to motivate me to seek outside help to process this acceleration of my decline. Fully aware that my perspective was off in some manner, I knew I needed help from someone. This process, external to my self-searching process, helped me regroup.

I applied to and entered graduate school with the conviction that it was what I was *meant* to do. I had not yet investigated the specifics of finances, where I would live, or self-care and support. At the time I applied, the program made no promises that I would be admitted to the Doctoral track. Somehow, I *knew* it was what I was supposed to do. I had confidence and optimism about the possibility of earning a Doctoral degree. In some ways, my determination baffled me. This conviction carried "Me" through and helped me focus and succeed in graduate school. Despite little energy, but excited about pursuing this degree, I made a personal commitment to journal, meditate, and pray to keep myself on track. These strategies kept me focused on earning my degree, the prize. Even though I did not always attend church, I practiced my "Spirit" life daily, as evident in references in my ongoing journal entries. In graduate school, I concentrated on my studies and my health, and kept *fighting* depression. In my journals, I mentioned "Faith" and "Spirit" in passing, over and over again, but here, my physical problems monopolized my thoughts, time, and energy.

It was mysterious to me why, at this point, I sought help with my physical problems, especially depression. Previously, I had felt it was my *responsibility* to deal with it all on my own. Wow, *how* unrealistic! I even prayed to "God" and "Spirit," while still ambivalent about whether "God" should take care of it all for me, or whether it was *my responsibility* to *fix* everything. Desperate appeals to "God" seemed like a possible solution to my ineffective personal efforts to help myself.

Later, in graduate school in Flagstaff, the physical problems that had consumed me led to my need for a hysterectomy. Then, as I faced the need to remove my womb, my desire to bear a child loomed larger than scar tissue and other debilitating physical maladies I had endured. My trusty psychiatrist, from a distance, encouraged me to use visualization to help redirect my fears and obsessions. Was "God" or "Spirit" with me? I could only appreciate that "God" was keeping people in my life to help me cope, and mark the time until my surgery. Though I was not tied to the Bible, an occasional verse entered my contemplation and provided meaning to some of my challenges:

> Isaiah 43:16: "I am the one who cut a path through the mighty ocean." This passage implored me to consider the powerful army of people who have provided light along the way. I recorded recognition of specific people who have been sources of some of that light, but I also appreciated that there would be more light along my way. "God" blessed me with these people who have made a huge difference in my life.

Though many of my journal entries documented my disconnection or desire for connection with "God" and "Spirit," my journals are also filled with ponderings about "God" and "Spirit," which included reassurance and promised connections. In August 1989, I thought I was on a new path of "Faith." Tears flowed as I reaffirmed myself:

> 08.10.1989: Day by day—can I keep up? Meditation can help me. I am a perfect miracle! Can I let "God" in? I want to transcend beyond my physical being, consumed by my physical problems. Father, grant me the peace of mind to be open to your love and care. I wish I didn't feel so needy.

During this time, "God's" tremendous creativity struck awe in me from Earth's creation to technological advances *ad infinitum*. I also celebrated my "Divine" curiosity, which sometimes gets me into trouble and other times fills me with exhilaration and wonder. In a time of contemplation, it occurred to me that I could let "God" in more if I periodically paused each day and noted the divinity of "God's" creation. In a tribute to these realizations, I wrote the following, in which, on this day, I paused to recognize and note the many gifts of "God" that manifested through my hands.

Father, your work is everywhere, yet I am not always cognizant of it. You know no limits and open the world of possibility. I want to look at the fruits of life you have given me and find the good in each.

Father, you have granted my hands so many gifts:
- *Caressing, cajoling, and making beautiful music with my flute*
- *Stitching fine clothing on a sewing machine*
- *Creating handmade art, crocheting, dried-flower cards*
- *Cooking to meet my physical needs*
- *Beautiful lettering*
- *The flow of my pen has allowed me to record my journey through life*
- *Endlessly give hugs*
- *Hands that glide across the keys of my computer help me complete my work*
- *Many ways to place my hands: in prayer, in openness, in cupping faces of others*
- *I decided I wanted to personally consider, accept, and appreciate the many gifts manifested through my hands*

At this particular time in my adventure, I experienced unbelievably marvelous revelations. I realized heaven is a dwelling place for the perfection of life, which always exists as a possibility. Heaven *is* here on Earth when I let "God" into my life. The kingdom of "God" is the peace and closeness I could gain in a relationship with "God." Throughout these ponderings, I became ready to and wanted to acknowledge the presence of "God Within."

I felt my whole concept of "God" and "Spirit" shift, grow, broaden, and engulf me completely. I wondered if it might fill some of the voids I felt if I let in the immensity of "God." St. Teresa of Avila described how, the more she emptied her life, the more room there was for "God Within." Some would call it a sacrifice, but, for her, it was renewal, creating openings for unknown possibilities and anticipation of the inspiration to come. I became aware of the many transitions in my life that seemed insurmountable at times and, yet, with reflection, revealed many great godsends that permeated my "Soul." These godsends, which I did not recognize at the time, burn bright in my memory today, ones that have proven essential to my survival over these many years in small—and tall—ways:

06.12.2011:

- ☙ *The courage to step into graduate school and find the financial support to achieve my Doctoral degree.*
- ☙ *My ultimate healing from endometriosis and my endurance to reach that point over many years.*
- ☙ *Moments of grace that pulled me through at repeated points in my life with depression.*
- ☙ *The blessings of relative health for my parents and sisters.*
- ☙ *Guiding my presence to the death of Grandma La Fave. I was the last family member to see her alive and gave her love and caring at the end of her life.*

- *The gift of my early experiences with understanding His grace through numerous theological perspectives as part of a course in Contemporary Religious Studies.*
- *The strength not to succumb to fundamentalism in Germany, to stand up for myself, and to stand confident in my faith.*
- *The special relationship with Rich and Marie, who embraced, guided, and accepted me for who I am when I was in high school.*

Over time, I have also realized that several times I have reveled in a sense of the "Union with God." Though these moments with "God" were often fleeting, the intensity and significance of their occurrences were undeniable milestones on my journey to "Spirit" and left invaluable imprints on my "Soul."

MAKING MY CONNECTION WITH "GOD"

How I related with my "God" came and went. Sometimes, I wished that "God Within Me" would wake up, and I would again feel the presence of "God." At other times, through rich, unexpected spiritual experiences, I felt connected to my "God."

Throughout my quest to connect with "God," the foundation of my "Spiritual Faith" was shaken mercilessly. Much of the time, in the depths of depression, I presumed that the connection was not there or not within my grasp. I struggled mightily over decades to make a connection and find the "Divine" in my life. I constantly asked "God," *What evidence of action or presence should I look for? What would my experience with the connection be like? How would I know I had reconnected? When would I feel the connection again?* Though I was sometimes clear about my connections, they waxed and waned dramatically from one time to the next.

> *11.07.2009: As I read stories of inspiration, I feel deeply pained and the helpless, hopeless despair is more profound as I lack my connection with God. It used to seem to be so simple. I trusted. I believed, I knew "God" and knew in moments of uncertainty that I would be fine, that things would work out.* **Now** *there is none of that. It is obvious to me that "God"* **does** *exist, but that He is just not accessible to me at this time. I continue to create openings for God, but I am unable to connect. It seems that, if I should be grieving anything, it should be all that I lost with the depression, not the loss of the presence of my God. I will forge on day-to-day in anticipation of the return of my link to the "Divine", the return of hope, the return of feelings and emotions (a range thereof), the return of inspiration, and a sense of future. I deserve your Love, "God," without conditions, with insight and all of the things I feel missing. Patience continues to be an issue.*

More recently, I have recognized that I needed to shift my understanding and the meaning of my "God"—to know that I am part of "God" and that "God" is within me. I had to accept myself unconditionally just as "God" accepts me unconditionally. I needed to reconnect with my heart since that is where "God" resides. My mind, on which I depend, is an important tool, but it is not *who* I am. I discovered that my sense of "Being" is in my heart and could bring me back to feel congruence with my "God." I continue to strive to allow thoughts to pass through and not sidetrack me from the reality of Who I am, the Essence of my "Being." That which cannot be put into words. An experience. A *way of being.*

I wondered if I quit trying so hard to make myself connect with "God," the process *might* unfold, and I would once again experience that connection with my "God." Though it was now apparent that "God" was within me, I did not feel or trust this consistently. And, true to me, I continued to ask questions; sometimes I begged, and sometimes I admonished myself for doubting. Often, I wandered aimlessly as I searched for a relationship with my "God." I did not yet trust that relationship would reliably and consistently be with me.

On numerous occasions, I pondered how I could share, or demonstrate, to others my personal evolution in how I connected with "God." I also wondered whether I needed to try to articulate the experience as a way to convince myself it was true. I now believe I used my head too much to reach the "God" deep inside of me. The "God Within" was waiting to surface despite my efforts. Without hesitation, I accept that my "Spirit" had always been open and ready to discover this truth, which I can now sometimes access. I dismissed my misconstrued notion of external connection with "God" and "Spirit" and realized the connection resided *within me.*

INTEGRATION OF THE "HOLY SPIRIT"

An integral part of my development of "God Within ME," evolved out of how I integrated my idea of "Holy Spirit." Father Richard Rohr noted that *"a paradox is something that initially appears to be inconsistent or contradictory but might not be a contradiction at all inside of a different frame or seen with a different eye."* My matured "Spiritual" foundation provided a different framework within which to integrate the concept of "Holy Spirit" and new ways to experience its integration into my journey to "God" and "Spirit."

Father Richard Rohr shared a meditation in his book *The Naked Now* designed to explore a litany to awaken and strengthen the presence of "God Within." Through this meditation, I perceived just how present the "Holy Spirit" lived within me, an undeniable connection of "God Within." I share just a few of my responses to some of the phrases Rohr suggests as a means to consider the existence of the "Holy Spirit." He provides a phrase and encourages contemplation on aspects of the "Holy Spirit".

Phrase	My Experience
Pure Gift of God	*Nothing is owed or expected; only receive it*
Inner Anointing	*When "God" dwells within, I am continuously anointed without any effort on my part*
Homing Device	*The "Holy Spirit" always guides me back to the center of my Being and the Being of "God Within"*
Knower of All Things	*I don't have to worry, because what I don't think I know is, in fact, already present within and most available when I stay in the present moment*
Stable Witness	*I know I will never be judged by the "Holy Spirit," which knows the depth of my goodness and drawbacks, but remains focused on the core of my Being*
"Divine" DNA	*Despite the "science" of DNA, "Divine" DNA augments the scientific, without necessary explanation, but with reminders of the inherent wisdom, knowledge, and direction from within*
Warmer of Hearts	*In the moments that seem to be filled with the deepest despair, warmth rises from within, opening space for the truth to emerge*

Father Rohr's words seemed to lift any embarrassment from me about sharing my journey, rather, it fueled my fire to continue to make time to experience and express my revelations about "God" and "Spirit." My relatively new awareness and knowledge exist without any need to proselytize, try to convince, prove or justify my journey. It exists as I share it. I leave a door ajar that offers engagement with the "Divine" in whatever way another person may choose. I realize many journeys of "Faith" and "Spirit" unfold over time like a stream, though one may have sudden "Aha!" moments as the adventure evolves! It is what the mystics describe as emptying to make space for more ways of filling up with the "Divine." It is an endless opportunity to make a connection with "God."

I learned as I emerged from the depression that, as I let go of my intellectual search for the "Divine," I became receptive to change. That shift occurred without any direct request, effort, or action from me. It just happened, and I needed only to recognize the "Divine" presence as it happened.

Upon review, *when* I felt "Union with God" became apparent. There were glimpses along the way that I did not fully recognize but became essential glimpses that "God" (*She*) was present. I opened to her being, experienced her, and believed I could survive great adversity. During my experience in the commune in Germany, I felt judged for not responding and *believing* as they did. Yet in the midst of all of this, I found myself "Soaring into the arms of Grace." As I experienced "Union with God," my personal evolution of "Faith" surprised me. The following Unions of "God Within" became clear after this, a more recent reflection.

During graduate school in Tucson, my doctor suspended all of my depression medications. Scared, I wondered what would happen. How could I survive? Would I have the fortitude to succeed? This process tapped internal strength I did not know existed. Where did that come from? I now believe "God Within" held me.

My rejection for admission to a Doctoral program at the U of A socked me in the gut. A flood of tears and even anger at the professors who made the decision surged through me. However, on this day before Thanksgiving, as I drove to Phoenix to be with my family, I had a sense that this held hidden opportunities and felt a swell of determination to move forward. I took a sky-high flight with the hunch that this was a gift. Immersed in certainty about who I was, my future, and the work I wanted to pursue, I felt blessed. Over a few days, many things unexpectedly converged that actualized a transition I would appreciate only in retrospect. Within a couple of weeks, I found myself bound for Flagstaff, Arizona, into a degree program that matched my exact interests and strengths. My "Soul" surged full of joy and the energy of "God Within."

Over the years, I recognized that the depths of depression still afforded me some small *twinkles* of "Union with God." There were moments when I felt obliterated, and, as I reflect, I acknowledge that these times emptied my "Spirit" yet opened my "Soul" to "God Within." It was hard to hold on to these brief bursts of elation and joy. Each time, fleeting reminders of unknown possibilities overcome me. My journals tell the story of a period of several years filled with endless searching, struggling, cleansing, and healing of my purged "Soul." These are all elements of the unfolding of "God Within."

In the writings of St. Teresa of Avila, she describes the evolution of prayer in life. During what she has labeled as the "5th Mansion in the Interior Castle," the Prayer of Union is present.

The experience of Union for St. Teresa peels away any conceptualization of the ability to love. The mind is described as suspended to live more completely in "God." St. Teresa describes the "Soul" as a silkworm. Before this union, the "Soul" is like a fat, ugly worm. Afterward, it blossoms like a beautiful butterfly. It doesn't even recognize itself. Its old self has died, and it is completely made new. These golden insights into my personal evolution gave me images that bolstered my appreciation of "God Within."

St. Teresa of Avila and her compadre, St. John of the Cross, described characteristics of the time of the *Prayer of Union with God*. Distractions fall away as memory and attention become fixed on "God," and the external world does not need to exist. It is not a time to try to figure things out or put experiences into words, rather, a time to indulge in the presence of "God Within." I passively received "mystical touches" from "God." At times, I felt a *wounding* of my "Soul." I attempted to explain what was happening despite the presence of pain and ecstasy. My temporary suspension of intellect and memory paved the way for total absorption in "God Within" and "Union with Spirit."

Rohr explains:

> p. 101: The kingdom of "God" is not about a place or an afterlife, but a way of seeing and thinking now. It is the naked now—the world without human kingdoms, ethnic communities, national boundaries, or social identifications.

MANIFESTATION OF "SPIRIT"

In 1997, I gave myself the previously mentioned gift of a retreat in Sedona, Arizona, for contemplation, solitude, and time for union with "Spirit." I promised myself no expectations for this time—just to open my "Soul" to the present moment to receive whatever would emerge. Aware of a waterfall deep within me, waiting to flow, I sensed that this deep, dark internal source or pool held many treasures. Unfortunately, I had an idea that, for my retreat, I needed to meet a set of preconceived requirements.

06.21.1997: Perhaps "quiet" means: setting aside all concerns about work, about family, about the credit-card problem, etc. I suppose there are ways in which I will never fully understand God's order. Many times, our plan does not fit with God's plan. Simplicity may be what is key to participating in the process. I know that even "negative" thoughts and feelings are there for a reason. The great question that remains in my mind is how to live the life of the contemplative in the midst of the world. I have always seen things differently from the "Group." I have been a solo voyager.

During my time in Sedona, the full moon illuminated the majestic Red Rocks that surrounded me. I imbibed in the spectacular magical glow of the moon's light. My "Spirit" took flight, and I floated on a cloud that lifted me above the heavy pall of depression. I knew the depression was still there, but I experienced relief, a smile on my face, and a creative flow of inspiration and imagination that had been missing. I believe my surroundings and the solitude, which gifted me with peacefulness and receptivity, inspired me. A few days of amazing multimedia art emerged effortlessly from my hands and mind, standing witness to my experience. To this day, framed pieces in my bedroom serve as visual reminders of this mystical time of "Union with God."

These private, intense times are woven throughout my "Soul's" evolution. A deepening—not a *mastery*—of the integration of "God Within" released fresh breaths of life even in times that felt hopeless. I absorbed these drops of awakening oil that endlessly expanded my capacity to keep going.

I cannot identify any particular experience as the pinnacle in the evolution of my "Faith" and "Spirit," however, many trips along the way held messages, insights, and refinements of my beliefs and understandings. Sometimes there were shifts in my core that did not make sense. With patience and acknowledgment, the wisdom that continued to emerge kept me going. I believed there were many adventures to come. They may not seem pleasant or beneficial at the moment, but the pause and reflection that follow offer a universe full of opportunities that await me. I am confident. I will continue to add to my vessel of "Spirit" and augment my sense of "God Within." The Union with "Spirit" continues to grow and morph into eternal enrichment that far exceeds my imagination.

✦ ✦ ✦

FINDING A "ME" I COULD EMBRACE AND TREAT WITH COMPASSION:

Growing and Blossoming Over Time

It is evident to me that I grew and continued to stretch the richness of my life in unlimited ways. In the midst of these various discoveries, I found a "Me" I could embrace and not beat up. I practiced and started to grasp the notion of self-compassion as a resource I had never considered. Some qualities that appeared for the first time continued to blossom and repeatedly bore new fruits. During the writing of this book, there were discoveries that I missed along the way that later seemed like new revelations. I explore my experience of *feeling different* from a pathological perspective to view my differences as things to be cultivated. I continue to discover ways in which my differences enhanced my sense of self. With those discoveries, I have deepened and elaborated on existing values that had always filled my heart.

My perspective of my *hamster wheel brain* transformed into an invaluable asset, in addition to its liability status. Instead of ignoring stresses as maladies of body and mind, I started to pay attention to them as worthwhile signals and reminders of what self-care I needed in a given moment. The development of self-compassion became an antidote to my tendencies to beat myself up. Along with that realization, I internalized that self-compassion is not *selfish*. The scale of balance and imbalance teetered drastically at times, however, the idea of balance went through an overhaul. The challenges along the way contributed to the development of my "Spirituality."

I've wondered what has contributed to the differences in my perception. Some obvious distinctions may reflect the impact of experience, emotional reactions, emotional needs, the significance of a situation, and social expectations. These factors may not be ones commonly explored as affecting *typical* development. Unfortunately, there is no easy explanation for why my perceptions often turn out to be different from those of people around me. Then there is my brain, its structure, and function. The more we have learned about the brain, the more we have understood the sheer complexity of thought and the virtual impossibility of simple, clear explanations of brain function.

DIFFERENCE PATHOLOGIZED TO DIFFERENCE EMBRACED

Among the many things I learned is that each of our brains is quite unique. It is divergent in physiological structure, varied in biochemical makeup, impacted by various life experiences and relationships, and full of strengths and challenges. The world sets *normality* from various views and beliefs, such that associated characteristics end up falling into a polarization—"Typical" or Pathological." Once I understood this dichotomous sorting, I took solace in my emerging recognition that we are all influenced by a mixture of factors that increase with the complexity of our differences. There were times when I thought, *I am different* and learned that that did not have to be viewed as unhealthy. I was the ten-year-old on Girl Scout campouts who sought out the adults to talk and interact with rather than my fellow scouts. At the same time, though encouraged to play with my age peers, I instead wanted the adults to acknowledge that I was different. Over time, I came to see my dissimilarities not as serious draw-backs but, rather, as blessed gifts to be explored and accepted.

My inborn curiosity led me down paths that I was not sup-posed to be attracted to: e.g., my age, what I was *supposed* to know, what was socially acceptable, my experiences as seen by others. I simply did not fit the expected molds or desired appearances for my chronological age. As my mother would say, "You are a unique and unrepeatable human being!" My *different brain* was a big part of that. Given the realm in which I thought and pondered, I often felt misunderstood when I asked questions that blossomed out of my curiosity. They were never meant to challenge or question others; it was about my unspoken, innocent desire for further acquisition of knowledge.

I was an innocent, curious, perceptive, articulate, and very verbal child. My brain was different in such a manner that it affected my perspective, observations, and internal explana-tions of what I heard and saw. Part of the approach to my view of the world was to bring up topics because I was inquisitive, but sometimes adults, in particular, thought I was challenging them or their authority. Some individuals were bothered and thrown into their own quandary about how I was coming up with *this stuff*. Others found my inquiries *concerning* and even *pathological*. At times, the reactions I got were off-putting and left me wondering what was wrong with the *innocent* question or comment I made.

Our different brains should be appreciated and celebrated! Having interests different from other people's is not something pathological; it is simply uncommon. Over the course of my life, I realized I thought differently from those around me. I was curious about how the brain worked. I wanted to know about the structures of the brain and the function of each part. I discovered that the "amygdala/hippocampus" team was key to the study of emotions. I found out there were many scientific studies examining these topics and their possible relationship with depression. What was even more fascinating was the study of the evolution of the integration of meditation into Western society. This led to the investigation of the brains of lifelong meditators, which demonstrated physiological/structural changes, as well as changes in brain-wave activity. There was a whole new world of knowledge to explore. The brain is an endless frontier that continuously leads to new discoveries and understandings.

Every child and adult needs to feel special to someone in some way or another. When one is different from the *norm*, there is a yearning to feel understood. All I really needed was an acknowledgment of who I was and appreciation and affirmation of my nosiness and precociousness. I was simply interested in things other than those that most children my age pursued.

A fascinating example of this kind of different thinking that society around us labeled *out of normative bounds* comes from the husband of a remarkably close friend. He was a curious child in third or fourth grade, trying to understand the Bible in Sunday school. He asked the question, "*What is the difference between a fairy tale and the Bible?*" He was kicked out of Sunday school and admonished by his parents. "Society" believed that the Bible was sacred, not to be questioned but respected. His thoughts were judged as having gone astray. That innocent question was treated as a transgression of some kind. His question was part of a much larger exploration, from which he launched one inquiry to try to clarify something he was trying to understand or figure out.

You may own the personal experience of individual differences, but you may also be aware of differing from what your community and society expect. As a teenager, while my younger sisters were getting into trouble for being too "physical" with their boyfriends on the couch, I was oblivious to guys. I briefly wondered why I did not seem interested in boys but decided I was okay with things as they were. I was very busy: played in the band, orchestra, and ensemble; made straight A's; organized ice-cream socials at church, with homemade ice cream and goodies to be donated; babysat to earn money to go to music camp; sewed my own clothing; made choir robes, with all of their intricacies; as the editor, led the creation of my high school yearbook; and impressed adults by what I was doing. My mom, youth-group leaders at church, and teachers (i.e., adults) praised me. I didn't think I *needed* friends, with everything I had to do. I don't recall feeling lonely. I didn't care whether I was wearing the most current style of clothing. I had made all of my own clothing with the money from the allowance my sisters and I were each given for back-to-school clothes. I just saw life differently from my socially adept and popular sisters.

RECOGNIZING MY ACTIVE BRAIN AS
BOTH AN ASSET AND A LIABILITY

I recognized that the thing I most valued about myself could also be a liability and that it was okay for these two polarized aspects to coexist. This proved to be a huge revelation—one that helped me better understand and be kinder to myself.

I do believe my intelligence hinders "Me" at times. Sometimes, I think too much about things, which can lead to quite implausible thoughts and ideas. This, in turn, creates anxiety and exacerbates my depression. Over time, I have falsely fallen into the trap of believing something to be an absolute truth, which then closes my mind and thinking to other possibilities or ideas. In the context of our highly intelligent and educated world, I have often tried to gather data to understand something by reading, researching, and looking on the internet. What I really needed was to make space for contemplation in the "Here and Now."

Another example: personal qualities outside of the norm fed my inquisitiveness and wonderment about my evolving world. How did that make me feel? What did I experience? Sometimes my inability to communicate to others what I was thinking left me spinning in my own imagination, distanced from them and unsure of myself. The wheels were always turning in my mind; sometimes, I wished I could shut them down, stop the thoughts, relax, or escape. So, my imagination *also* showed itself to be an asset *and* a liability.

By now, you know I am a *thinker* and *problem-solver*, but these qualities can take me in different directions and overwhelm me. As I have said many times before, sometimes I wished I could turn my brain off! Actually, I just wanted to slow down my thoughts or shut them down temporarily. At times, my brain has served me well, as a useful tool to help me work through some tricky situations and thoughts. But other times, it led me to throttle myself with a slew of questions: What is wrong with me? Why can't I figure this out or turn the thoughts off?

Divergent thinking and problem-solving can be exhilarating, productive, and beneficial. Divergent thinking can also pull me under when I generate, within these thoughts, too many negative outcomes. I have learned to recognize my flight down a rabbit hole is of my own doing, which means there is the potential for me to *undo* it and open new doors full of possibilities.

Through the cumulative impact of my intellectual and emotional journeys, I integrated what I learned, which expanded what I believed I already *knew*. This swelling of such insights enriches all areas of my life. That said, my desire to incorporate all of these factors is a gargantuan exercise and can swallow me up and tear me away from the present moment. So, I must understand that such diversions into flights of thought can invigorate me, frustrate me, or even leave me feeling lost.

I now embrace that my flourishing mind has broadened my views of my thoughts. But I am also clear about my mind's liabilities in some contexts. As a consequence, I am so much closer to achieving a balance between how I view the "assets" and "liabilities" I experience. In addition, I am able to better steer my mind's flights toward the realm of assets.

SHIFT FROM SELF-FLAGELLATION TO THE ACKNOWLEDGMENT OF SUCCESS AND THE PRACTICE OF SELF-COMPASSION

Huge, though vacillating, characteristics of change that I have repeatedly encountered have put me on a tightrope, on which I try to minimize self-flagellation and acknowledge my successes. I regularly look to many resources to educate myself about life habits, yet my actions are incongruent with what I know might help me achieve more balance in my life.

> *I know what I should eat, but I just took something that was quick and easy. I still want to eat it, but I know it is not in my best interest! I am on the verge of tears and really stressed out. I ate tortilla chips instead of a salad. I "wanted" more chips but decided there was no physical reason for wanting or needing them. Instead, I ate chocolate. I cannot justify or explain my reactions.*

This series of choices set the perfect scene for me to beat up on myself. In the moment of that experience, all I saw were the *failures* in my choices and thinking. As I stood back and put on a different set of lenses, I saw things in another way.

- ❦ I did not impulsively just start eating. I checked with my awareness and acknowledgment of the dilemma of what to eat in that moment.
- ❦ I took a moment to consider if I was actually hungry.
- ❦ I resisted the impulse to eat more, given my previously described awareness.

- ☙ I stepped back and realized I was reacting to a very stressful experience and needed to be patient with myself in moments of vulnerability.
- ☙ I did not binge on something unhealthy. Those who binge are likely to eat a whole half gallon of ice cream or a whole bag of potato chips. I am fortunate that I have never binged.
- ☙ I carefully paid attention and prepared appropriate portions (including limiting the amount of chocolate).

Why has this been so hard for me? I want to be patient with myself *and* succeed at something new and different. I supposedly *know* enough to make healthy personal decisions, but my actions are not necessarily congruent with that knowledge. I hurt no one except me in the process. This is a dilemma I have regularly faced. Do I recognize, appreciate, and celebrate aspects of the choices I make, or do I beat myself over the head for *failing* to follow through? I have made great progress in realizing how to appreciate the smallest steps I take. And I have begun to recognize how essential they are to treating myself with compassion, even without external praise and recognition.

TRANSFORMATION FROM STRESS SIGNALS IGNORED TO THOUGHT AND BODY SIGNALS RECOGNIZED AND MANAGED

Even though I have regularly practiced and combined meditation, relaxation, and self-compassion, I am still vulnerable to stress. Why? I struggle with myself when I believe I have been caught off guard yet intellectually recognize that I feel stressed. The following is an example of my awareness of stress that has frequently sparked unnecessary anxiety. Historically, I have minimized or denied I was vulnerable to stress instead of acknowledging it and befriending myself.

I do not know what is happening. I had a very stressful morning with a provider who was attempting to facilitate bringing me online to their platform; the provider's endeavors went on for one and one-half hours. I tried and tried and could not breathe through the waiting. It was making me very anxious.

I tried to work with my breathing to help me relax. I told myself it was not the "end of the world" if this did not get resolved. At the same time, I knew I could not do the work the organization wanted without the resolution of this problem. I questioned why I was not able to follow the directions I was given; surely, it was my fault. My attention to this tech issue precluded work I had scheduled to do with parents of genuine clients. Actually, I had responded to the realities of the situation, yet I still turned on myself. Multiple elements contributed to my stress reaction. Boy, was I worked up!

It is essential for me to know and acknowledge the physical signs of stress in me. My feet twitch and swing. Anxiety creeps up my throat and tightens it. Time seems suspended. Things take forever!!! A headache may start to develop. I find I am quite thirsty. I may crave chocolate or comfort food. How many screaming physical signs are required for me to admit I am stressed? My breath becomes shallow and feeds the anxiety. Various muscles in my body tense up. It has taken some time, but I have learned that, when I become aware of these physical signals of stress, I need to be patient with and not punish myself. Self-compassion asks little—just deep breaths and a brief meditation for me to come back to the present moment. Today I understand that *stressing out* and self-compassion are not compatible. And I now know that I can push the stress feelings out of the way with these practices. I can engage them, without being obvious, anytime and anywhere, to gently bring myself back into balance.

SOME AREAS STILL CHALLENGE "ME" AND DEFY EXPLANATION

Life is full of different journeys that overlap, are interwoven, and provide insights and benefits for a variety of issues. My eating as it affects my weight has been and continues to be an ever-present and consternating challenge that defies the many explanations I have considered over the years. I don't have any answers for weight loss, but I have learned—through the process—lessons that extend well beyond how to eat or what to eat to lose weight. I move through a labyrinth of thoughts and related matters required for me to succeed. I may *think* I have learned, but I may not actually understand. Why do I initially bludgeon myself, rather than focus on my strengths in my ongoing persistence to work on this issue and others?

I have begun to realize the process of change is ongoing. I will never *arrive* at complete mastery of handling my weight or any other vital life issue. However, adaptation and assimilation are reasonable steps. My choice is to welcome ever-present opportunities to change and grow. Realistically, each and every step is a gift, though it may not feel that way in the moment. Maintaining a healthy weight is just one example of a process that is filled with ideas and roads for exploration. Moments of disenchantment are sometimes just the kick in the butt I need to shift my choices related to when I eat, what I eat, how I eat, and whether I choose self-compassion. I am now clear that, to change, break, or undo habits is a forever process! And guess what? When I am patient with myself and step back from the fray of a stressful situation, I *do* take steps in a healthier direction.

TO TAKE CARE OF SELF IS *NOT SELFISH*

As I have recognized and paid attention to making choices for my personal well-being, I have worried that others would view me as selfish. I worried that they would not feel positive about me.

Emphasis on self-care in my life has been a huge lesson, and I have been a slow believer. I *still* struggle with self-care because I associate it with selfishness. I don't want to be seen as selfish. Surely the journey to care for my parents was not selfish. It was one example of my deep love, concern, and gratitude for my parents, who cared for me.

On one occasion, I was dealing with the demands of caring for my mother, which drained my energy even for things I *wanted* to do. In the midst of that, I did not feel any pleasure. My sleep was disturbed, and my energy and coping ability were sucked right out of me. As I reflected on my participation in caregiving, I realized I was exhausted in body, mind, and "Soul." I was angry about the solitary burden of my mother's care. I told myself I should not feel guilty about my anger because I had agreed to care for her.

One of the positive outcomes of this trying time was when I stepped out and put myself first in the form of claiming more time for my professional passion and writing this book. With this step, I practiced self-compassion and confronted my fear of judgment by my sisters for reaching my personal limits.

Finally, this expression of my frustration was freeing, and I *knew* I had done the best thing for myself. I felt the yoke of weight moving away, and I turned my attention to whatever came next. This was *not* selfish. I had to take care of myself. At this moment, I reined in my perspective of self-preservation with pride and pleasure. I moved into action toward self-care, and I knew I had not done it all alone. Nuggets of wisdom from my "Perspective Mentors" about this dilemma permeated my heartless "Soul" to bring me back to my strengths and insights.

I now realize that, when I'm out of sync with myself, I need to integrate into my daily life those things that are essential for my long-term health, like diet and exercise. For example, I know that, when I exercise, it helps decrease my feelings of depression, and it otherwise engages my mind. Periodically, I reassess how I spend my time. I often make a pie chart that serves as a reminder to refocus on balance.

I must revise my image of quantity of work being a reflection of who I am and my capabilities. I need to give energy to the quality of what I do. In spite of the physical and emotional limitations, I can still have an impact on others and provide care of myself which might not happen without my stretching.

I have repeatedly addressed the issue of balance throughout my writings:

Time for myself. In my journals, I have often asked whether I am working too much, resulting in an imbalance between my personal and professional lives. One entry included a vision to step out of my circle of work and soak up the existence of a large, expansive world waiting to be explored. I must periodically pause to celebrate my successes—a new behavior for me. I intentionally decided that, to value the whole of my personal life, I must relegate work to a lesser role. Peace of mind is more likely when I make time for "Spirituality" and remember my values. When I acknowledge my personal needs, I am able to relax and focus on myself in a positive manner.

Time and accomplishments come into perspective, and I am better able to appreciate each day when I strive to see the multitude of perceived demands and needs that I face.

The past six months have really challenged my ability to balance time to care for myself and meet my needs spiritually, emotionally, and physically. Mother's wrist fracture, selling our house, buying a new house, trying to work, Mom feeling less able to do things. (June 2016)

Finding and maintaining balance is an ongoing dilemma. It is a constant test of patience as I confront my desire to be in charge or *in control* of what is going on in my life. To be in charge of my life, of course, is an illusion; it is essential for me to step back and make room for more patience. When I am able to enter reflection, prayer, meditation, or contemplation, I can sustain patience. By staying present in the moment, my receptiveness to "Spirit" multiplies and increases the chances of *feeling* that important part of my life. I worry less about things to do for others and pay attention to taking care of myself.

A SHIFT FROM IMBALANCE TO BALANCE
BY FOCUSING ON SELF-CARE NEEDS

Balance has been an awkward thing to find because my whole previous approach to life needed revamping. Balance continues to be a perpetual topic of thought, discussion, and consideration in my self-dialogue and with others. From this work, I recognized that, before my most serious episode of depression, I had immersed myself almost 100% in my work (teaching job). When I was not doing that, I was always thinking about what I could do for others (very often creating gifts/art).

Naively, I viewed work as the number-one priority, to the exclusion of activities that brought me pleasure. Making gifts for others is something I choose to do because it brings me joy. Through thoughtfulness and nurturing, I aspire to give hope to others. With time, I decided I wanted to invest in my *self-care* needs, too! In a sense, I came to understand that there is more to life than just working and doing for others—there is also *being*. Living in *being* mode brings me into the present moment wherever I am or in whatever I am engaged. This ultimately increases the richness of everything I do. It does not cost a dime and is priceless at the same time.

Increased awareness of "well-established" ways of dealing with choosing priorities and how to shift those choices to bring more balance into my life is just a starting point. To be aware of the research on weight gain and loss is a vital first step, but establishing solid change in behaviors is where the work starts. Change demands fortitude on many levels, which include questions such as: "Is that good for me?" "How will a particularly healthy or unhealthy choice affect how I feel physically?" "What are the consequences of doing/not doing something?" There are *many* questions to "think" about, but, ultimately, I must take action. There are times when I assume I have "learned" about some aspect of life. But it ends up in my thoughts, without me fully understanding or implementing the lessons I assumed I understood. The problem for me is that I *think* I know and understand what to do for myself; then, making it happen becomes a challenge.

CHALLENGES AND PRACTICES ALONG THE WAY THAT FED THE DEVELOPMENT OF MY "SPIRITUALITY"

"Spirituality" is one of the most complex aspects of my life and insists on constant broadening and narrowing of my perceptions. Wondering why I felt different from those around me was one piece of the puzzle. As I pondered lessons learned about different aspects of life, they spilled over into my "Spirituality," expanding and enriching it, which continued to evolve. Mindfulness has helped reduce the clatter of negativity and runaway thoughts in my mind and, at the same time, breathed fresh air into my being. That fresh air, in turn, provided enrichment of my practice of "Spirituality." As I practiced self-compassion, I tossed out a lot of unnecessary and unhelpful thoughts and ideas, which made room for the further blossoming of my "Spirituality." My growth to embrace myself and the glorious self-compassion that accompanied it, then, have further pollinated my flourishing "Spirit."

SUMMARY

Clearly, change is a multifaceted, ever-morphing process that sometimes demands that I stop, ponder, evaluate, and choose the next direction. As I embrace "Me," the options mushroom, defy explanation, and sometimes overwhelm me. Even if I have an automatic reaction to an idea, I now have more insight into the origin of my thoughts. I breathe, and the stress of a robotic response dissipates. The evolution of change does not always feel like something I want to do, yet I *know* it will enrich me. If I don't assess and make personal judgments about my reactions, it frees me to indulge in new adventures. My frame of reference for my thoughts keeps expanding in ways that drown out previous dichotomous views of myself and release me into infinite possibilities. This unique perspective allows me to indulge in my experience and appreciate how it fits into the balance of my self-care. The presence of "Spirit" serves as a constant reminder to let go of hesitation and fear, and to trust whatever path is budding.

✦ ✦ ✦

THE PERSPECTIVE OF
LIVED EXPERIENCE

On my journey, I realized my lived experiences grounded my outlook at many points in time. My personal preferences, thoughts, emotions, physical needs, "Spiritual" evolution, and intellectual views have affected me and my depression. They contributed to how I considered my everyday lived experiences. My changing understandings, spur-of-the-moment judgments, rationalizations, personal causal explanations, and over-generalizations influenced my long-held foundational perspective. Various sources of support provided additional contributions of food for thought for me to consider.

However, doubts and questions filled me as I moved through the extremely slow process of various treatments and the metamorphosis of my "Soul." I had tried to come up with an elusive *perfect* solution to my anguish. Failing to find that perfection, I did not respect myself, felt inadequate, discounted my emotions and experiences, and disparaged my thoughts.

In retrospect, my desire to *feel* anything besides despair and witness my "Spiritual" life again impeded my movement. Slowly, I came to recognize that my perspective and my discontent were related. For example, when moved by something, I lacked the physiological sensations I had previously experienced. From my perspective, this felt devastating. I missed the sensation of a tingle that went up my spine when I heard a piece of music, experienced an inspiring event, or was touched by something I read. I wanted to feel this way again, but my efforts to return to perceived inspiration did not spark feelings. With this intense desire for something not available to me, I knew I needed help.

HOW KEY POINTS OF IMPACT SHIFTED AND MATURED MY PERSPECTIVE

Critically, my intellectual gyrations left me no space to pay attention to the physical sensations of my body. A vital ingredient of my *feeling* is what is called the *embodiment*, or physical sensations that are not based on thoughts yet are crucial to survival. Without the physical sensations attached, my mind created thoughts and theoretical explanations that did not bring me any closer to my feelings.

THE HISTORICAL EFFECTS OF TENETS OF CBT

The emergence of Cognitive Behavioral Therapy (CBT) in the 1970s affected multiple aspects of my thinking. In my early 20s, my therapist had me read *A Guide to Rational Living*, by

Albert Ellis, as a focus of therapy. I tried to apply the essential element of CBT to my thoughts and cognitions. Ellis says that my cognitions—my thoughts—affect my behavior and feelings. *After all, if I just change my thoughts, I should feel better!* Because my efforts didn't succeed, I made judgments on myself that pathologized my experience before I even explored it. The psychiatrists in the DBS study told me my depression was not just my thoughts and that, if I could have changed my thoughts, I would have done it a long time ago.

Part of my persistence to keep trying depended on my frame of reference in a given situation or on a particular day. In my attempts to apply the ideas from the CBT, I did not consider the abundance of persistent influences in my life. My thoughts and lived experiences included features such as beliefs, education, childhood, morals, self-concept, "Faith," mental state, and values. Though I knew this in my gut, when I experienced something, I tended to make a judgment about myself, my emotions, and how I felt. My assessment of what had been affecting me during this time did not include these aspects of my history.

I also learned that *"Being Is More Important Than Doing."* Though I was a slow learner, the practices I eventually implemented gave me the space to focus on *being*. The notion that *doing* would accomplish anything I wanted or needed faded in the face of just *being*. Staying present in the moment, with mindfulness, meditation, and *doing nothing* radically altered the focus of my efforts, and opened unimaginable insights. Personal care, self-compassion, and time for solitude moved up the ladder of importance as means to just "Be."

THE ROLE OF SUPPORTS

Surviving depression requires tons of different types and sources of support. Social support systems are essential to everyone's life. Family and friends seem like givens, but a much broader net is needed. The number of different everyday-living demands I faced at a given time also affected my ability to appreciate and receive any type of support. Some of the most intimate and important relationships had an intensity that made it seem like they could never be replaced. I discovered that each relationship and support system endows unique gifts.

My therapist alone is inadequate for thorough healing and an enriched quality of life. My therapist is vital, as I previously described. In reality, what may seem inconsequential supports have an impact and can enhance or detract from the broad entirety of my care. Medical providers are not only doctors and nurses, but support staff, billing offices, and insurance companies. Spiritual leaders may encompass formal religious leaders, alternative spiritual sources, and even a religious community.

Episodes of depression proved so dire and lasted so long that I doubted I could regain my life in any meaningful way. When I shared my points of view with my "Perspective Mentors," they listened. They even provided me with new ways to hang on to the edge of the precipice of deeper depression, toward which I felt headed. After affirming my lived experience, they offered me new ways to see or think about my current situation. Often these shifts in perception and perspective felt important, but I could not immediately implement them, despite my expectation that I should. I discovered that, if I even *momentarily* pondered simple reframes, they could create space to move on toward restoration. They were ideas that brought flashes of hope.

I constantly talked about the lack of quality in my life. I found that sharing my deeply personal perspective with people other than my "Perspective Mentors" was fraught with communication barriers. Repeatedly, I grappled with how I could possibly help someone else understand the numbness and comprehend that I faced *the end of the road*. It proved especially hard when well-intentioned people who had not taken the time to understand me wanted to dialogue with me from their personal life experiences and strategies, which they found helpful but were unrelated to my situation.

I required trusted viewers from outside of my life and individual therapy to reel me to a point where I could refine my thoughts on a given day. My "Perspective Mentors" pointed out, affirmed, and celebrated my gifts, and respected my "Spiritual" assets. Though they were physically absent from me, I always felt the presence of these precious resources. I knew it was important for persons outside myself to regularly reaffirm my ingrained, elegant essence and insights. While I often felt incompetent or ineffective, reminders of my strengths kept me going and carried me far.

Even today, I often make a request of my "Perspective Mentors" to validate where I am, emotionally, psychologically, and spiritually. Marilyn Kieffer-Andrews, RNP, PhD (MKA), my primary "Perspective Angel," critically intervened many times. Her observations and suggestions reassured me and even briefly sustained me. Repeatedly she validated expressions of my experiences and asked questions for me to consider regarding expressed thoughts. It was as though she was the link between

"God" and me—and a flicker of hope for change. This frequently helped me shift my views in a different direction.

But how was I supposed to measure getting better? It was a nagging question that preoccupied me. Was I standing in my own way? Did a vicious circle trap me that needed to be blasted open? How did I perceive this question? People often asked me whether I was feeling better. I still get this question from the doctors in the DBS study, my family, my friends, and my therapist. I endlessly searched for an answer that never surfaced. But I felt an inkling that kept telling me to persevere with unwavering patience. The source of the message was not clear, though I often believed and hoped it was "God."

I am quite close to my family members and fortunate to feel accepted even when I did not make sense. My family learned about depression up close and personal. Each individual dealt with their personal reactions to my depression.

One of the most salient examples of communication difficulties arose for me when Dr. Kieffer-Andrews called the family meeting that I discussed earlier. She emphasized that I could not just *snap out of it*. She explained that part of the illness was my inability to express my emotions and feelings. She suggested that the family listen, love me, accept me, be patient with me, and be present. It would be beneficial to try to avoid specific expectations of me. She encouraged them to respect my limitations in receiving and responding to recommendations and suggestions they might offer. She relayed my gratitude and appreciation for their invaluable expressions of love, care, and concern. She also explained that my lack of responses was by no means a rejection of what they offered.

Consistent contact and overall availability of friends and various supports made a difference. On one hand, I wanted to remain respectful of the time in the lives of close friends. On the other hand, my grave desperation had an urgency I could not suppress. I appreciated not only ease of access but models of clear personal boundaries, which increased my appreciation and high regard for them. With some individuals, we had regularly scheduled times to get together, which provided predictability and reassurance of contact. There did not have to be a specific plan or goal for the get-together. Just being present with another person provided comfort. I appreciated that each individual had unique personal insights that they shared with me. Each friend provided care that strengthened the scaffold I needed to get through. It is impossible to adequately express my gratitude for each of these precious souls.

A most amazing gathering of friends occurred right before I left for Atlanta. A very close family friend who is a Certified Celebrant created a sendoff Healing Journey Ceremony for me. Those who came included close personal friends, long-term family friends, colleagues, spiritual partners, spiritual leaders, and teachers on the journey I was on. I *knew* that "Spirit" was present, though I did not feel it. The ceremony was attended by friends who each brought a special bead that went into a necklace I took with me. There were affirmations from each person, and I was surrounded by an unimaginable sea of love. I could not be more grateful. They were integral elements of my support network.

THE MEANDERING EXPERIENCE OF "GOD WITHIN"

Given "Faith" as a constant focus on my journey, I sold myself short about how well I coped with my depression and integrated my understanding of "God Within." I availed myself of ministers and other individuals who advocated for a "Spiritual" component to my perspective of life. Certainly, the minister who led the church I grew up in had a significant impact on the evolution of my perspective. He listened carefully and asked difficult questions to stimulate thought and personal reflection. It became obvious to me that my "Faith" served as motivation to participate in the world with integrity and a sense of the greater good as the goal.

Without a sense of the "Divine" to fall back on or make me feel safe, the emptiness felt infinite; it did not seem possible to bring any meaning, appetite, or interest to my life. The physical sensations attached to emotion, another acute aspect of my perspective, were also impacted by my emotional connection with "Spirit." My relationship with the "Divine" expanded as my perspective evolved. I talk about this transformation in depth in the section of this book I have designated as the "Dark Night of the Soul."

Periodically, I resorted to expecting "God" to make things better and heal me. These expectations did not serve any useful purpose but reminded me of another valuable resource always available for me to access.

02.11.2010: Lord, I feel like I need to let go and let you run the show. I feel like my mind, my "Soul," my heart, and my emotions have all been stripped from me by this disease. It isn't even control that I want; it is relief that I seek, the ability to experience and trust my inner essence. To not feel imprisoned by depression. To feel like my life is not at a virtual standstill.

For answers about what I should do, I realized that my search for "God" meant becoming immersed in life. I came to understand that feeling "God's" absence is part of the process. It is impossible to see the light of insight and "Spirit" without the contrast of the darkness, when it feels like there is no "God." I hoped a reconnection with "Soul" and "Spirit" would help my frame of mind and perspective.

Sources of religious and spiritual support are infinite, with constant opportunities, and a snowballing effect that enriches me. I learned that, if I maintained a thirsty mind and willingness to explore many practices and ideas, this kept the evolution of my "Spirituality" fresh and expansive.

Even though I did not feel "Spirit," I somehow endured side trips with determination. With or without an awareness of obvious "Spiritual" feelings, I seemed to believe they were present. At some point, I started to attend to "God" in my interior. This demonstrated a shift from helplessness to my ability to consider healthier trajectories.

In time and with perspective, I realized and knew that "Spirit" is always present in my inner essence. I learned to trust that the unscheduled events of my life are a form of "Spiritual" direction. Maybe my highest intention—of reconnecting with "God"—could spark the unfolding of my future. Was it really possible to think that my exploration, discovery, and openness to the mystery of my "Spiritual" life would direct me somewhere toward a different perspective on depression?

I want help, but I don't know what I need or want.
    Could I integrate depression as a respected part of me, not in possession of me?

Things happen in "God's" good time, and "God's" direction will come. I wanted to accept whatever "God" had in store for the sake of my own "Spiritual" development. My previous experiences of feeling "God Within" reassured me.

ANOTHER SIGN OF THE TIMES

Throughout much of my journey, my concept of "the time frame for change" haunted me. Time often felt like it crawled at a snail's pace, yet painstaking reflection only momentarily revealed a change to me. Unfolding change takes time. Just as we should not try to help the butterfly burst from its cocoon, when it needs the struggle to gain strength in its wings, I came to understand that I should not pressure or force myself into a rush to change. I learned I had to allow the process of change to unfurl and reveal new directions carefully and meaningfully. Likewise, just as the blooming of a flower cannot be accelerated, I required trust, endurance, and an appreciation for change from various sources of support to take place in order for me to move along and bloom. I had to nurture a willingness to live in the unknown and accept the notion that I needed help with perspective on an ongoing basis.

Initially, I either had expectations that "God" would fix everything, or I assumed that I was not doing enough to realize the strength I carried in my heart. Acknowledgment, awareness, and affirmation of my beautiful "Spirit" were required to stabilize my perspective and gave *change* the time that it was due.

SUMMARY

The biggest change I noticed over cycles of depression was a return to a prior level of independence and living, after being left virtually useless and unable to function. Once again, however, feelings were missing from the formula. The fluctuations in my stamina and the ability to maintain personal care were signs of improvement.

I asked my therapist of more than twenty years, "How did I function with depression before all of this [the most severe multi-year episode I had?" Prevention. She replied that I made sure I got enough sleep, ate right, exercised, took my medications, prayed, reflectively journaled, and meditated—all things I must constantly integrate into my daily routines for the rest of my life.

I believed somewhere in my "Soul," I could eventually feel calmer, reassured, undergirded, safer, warmer, and physically relaxed. The feelings of destruction and nowhere else to turn nudged me to recognize, open up, and explore possibilities for transformation. The trials I faced, in addition to depression, served as random steppingstones on a path to oneness with "Spirit." I discovered that the discomfort I often felt actually became a powerful catalyst for change. Over time, my perspective expanded and became more flexible. And as my self-confidence and self-respect grew, so did my "Soul," "Spirit," and "Faith" in "God."

PERSPECTIVE REFLECTION

On some level, I realized my assessments of my frame of mind were very different from those of people I highly respected. I did not understand what was affecting my perspective in many situations. Reflections from those closest to me mirrored my life circumstances, past experiences, and feelings, which helped me nudge and shift my perspective.

My personal goals, no matter the appropriateness, impact how I view a situation or feeling. If my goal is to *feel better*, what matters is what that means to "Me," which becomes my frame of reference for experiences. Sometimes my perspective accurately expressed my distress, loneliness, and pain. At these times, I did not have words to express my true lived experience. Eventually, I asked for help, and that made a difference.

Sometimes, though, when my interpretations were not accurate or realistic, I erroneously thought otherwise. I learned to shift my perspective when those around me asked me to see something in a different light. With time, I realized that sometimes my perspective contributed to my misery, but I initially could not figure out how to change it. Most salient was the fact that, when I learned how to change my perspective, with others' input, I significantly changed the meaning of life events and experiences for me.

Ultimately, the growth I achieved created more accurate and flexible perspectives. In turn, I was led to experience healthier thoughts and feelings about my lived life. I was able to see events through a different lens, which helped me find my way. This process opened doors to expand my vision for the future of my life.

✦ ✦ ✦

KEY INSIGHTS FROM MY
PERSONAL JOURNEY

I expect that there aren't any easy answers or sudden transfor-mations in what I share. The thoughts I share reflect years of personal searching and growth. They reflect my own evolution. There is soooo much to learn on the journey of life. Patience is absolutely necessary and something I strive to practice constantly. Give yourself the gift of patience [with yourself]!

I wanted to summarize and articulate the big picture of what I gained. I realized time is on my side as long as I make and take it for myself. I need to listen to my heart, mind, body and "Soul" and remain open to discovery. I am not writing a prescription for you; I'm simply sharing my experience. Previously, I seemed to be able to see my future only in the context of my professional work, but time taught me that there is much more to my life and future.

GIVE "ME" TIME

The more I am present in the moment, the better I function and feel. I avoid expectations of myself. The things that help me manage the passage of time include relaxation or meditation; listening to music I like; doing creative activities to express my thoughts and feelings; taking a drive; watching a very funny or sad movie or program, etc. I *know* the practice of self-compassion and being gentle with myself are indispensable. Three cleansing breaths are my constant companion, available anytime, anywhere.

Guided meditation distracts me from worry for a little while. I always thought life was so complex, and now I realize it's really quite simple.

JOURNALING

Often once I get started writing, I am amazed at how much I have expressed and what I did not even realize was on my mind. Journaling allows me to enter into an exploration of thoughts I never considered. The journal-writing process for me is about: reflection, processing, remembering, a realization of what I have learned or accomplished, and reminders of significant changes I have made in my life. Entries can be a burst of insight/energy propelling me along in my process. There have been times I have written to myself as reminders of important insights. My writing is a treasure trove of self-expression.

I have shared multiple journal entries because they some-times express something I don't feel I can share with another person, or I want to try out and play with my thoughts. I truly appreciate what I have learned about myself through the process of journal writing. I have learned to just write, without any thoughts about grammar, choice of words, sentence structure, or other censorship of what goes on paper. There is *not* a best or most appropriate way to journal. It is vital to remind myself of how significant the changes have been in my life. What may seem small or trivial to others can be a burst of insight/energy that propels me along in my journey.

THE TREASURES OF A MEANINGFUL SUPPORT GROUP

I recently had lunch with my cancer support group, and someone noted we had *already* been together for eleven years. We share an understanding of the challenges only other cancer patients experience. Love abounds, and we are there for vital life events such as the recurrence of cancer, deaths of parents, getting through caregiving, new health challenges, celebrations galore, and fun to boot. These amazing women continue to enrich my life and share so much life wisdom. We have very different experiences, beliefs, work experiences, values, and opinions, but infinite acceptance abounds.

I NEVER QUIT LEARNING

My endless pursuit of wisdom has taken on a dramatic shift in focus. I have realized that books or research don't reflect the whole picture of life. Without ongoing attention to body, mind, "Soul," and "Spirit" as integral parts of the puzzle I am, written knowledge is useless. I am still curious and want to keep learning. Reading sometimes provides me companionship and even comfort. It might be an affirmation of personal experience, words of hope and encouragement, or specific approaches and strategies to wellness and treatment.

I continue to wonder how often and for how long depression will continue as part of my life. As previously noted, I realize I am unlikely to be *done with it*. Fortunately, the course of time has taught me to embrace depression as part of who I am. I don't feel I have to conquer it, since I know that the chemistry of my brain isn't likely to completely change.

PATIENCE

My learning and practice of patience are eternal. Repeatedly, about the time I think I have something mastered, another life event showers down on me. There are new lessons, directions, and considerations for exploring patience that continue to refine and expand this indispensable ability. I am grateful for the tools I have gained to nurture my patience with myself. I wait with positive expectations for opportunities to continue to expand my experience and understanding of patience.

WHAT ABOUT THERAPY?

For whatever reason(s), I thought that, if I initiated a therapeutic relationship with someone as their client, I was making a commitment I could not break. I learned that not every therapist is meant to work with every person! It is important to be aware of and know when to trust my gut reactions to people and first impressions. These things do not always make me *right* or ensure the best decision, but they can help. Sometimes it is important to try a couple of sessions with someone even if I am initially uncomfortable, but I am under *no* obligation to stay with that therapist.

It is vital to explore the philosophy and treatment methods of a therapist and consider whether those ideas fit me. Are there any things about what is said that strike a note of caution in me? Treatment is not just about being comfortable; in fact, moving out of my comfort zone has been revealing. I know myself well enough that, if a therapist is driven by a *fundamentalist* religious approach, this is not for me.

Another very important consideration is communication with a therapist. Do I want to be told what to do and how to do it? Do I want a partner in a therapist or be under the thumb of a dominant-parent type? Do I want to be asked thoughtful questions to ponder, or do I want "answers" and/or directives? I want to be aware of my intellectual, emotional, *and* visceral reactions to the therapist when interacting with her. The bottom line is that I am under absolutely no obligation to continue with a therapist if I don't think the relationship is potentially beneficial. This can mean a trial-and-error process, but it is an investment in my mental health.

I am invested in my own well-being. What I know is that the challenges I have faced remain part of the tapestry of my life. They have taught me very valuable lessons again and again, and often offer new insights and jewels with time. Fortunately, as I mentioned earlier, the course of time has taught me to embrace depression as part of who I am; I don't feel I have to *conquer* it. I embrace *all* of the complexity of depression that encompasses me physically, intellectually, biologically, spiritually, and experientially.

WHO COULD ASK FOR MORE?

Certainly, this is an ongoing journey that will continue throughout my life. However, the insights and tools I have already gained bode well for my future. I have been blessed in so many ways. I am sure there is much more to learn and enrich me. The set of strategies I have developed is ingrained in me such that I feel confident about their long-term benefits for thriving, even in the face of depression. I expect that these lessons learned will only continue to expand and become stronger as I continue to evolve.

✦ ✦ ✦

AFTERWORD

What a journey this continues to be! I feel so blessed that I have had the opportunity to share this trek and hope my tenacity shines through.

My odyssey is not over, and who knows what lies ahead? I have regained many abilities and insights I thought were gone, for which I am extremely grateful.

While this book has been many years in the making, the process of writing has been quite healing. It has not always been easy to read my depictions of quite painful times. Yet, it has helped me appreciate the gravity of the impact of depression on me. I'm astonished at how I have learned to handle the struggles and thrive. When I revisited my journals, though it wasn't easy, I gained great insights into my journey and an appreciation of my perseverance and resilience, despite my desperation. My journey over all these years deepened my understanding of the manifestations of "Spirit" in my life.

I accept that I am unlikely ever to be free of depression, but the vessel where it resides deep inside has become malleable and manageable. I am overwhelmed sometimes, but the immobilization typically lasts only a few hours or, at most, a couple of days. I am much less likely to panic when these times approach because I have repeatedly weathered them, survived, and emerged stronger.

I found during the winding and evolutionary road of my "Spiritual" life an underlying presence of an eternal source of reassurance and feelings of hope—even in its absence. My "Spirituality" is one of the richest parts of my life and never ceases to embellish and heighten my lived experience. This creates infinite space for exploration and discovery of the greatness of "God" and "Spirit Within."

When I asked family and friends how they experienced me when I was deeply depressed, their answers to my questions amazed me. I could not believe the number of individuals who "knew" I would eventually get better, and the fact that they stayed with me throughout blew me away!

One friend and colleague repeatedly came up with ways for me to stay in touch with my professional gifts and help me hold on to that very personal and precious part of my life. Determined, she made sure that I would not lose sight of my strengths and worth as a teacher and psychologist. At any given moment, she knew where I *lived* and always treated me gently and with sensitivity. I can't express how appreciative I feel for all of her efforts.

As we looked back over the years, she expressed how she intentionally created purpose, determination, and support to help me succeed. My ability to express what I needed or could not handle at any given time required me to let others into my life. In order to do this, I learned to trust and risk reaching out to others.

My sense of "Spirit Within" fluctuated widely over the years. While I depicted it as coming and going, it became my belief that "Spirit" is *always* with me, despite my momentary feelings of absence. The following piece expresses my conviction.

Knowing

2-13-2022

I have often and repeatedly said I KNOW something deep inside.

It doesn't demand "proof" that something tangible exists.

It is, for all intents and purposes, not "Unknown" or doubted or debatable.

It is something deep inside that I may be unable to describe, but I am certain of its presence.

It is not "concrete knowledge."

It is self-affirming, and exhilarating, without question of its existence.

It is a firm foundation of "Spirit" that undergirds me and reminds me that some of what I experience is present without awareness or need for acknowledgment.

It is present without effort; I accept the simplicity of awareness of its presence, which does not have to be examined or explained.

This KNOWING exudes freedom from my analytic mind and the need for a concrete explanation.

It need not be questioned, because it is a deep expression of an emotion that doesn't have to be proven, documented, or even subjected to describe with words.

There is no doubt that it exists.

Sometimes I think KNOWING is the presence of "Spirit" that needs no questioning.

TRUST, A PRESENCE, A GIFT

Its presence provides a sense of stability in even the most difficult or threatening moments.

This KNOWING is palpable, despite no evidence of its existence.

It is comforting and consoling—qualities that also escape description with words.

KNOWING is filled with unspoken insight that provides reassurance.

KNOWING is not conceivable and may not make sense.

KNOWING has deep roots in my heart and "Soul" that are undeniable.

In my gut, I am sure of the existence of something greater than myself.

KNOWING frees me to be present in the moment, without any strings attached.

I cannot adequately express the depth and breadth of my gratitude for the multitude of people and lived experiences that have influenced me. I am flourishing and blooming brighter and bolder every day. I can hardly wait to see where I go from here!

✦ ✦ ✦

NOTES

Prelude to My Journey

1. AzEIP—Arizona Early Intervention Program, State of Arizona services delivered in the family home for children younger than three and their families.
2. The Endometriosis Association—comprehensive resource for details about the disease, medical information, possible treatments, current research, and support groups. https://www.endometriosisassn.org.

My Subjective Experience of Depression

1. NIMH reports the prevalence of major depression as of 2020 in the United States. A basic overview of depression. https://www.nimh.nih.gov/health/statistics/major-depression.
2. Styron, *Darkness Visible: A Memoir of Madness* a seminal book on the personal experience of depression.

3. "A Depression Switch" article on Deep Brain Stimulation. More specific information about the procedure and research for those interested.

4. Helen Mayberg, MD—a neurologist, her professional focus on studying treatment-resistant depression. A pioneer in Deep Brain Stimulation, she is the lead investigator on the DBS study in which I participate.

5. "Psychache" defined by Edwin Schneidman, Ph.D.—studied suicide and developed the term to define the state of severe depression and/or suicide. *Suicide as Psychache: A Clinical Approach to Self-Destructive Behavior.* Northvale, NJ: Jason Aronson, Inc., 1995.

6. Mother Teresa is a fountain of insight and inspiration. Her book *No Greater Love.* Novato, CA: New World Library, 1989, shares her wisdom.

7. Alzheimer's and Dementia not always clearly defined and delineated, the Centers for Disease Control and Prevention. https://www.cdc.gov/aging/aginginfo/alzheimers.htm.

8. Electroconvulsive Therapy (ECT)—care for a variety of mental illnesses. The Mayo Clinic provides a concise discussion of ECT. https://www.mayoclinic.org/tests-procedures/electroconvulsive-therapy.

Staying Present in the Moment

1. Sharon Salzberg, author, workshop leader, recorded CDs and offers new insights and meditations for meditation practice. *Lovingkindness* and *Real Love: The Art of Mindful Connection.*

2. Thomas Moore writes about spirituality and integration into daily life. His book *A Religion of One's Own: A Guide*

to Creating a Personal Spirituality in a Secular World unveils his spiritual journey from his life as a Catholic priest, to psychotherapist and author.

3. Dan Siegel, MD—shares practice, research, writing, and academics integrated into a field of interpersonal neurobiology and mindfulness.

4. Zindel Segal, Ph.D.—the impact of mindfulness on the treatment of depression. Has contributed to the development of Mindfulness-Based Cognitive Behavior Therapy for depression.

5. Mindfulness-Based Stress Reduction (MBSR) was created by Jon Kabat Zinn, Ph.D. This mindfulness-based approach treats a variety of illnesses around the world. A student of yoga and renowned Buddhist masters, Zinn set up the Cambridge Zen Center.

6. Judson Brewer, MD, Ph.D.—a psychiatrist/neuroscientist used fMRI to study the role of the brain in mindfulness. His programs address mindfulness, habit change, anxiety, smoking, stress and eating. Two online applications *Unwinding Anxiety* and *Eat Right Now.*

7. Jack Kornfield, Ph.D., Buddhist monk and teacher—contributed widely to the experience of mindfulness in the west. He founded the *Insight Meditation Society* and the *Spiritrock Center* in California.

8. Sharon Salzberg and Joseph Goldstein, teachers of Buddhist meditation—authored *"Insight Meditation: A Step-By-Step Guide to Meditation."*

9. Carolyn Myss' audio tape *Spiritual Madness: The Necessity of Meeting God in Darkness,* by Sounds True, discusses "mystics without monasteries." Her workshops, podcasts and many books elaborate on the topic. https://www.azquotes.com/quote/1111536.

10. *Daily Word & Guideposts* in Suggested Reading and Resources.
11. The Merritt Retreat Center and Lodge in Payson, Arizona—sponsors personal and group retreats for renewal and empowerment. mcenteraz@gmail.com.

Dark Nights of the "Soul"

1. Brainy Quotes Julia Cameron, well-known artist, author and teacher, best known for her book, *The Artist's Way* about creativity. Noted from: Write Quotes.BrainyQuote.com. https://www.brainyquote.com/topics/write-quotes, accessed November 9, 2022.
2. St. John of the Cross, https://www.goodreads.com. Juan de la Cruz, Quotes, *Quotable Quote*, accessed November 9, 2022. https://www.goodreads.com/author/quotes/1911605.Juan _de_la_Cruz.
3. St. Teresa of Avila, written about by Caroline Myss and Mirabai Starr, who tell the story and share the wisdom of this very influential woman.
4. Ram Dass—https://www.goodreads.com/author/quotes/14525 .Ram_Dass, accessed September 28, 2022.
5. Hazrat Inayat Khan—an Indian Muslim Sufi teacher https://www.inspiringquotes.us/author/author/3500-vilayat -inayat-khan,
6. Caroline Myss. AZQuotes.com, Wind and Fly LTD, 2022. https://www.azquotes.com/author/19450-Caroline_Myss, accessed September 19, 2022.
7. Caroline Myss, regarding the Dark Night of the Soul. https:// www.azquotes.com/quote/1358746, accessed November 5, 2022.

Life Experiences Affect My Thoughts

1. Division 12, American Psychological Association. "What Is Cognitive Behavioral Therapy?" *PTSD Clinical Practice Guideline.* American Psychological Association, 2017. https://www.apa.org/ptsd-guideline, accessed October 29, 2022.

Responsibility

1. DSM-5—American Psychiatric Association Ed. *Diagnostic and Statistical Manual of Mental Disorders (DSM-5).* Washington DC: American Psychiatric Association, 2013.
2. Education and discussion of biochemistry and depression. Nancy Schimelpfening, "The Chemistry of Depression: What Is the Biochemical Basis of Depression?" https://www.verywellmind.com/the-chemistry-of-depression-1065137, accessed on November, 11, 2022.
3. If you are curious about AI's, The American Cancer Society provides in-depth information. https://www.cancer.org/cancer/breast-cancer/risk-and-prevention/aromatase-inhibitors-for-lowering-breast-cancer-risk.
4. Ram Dass https://www.quotes.thefamouspeople.com/ram-dass-2617.
5. Depak Chopra— *Jesus: A Story of Enlightenment.* New York: Harper One, 2008.

Holistic Explorations of Treatment Options

1. The printed book *Physician's Desk Reference for Medications* has been renamed *Prescriber's Digital Reference* (now available for free online). A premier reference for drugs, with prescribing information from the actual manufacturers. https://www.pdr.net.

2. Resources for understanding different drug categories can be found in the *Merck Manual Consumer Version*. Online. https://www.merckmanuals.com/home.

3. National Center for Complementary and Integrative Health, US Dept of Health and Human Services, description, discussion, and treatment approaches. https://www.nccih.nih.gov/health/complementary-alternative-or-integrative-health-whats-in-a-name.

4. Traditional Chinese Medicine, https://www.nccih.nih.gov/health/traditional-chinese-medicine-what-you-need-to-know.

5. Overview of yoga, benefits, examples, and application for different groups of individuals, https://www.nccih.nih.gov/health/yoga-what-you-need-to-know.

6. Tai Chi, https://www.nccih.nih.gov/health/tai-chi-what-you-need-to-know.

7. Homeopathy, https://www.nccih.nih.gov/health/homeopathy.

8. Relaxation Techniques, https://www.nccih.nih.gov/health/relaxation-techniques-what-you-need-to-know.

9. Reiki, https://www.nccih.nih.gov/health/reiki.

My Desperate Choices

1. Electroconvulsive Therapy (ECT) care for a variety of types of mental illnesses. The Mayo Clinic provides a concise discussion of ECT. https://www.mayoclinic.org/tests-procedures/electroconvulsive-therapy

2. Gabor Gazdag and Gabor S. Ungvari, "Electroconvulsive therapy: 80 years old and still going strong," *World Journal of Psychiatry*. 2019 Jan 4;9(1): 1–6, https://doi: 10.5498/wjp.v9.i1.1. PMID: 30631748; PMCID: PMC6323557.

3. In *Experimental and Therapeutic Medicine*, Trifu, S., Sevenco, A., Stanescu, M., Miruna Dragoi, A., and Bogdan Cristea, M. "Efficacy of electroconvulsive therapy as a potential first-choice treatment in treatment-resistant depression (Review)". *Experimental and Therapeutic Medicine*. 2021 Nov; 22(5): 1281. Published online 2021 Sep 9, https://doi: 10.3892/etm.2021.10716. PMID: 34630636; PMCID: PMC8461517.

4. "A Depression Switch" is an article regarding Deep Brain Stimulation. Information about the procedure and research. Link to interview is in the resources section.

5. Information about the Atlanta Hospital Hospitality House (AHHH) can be found on their website https://www.atlhhh.org.

6. See website LifeStance Health, for information about neuropsychological testing. https://www.mygbhp.com/service/neuropsychological-testing.

7. MRI = Magnetic Resonance Imaging, CT Scan = Computerized Tomography, EEG = Electroencephalogram. For more information, search by test.

Talk Therapy

1. EMDR refers to Eye Movement Desensitization and Reprocessing, https://www.emdr.com.

2. CBT refers to Cognitive Behavioral Therapy, discussed online. The American Psychological Association has detailed information at https://www.apa.org/ptsd-guideline/patients-and-families/cognitive-behavioral.

3. Humanistic/Experiential Therapies—are detailed on the website Psychotherapy Matters, https://www.psychotherapymatters.com/faq/humanistic-experiential.

4. Maslow, "A Theory of Human Motivation." *Psychological Review*, 50(4)1943, 370396, http://psychclassics.yorku.ca /Maslow/motivation.

5. Behavior Therapy is defined by specific strategies. https: //dictionary.apa.org/behavior-therapy.

6. Acronyms for degrees: PhD—Doctor of Philosophy; EdD— Doctor of Education; PsyD—Doctor of Psychology; MD— Doctor of Medicine; DO—Doctor of Osteopathic Medicine; DSci—Doctor of Science; LCSW—Licensed Clinical Social Worker; NP—Nurse Practitioner; MFC—Marriage and Family Counselor; PA—Physician's Assistant.

7. The website "Got Questions" describes Spiritual Direction—"*It has become popular in modern society to be spiritual, but not religious. 'Spiritual' usually means that a person is in touch with his or her own spirit, the spirits of others, and some (personal or impersonal) Higher Power or Spirit that inhabits (and perhaps empowers) the universe. To do this, one does not need to be part of an organized religion or believe any specific doctrines about God, sin, salvation, heaven, hell, or Jesus . . .*" https://www .gotquestions.org/spiritual-direction.html.

Paths to Union with "Spirit"

1. Kenneth Kendler, "Religion, Psychopathology, and Substance Use and Abuse: A Multimeasure, Genetic-epidemiologic Study," *American Journal of Psychiatry,* 154(3): (1997), 322–329.

2. Rohr, Richard, *The Naked Now: Learning to See as the Mystics See,* New York: Crossroad Publishing, 2009, p. 146.

3. Saint Teresa of Avila, *The Interior Castle, St. Teresa of Avila*. Translated by Mirabai Starr. New York: Riverhead Books, 2004.

Finding a Me I Could Embrace

1. Amygdala and hippocampus are emotional parts of the brain. https://www.differencebetween.net/science/difference -between-amygdala-and-hippocampus/. Olivia Guy-Evans, *Simply Psychology,* authored the amygdala, May 09, 2021, https://www.simplypsychology.org/amygdala.html, and the hippocampus, June 16, 2021. https://www.simplypsychology .org/hippocampus.html.

SUGGESTED READING AND RESOURCES

Ackerman, Angela and Puglisi, Becca. *The Emotion Thesaurus: A Writer's Guide to Character Expression, Second Edition*. United States: JADD Publishing, 2019.

American Psychiatric Association Ed. *Diagnostic and Statistical Manual of Mental Disorders (DSM-5)*. Washington, DC: American Psychiatric Association, 2013.

Brach, Tara. *True Refuge: Finding Peace and Freedom in Your Own Awakened Heart*. New York: Bantam, 2016.

Brewer, Judson. *The Craving Mind: From Cigarettes to Smartphones to Love—Why We Get Hooked and How We Can Break Bad Habits*. New Haven: Yale University Press, 2017.

Brown, Brené. *Atlas of the Heart: Mapping Meaningful Connection and the Language of Human Experience*. New York: Random House, 2021.

Brown, Brené. *Radical Compassion: Learning to Love Yourself and Your World with the Practice of RAIN*. New York: Penguin Books, 2020.

Campbell-Rasmus, Juanita. *Learning to Be: Finding Your Center After the Bottom Falls Out*. Grove, IL: InterVarsity Press, 2020.

Cameron, Julia. "Dark Night of the Soul." *A to Z Quotes*

Canavan, Alison. *Minding Mum: It's Time to Take Care of You*. Dublin, Ireland: Gill Books, 2016.

Carlson, Richard, and Bailey, Joseph. *Slowing Down the Speed of Life*. New York: Harper Collins, 1997.

Chittister, Joan. *Between the Dark and the Daylight: Embracing the Contradictions of Life*. New York: Penguin Random House, 2015.

Chittister, Joan. *The Breath of the Soul: Reflections on Prayer*. New London, CT: Twenty-Third Publications, 2009.

Chittister, Joan. *The Gift of Years: Growing Older Gracefully*. New York: Blue Bridge Books, 2010.

Chittister, Joan. *Radical Spirit: 12 Ways to Live a Free and Authentic Life*. New York: Convergent, 2017.

Chodron, Pema. *The Places That Scare You: A Guide to Fearlessness in Difficult Times*. Boston: Shambhala, 2007.

Chopra, Deepak. *Jesus: A Story of Enlightenment*. New York: Harper Collins, 2009.

Coburn, Nadia. "Seven Steps to Embracing Your Full Story" *Spirituality & Health*. September/October 2018: pp. 29–32.

Cronkite, Kathy. *On the Edge of Darkness*. New York: Dell Publishing, 1995.

Crowell, Andrea, Riva-Posse, Patricio, Holtzheimer, Paul, Garlow, Steven J, Kelley, Mary, Gross, Robert, Denison, Lydia, Quinn, Sinead, and Mayberg, Helen. "Long-Term Outcomes of Subcallosal Cingulate Deep Brain Stimulation for Treatment-Resistant Depression." *American Journal of Psychiatry.* Advance Online Publication (https//doi.org/10.1176/appi .ajp.2019.18121427: 1–10. 10.4.2019.

Daily Word. Unity Village, MO: Unity World.

Dass, Ram. *Still Here: Embracing Aging, Changing, and Dying.* New York: Penguin Books, 2001.

Davidson, Richard J and Begley, Sharon. *The Emotional Life of Your Brain.* New York: Hudson St. Press, 2012

Dockett, Lauren. *The Deepest Blue: How Women Face and Overcome Depression.* New York: New Harbinger, 2001.

Ellis, Albert and Harper, Robert. *A New Guide to Rational Living.* New York: Prentice-Hall, 1975.

Flanagan-Hyde, Sharon. *Forget They Were Ever Born.* Sharon Flanagan-Hyde, 2019.

Frankl, Victor. *Man's Search for Meaning.* Boston: Beacon Press, 1953.

Gandhi, Mohandas K. and Gandhi, Mahatma. *Autobiography: The Story of My Experiments with Truth.* New York: Dover Publications, Inc., 1983.

Germer, Christopher. *The Mindful Path to Self-Compassion.* New York: Guilford, 2009.

Gazdag G, Ungvari GS. "Electroconvulsive therapy: 80 years old and still going strong." *World Journal of Psychiatry.* 2019

Jan 4;9(1):1–6. doi: 10.5498/wjp.v9.i1.1. PMID: 30631748; PMCID: PMC6323557.

Goleman, Daniel. *Healing Emotions: Conversations with the Dalai Lama on Mindfulness, Emotions, and Health.* Boston: Shambhala, 1997.

Goleman, Daniel and Davidson, Richard J. *Altered Traits: Science Reveals How Medication Changes Your Mind, Brain, and Body.* Somerville, MA: Wisdom, 2017.

Goldstein, Joseph. *Mindfulness: A Practical Guide to Awakening.* Boulder, CO: Sounds True, 2013.

Guideposts. Danbury, CT: Zondervan Books, 2022.

Gunaratana, Bahante. "Mindfulness." *The Science and Art of Meditation: How to Deepen and Personalize Your Practice.* Woodbury, MN: Llewellyn Press, 2020. P. 133–142.

Hahn, Thich Nhat. *No Mud, No Lotus: The Art of Transforming Suffering.* Berkeley, CA: Parallax Press, 2014.

Hahn, Thich Nhat. *Peace in Every Step: The Path of Mindfulness in Every Step.* New York: Bantam Books, 1991.

Hillman, James. *A Blue Fire: Selected Writings by James Hillman.* New York: Harper Collins, 1989.

Hillman, James. *The Soul's Code: In Search of Character and Calling.* New York: Random House, 1996.

James, William. *Psychology.* New York: Henry Holt and Company, 1892

John of the Cross, Saint. *Dark Night of the Soul, St. John of the Cross.* Translated by Mirabai Starr. New York: Riverhead Books, 2002.

Kabat-Zinn, Jon. *Meditation is Not What You Think: Mindfulness and Why It is So Important*. New York: Hachette Book Group, 2018.

Kabat-Zinn, Jon. *Falling Awake: How to Practice Mindfulness in Everyday Life*. New York: Hachette Book Group, 2018.

Kabat-Zinn, Jon. *Full Catastrophe Living: Using the Wisdom of Your Body and Mind to Face Stress, Pain, and Illness* (revised and updated edition). New York: Random House, 2013.

Kabat-Zinn, Jon. *The Healing Power of Mindfulness: A New Way of Being*. New York: Hachette Book Group, 2018.

Kahnweiler, Jennifer B. *Quiet Influence: The Introvert's Guide to Making a Difference*. San Francisco: Berrett-Koehler Publishers, 2013.

Karasu, Toksov Byram. *The Art of Serenity: The Path to a Joyful Life in the Best and Worst of Times*. New York: Simon and Schuster, 2003.

Keating, Father Thomas. *The Contemplative Journey: Volume 1: Contemplation and Transformation from Christianity's Mystical Tradition*. Boulder, CO: Sounds True, 2005.

Kendler, Kenneth. "Religion, Psychopathology, and Substance Use and Abuse: A Multimeasure, Genetic-epidemiologic Study. *American Journal of Psychiatry* 154(3): (1997) pp. 322–329.

Kornfield, Jack. *A Path with Heart: A Guide through the Perils and Promises of Spiritual Life*. New York: Bantam, 2009.

Kubler-Ross, Elisabeth. *On Death and Dying: What the Dying Have to Teach Doctors, Nurses, Clergy, and Their Own Families*. New York: Routledge. 2009.

Maslow, Abraham. *Toward a Psychology of Being.* New York: John Wiley and Sons, 1968

Matousek, Mark. *Writing to Awaken: A Journey of Truth, Transformation, & Self-discovery.* Oakland, CA, New Harbinger Publications: Reveal Press, 2017.

Mayberg, Helen. "A Depression Switch" David Dobbs. *The New York Times Magazine,* (6)p. 50, Interview Date April 2, 2006. Online. www.nytimes.com/2006/04/02 /magazine/a-depression-switch

Miller, Lisa. *The Awakened Brain: The New Science of Spirituality and Our Quest for an Inspired Life.* New York: Random House, 2021.

Mlodinow, Leonard. *Emotional: How Feelings Shape Our Thinking.* New York: Pantheon Books, 2022.

Moezzi, Melody. *The Rumi Prescription: How an Ancient Mystic Poet Changed My Modern Manic Life.* New York: Penguin Random House, 2021.

Moore, Thomas. *A Religion of One's Own: A Guide to Creating a Personal Spirituality in a Secular World.* New York: Penguin Random House, 2015.

Moore, Thomas. *Care of the Soul: A Guide for Cultivating Depth and Sacredness in Everyday Life.* New York: Harper Collins Publishers, 1992.

Moore, Thomas. *Dark Nights of the Soul: A Guide to Finding Your Way Through Life's Ordeals.* New York: Penguin Random House, 2005.

Moore, Thomas. *The Soul's Religion: Cultivating a Profoundly Spiritual Way of Life.* New York: Harper Collins Publishers, 2009.

Mother Teresa. *No Greater Love*. Novato, CA: New World Library, 1989.

Myss, Caroline. *Anatomy of the Spirit: The Severn Stages of Power and Healing*. New York: Harmony Books, 1996.

Myss, Caroline. *Entering the Castle: Finding the Inner Path to God and Your Soul's Purpose*. New York: Free Press, 2007.

Myss, Caroline. *Sacred Contracts: Awakening Your Divine Spirit*. New York: Harmony Books, 2002.

Myss, Caroline. *Spiritual Madness*. Colorado: Sounds True, 1997.

Ostaseski, Frank. *The Five Invitations: Discovering What Death Can Teach Us About Living Fully*. New York: Flatiron Books, 2017.

2016 Physician's Desk Reference, 70th Edition. Publisher: PDR Network, 2015. This is now *Prescriber's Digital Reference* available for free online @ www.pdr.net.

Nouwen, Henri J.M. *Here and Now: Living in the Spirit*. New York: The Crossroad Publishing Company, 1994

Redfield Jamison, Kay. *An Unquiet Mind*. New York: Random House, 1996.

Remen, Rachel Naomi. *Kitchen Table Wisdom: Stories That Heal*. New York: The Penguin Group, 2006.

Rohr, Richard. *Falling Upward: A Spirituality for the Two Halves of Life*. San Francisco: Jossey-Bass, 2013.

Rohr, Richard. *The Naked Now: Learning to See as the Mystics See*. New York: Crossroad Publishing, 2009

Salzberg, Sharon. *Lovingkindness*. Boston: Shambhala, 1995.

Salzberg, Sharon and Joseph Goldstein, *"Insight Meditation: A Step-by-Step Guide to Meditation,"* Colorado: Sounds True, 2002. This is a kit that includes an In-Depth Workbook, Study Cards and 2 Compact Discs. (Available @ Amazon and Sounds True)

Salzberg, Sharon. *Real Love: The Art of Mindful Connection.* New York: Flatiron Books, 2017.

Segal, Zindel, Williams, Mark, and Teasdale, John. *Mindfulness-Based Cognitive Behavior Therapy for Depression.* New York: Guilford Press, 2012

Siegel, Daniel. *The Mindful Brain: Reflection and Attunement in the Cultivation of Well-being.* New York: W.W. Norton, 2007.

Siegel, Daniel. "Reflections on the Mindful Brain" pp. 61–83. *Measuring the Immeasurable.* Boulder, CO: Sounds True, 2008.

Silverman, Amy. *My Heart Can't Even Believe It.* Bethesda, MD: Woodbine House, 2016.

Schneidman, Edwin S. "Commentary: Suicide as Psychache." *Journal of Nervous and Mental Disease, 181(3), 145–147.* 1993. https://doi.org/10.1097/00005053-199303000-00001

Starr, Mirabai. *Caravan of No Despair: A Memoir of Loss and Transformation.* Boulder, CO: Sounds True, 2015.

Starr, Mirabai. *Wild Mercy: Living the Fierce and Tender Wisdom of the Women Mystics.* Boulder, CO: Sounds True, 2019.

Styron, William. *Darkness Visible: A Memoir of Madness.* New York: Modern Library, 2007.

Teresa of Avila, Saint. *The Interior Castle, St. Teresa of Avila.* Translated by Mirabai Starr. New York: Riverhead Books, 2004.

Thompson, Tracy. *The Beast: A Journey Through Depression.* New York: Plume, 1996.

Wadhwa, Hitendra. *Inner Mastery, Outer Impact: How Your Five Core Energies Hold the Key to Success.* New York: Hachette Book Group, 2022.

Williams, Mark, Teasdale, John, and Segal, Zindel. *The Mindful Way Through Depression: Freeing Yourself from Chronic Unhappiness.* New York: The Guilford Press, 2007.

Wiseman, Neil B. "Make Time Your Friend: Do Something Wonderful with Every Day." *Growing Your Soul: Practical Steps to Increase Your Spirituality.* Baker Publishing Group, MI, 1996 pp. 123–148.

Zukav, Gary. *The Seat of the Soul.* New York: Simon and Schuster, 2014.

Zukav, Gary. *Soul to Soul Meditations: Daily Reflections for Spiritual Growth.* New York: Free Press, 2012.

ACKNOWLEDGMENTS

The richness of this book would not have been possible without the efforts and impact of many. It is impossible to *rank order* the significance of these contributors, because their unique input has come in a variety of manners at different times. The kinds of ideas and insights they share weave in and out over the course of my life. Some contacts included a single powerful event, thought, or idea. Others brought support in a broad number of actions, expressions of love, and inspiration throughout my existence.

Inspiration related to my depression and spiritual evolution came from friends, colleagues, providers, and groups. Personal friends provided unspoken acts of care and blessings I may not always have acknowledged.

Certainly, a very key figure has been my therapist of more than twenty years, Dr. Marilyn Kieffer-Andrews, Psychiatric Mental Health Nurse Practitioner, who has been a lifeline of continuous learning, inspiration, and growth.

The long list of personal friends is in alphabetical order; it is not exhaustive, and I apologize for anyone specific I may not have included: Myla Bobrow & Brian Meek, Karen Borggren, Kristin Rogers Chase, Dr. Teri Gallenstein, Elaine Groppenbacher, Pastor Ken Heinzelman, Reverend Robin Kreider, Dr. Terry Matteo, Sandie Miller, Dr. Beth Onufrak, Marilyn Rampley, Dr. Yvonne Saffron, Rich & Marie Schreiber, Dr. William O. Smith, Dr. Jeanie Thomson, Ida Vigil, and my Navajo Sister Carlene Wauneka.

While we each have professionals who have cared for us in one manner or another, I want to mention a few specific individuals. The doctors at the Emory University DBS Study, Helen Mayberg, MD, and Patricio Riva-Posse, MD, treated me with care and concern as an individual, not just a subject of their study. Sources of exceptional medical care in Phoenix included Harris Murley, MD, Lawrence Kasper, MD, Maureen Hamel-Schwartz, PA, and Coralee H. McKay, MD. There are also several massage therapists who provided a variety of approaches, acupuncture, Reiki, acupressure, and aromatherapy.

Several groups have given infinite support. Members of Shadow Rock Congregational church have supported my family and me, spiritually and physically. My professionally creative sisters—the "Solopreneurs" (Dr. Beth Onufrak, Jan Katzen, and Tina Kanelos Jones) serve as inspiration for each other professionally and personally. My "(Cancer) Survivor Sisters" have seen each other through many physical, emotional, and unique needs for more than eleven years (Karen Borggren, Cyndy Gaughan, Dorothy Hailey, Meredith Lee, and Bobbie Thayer). The staff and volunteers at the Atlanta Hospital Hospitality House in Georgia have been my family and home away from home for more than fifteen years as I have received DBS care.

The basic foundation of my life is the love and care of my family. My parents, Bob and Eileen Hoard, were models for these attributes. My sisters Robin Damore, Michelle Schwartz, Kristen Hoard, and adopted sisters Jessi Brooks and Pam Reinke each continue to share their unique gifts. Our extended family of in-laws (Dennis Damore Family and Peter Schwartz), nieces and nephews (Andrea Marie Breiling, Madeline Ann Damore, Maxine Eileen Kinison, Robert Cassidy Damore, and Jude Dennis Pierce) enrich each of us. My paternal grandmother, Nana Amy LaFave, taught me different ways to pray, getting down on her knees every night until she was in her 80s. Our family neighbors of more than fifty years (The Kesslers—Kathryn Allen, Linda Hohl, Mary Barth, Patti Moore, Margie Merrill) are sisters whom we affectionately refer to as the group of "Blessed Beyond the Alley."

Ultimately, there have been key partners in the literal development of this book and include readers who provided feedback as the book emerged: Dr. Jeanie Thomson, Dr. Beth Onufrak, Lisa Friedberg, Jan Katzen, Denny Damore, Tina Kanelos Jones, Marilyn Rampley, and Cassidy Damore.

Last but certainly not least, in fact, indispensable, the team from 1106 Design (www.1106design.com) who guided me to get ready to publish, Michele DeFilippo, Ronda Rawlins, Jerome McLain, and other professionals were invaluable.

ABOUT THE AUTHOR

Cindy Hoard is a student and patient of treatment-resistant depression. She has undergone a wide range of treatments, therapies and activities to help herself over many years. As a consumer of many sources of information, research and modalities she has been an active participant in her own care. Over 40 years she documented her journey, expressed her reactions to lived experiences and kept a history of her progress in journals.

Dr. Cindy is a retired child psychologist and former special education teacher who has worked primarily with children birth to age six and their families in a variety of settings and cultures. She has worked with Head Start and Early Intervention

Programs for over 20 years, truly her passion. She has had an amazing variety of experiences and has continued to learn from the children and families she has served.

A vital element of this odyssey has been the evolution, rollercoaster and maturation of the Spiritual dimension of her life. Dr. Cindy integrates aspects of formal religion, world religions, meditation, and mindfulness as integral to all facets of her life. Daily practices are essential to the maintenance of her calm and peacefulness.

Cindy enjoys a variety of creative projects such as quilts, cooking, needlework, making cards with dried flowers and multimedia pieces of art. She enjoys music, singing and playing the flute and loves personal retreats in rich natural settings.

Made in the USA
Las Vegas, NV
15 June 2023